A BIBLIOGRAPHIC GUIDE TO EDUCATIONAL RESEARCH

SECOND EDITION

Dorothea M. Berry

The Scarecrow Press, Inc.
Metuchen, N.J., & London
1980

Library of Congress Cataloging in Publication Data

Berry, Dorothea M
   A bibliographic guide to educational research.

   Includes indexes.
   1. Education--Bibliography. 2. Reference books
--Education. I. Title.
Z5811.B39   1980   [LB17]   016.37   80-20191
ISBN 0-8108-1351-3

To

Dr. Jack D. Mezirow

PREFACE TO THE FIRST EDITION

This bibliographic manual is the outgrowth of instruction in the use of reference materials in the field of education given to classes at the University of California, Riverside, over a period of several years. It is intended to serve as a concise guide to assist students in education courses to make effective use of the resources of the library of their college or university. In order to carry out library research efficiently, students need to know what materials are available, how and where to find them, and how to use them. This manual lists and describes important sources and gives information that will enable students to work independently and efficiently. It may also be found useful in courses in the literature of educational research. It should be of value to college librarians as a reference guide. Some sections, particularly the listings of special types of materials, will be of interest to teachers and school librarians.

More than 500 references, with descriptive annotations, are included. Emphasis has been given to recently published sources. Sections I through VI cover different types of material--books, periodicals, research studies, government publications, pamphlets, and special types, such as children's literature, textbooks, tests, audiovisual materials, and programmed instruction and computer-assisted instruction materials. Bibliographies and indexes are listed and described as means of locating these materials.

Other types of reference sources, including encyclopedias, dictionaries, handbooks, statistical sources, yearbooks, directories, and biographical sources, are listed with annotations in Section VII. Section VIII lists handbooks on the methodology of educational research, and on form and style in research papers.

I am grateful to Jan Sielen for her excellent typing of the manuscript. I am grateful also to Estella Rivera and to Roxanne Starbuck for their valuable assistance in typing additions and the indexes.

Dorothea M. Berry
Education Services Librarian
University of California, Riverside

PREFACE TO THE SECOND EDITION

The second edition of this bibliographic guide is considerably enlarged with the addition of new titles and new editions published 1975-1979 and expansion of the coverage of material published prior to 1975. The second edition includes 772 entries compared with 504 in the first edition. A total of 140 entries from the first edition have been deleted; 408 new titles have been added, plus new editions of 87 titles previously cited. New annotations have been written for recent editions of more than 30 annual and biennial publications cited in the first edition. Annotations for many titles retained from the first edition have been revised and expanded to give fuller information.

Most of the titles included were published between 1970 and 1979, with emphasis on those published since 1975. Some titles published before 1970 are included because of their historical value or quality, or because there are no recent publications to replace them. All items included are in the English language. A few bilingual or multilingual publications, such as some UNESCO titles, are included. Most publications are American, but many British and some Canadian and Australian publications are included. Annotations are descriptive rather than evaluative. Inclusion of an item indicates it is considered to be useful.

In the second edition more attention has been given to international and comparative education, bilingual and multicultural education, education of minorities, special education, and vocational education. A separate section on ERIC documents and computer searching of ERIC materials has been added in Part III. A new section of bibliographies of instructional materials, print and nonprint, has been added in Part V. New subsections have been added in the sections on subject bibliographies, periodical indexes, children's literature, and directories. A brief section on pamphlets in the first edition has been deleted since pamphlets of substantial value are treated as books in most libraries. Cross-references have been added for works covering more than one subject or appropriate for more than one category. An annotated list of other bibliographies of reference materials in the field of education has been added as an appendix.

The guide's selectivity, inclusion of material in the English language only, emphasis on recently published materials, descriptive information on entries, and organization of materials contribute to making library research easier and more effective. It has been useful to graduate and undergraduate students for independent research, as a guide in courses in the literature of educational research, and as a reference tool and checklist for college and university librarians, children's librarians, school librarians, teachers, and administrators.

I am grateful for the use of the resources and services of the library of the University of California, Riverside. Many members of the staff of this library have contributed much to the completion of this project through their friendly, courteous, and efficient service. To each of them I am grateful. I am also grateful to several members of the faculty of the School of Education of the University of California, Riverside, and to others for their encouraging comments on the first edition.

Dorothea M. Berry

CONTENTS

INTRODUCTION

This guide is an annotated bibliography of sources useful or essential for research in the field of education. Its purpose is to make the user aware of the sources available for finding different types of materials on various subjects, and to make research easier and more effective. Emphasis is on basic sources and recently published works representative of various aspects of the field. Arrangement is by type of material. Different types of publications on a specific subject are brought together by the subject index. Author-editor and title indexes are also provided.

Part I is concerned with bibliographies as a means of finding books on particular subjects. It includes a discussion of the card catalog, and listings of library catalogs in book form, trade bibliographies, bibliographies covering the entire field of education, and bibliographies on specific aspects of the field.

Part II lists comprehensive, general directories of periodicals, directories of education periodicals, and indexes and abstract journals as means of access to articles on education and education-related subjects published in periodicals, with emphasis on professional journals.

Part III includes an explanation of the Educational Resources Information Center and of computer searching for ERIC materials, and lists of sources for ERIC documents, theses and dissertations, and other types of research studies.

Part IV lists bibliographies and indexes of government publications--federal, state, and UNESCO--concerning education.

Part V covers bibliographies and indexes for special types of materials, including literature for children and young adults, textbooks, instructional materials, and tests and measurements. The section on literature for children and young adults is subdivided into bibliographies about children's literature, general bibliographies of books for children and young adults, bibliographies of books on special subjects and problems, bibliographies of reference books and periodicals, and indexes. The section on instructional materials includes both print and nonprint materials, and includes subsections for media selection aids, directories, and lists of media by types and subjects.

1

Parts VI and VII differ from the first five parts in that they list sources of information rather than guides to other publications. Part VI includes encyclopedias, dictionaries, thesauri, handbooks, statistical sources, directories, yearbooks, and biographical sources. Part VII is a selective list of books on the methodology of educational research, and manuals on form and style in research papers.

The Appendix lists other guides to reference materials in the field of education.

Sources used for research will vary according to the subject, purpose, and level of research. The undergraduate preparing a paper may find it sufficient to read an article in an encyclopedia of education for an overview of the subject, and a few recent books and articles found through the card catalog and periodical indexes or abstract journals. The graduate student will need more specialized materials found through bibliographies on special subjects, research studies, and possibly historical, statistical, and biographical material.

The professional educator may need extensive bibliographies on specific areas, such as special education, multicultural education, or adult education, or specific information, such as statistics or directory-type information.

If the researcher is compiling a bibliography, he or she can use several sources, such as the card catalog, library catalogs in book form, trade bibliographies, published bibliographies on the subject of interest, indexes to periodical literature, or lists of references given in books or with articles in encyclopedias and journals. If an extensive bibliography is needed, or if time for research is limited, computer searching may be desirable. Many libraries have services whereby printed lists of references may be obtained to fit the exact needs of the researcher. A trained search analyst handles requests. Charges for this service vary according to the length of the bibliography and the time required for the search. An explanation of computer searching for ERIC materials is given in Part III. Many libraries also offer computer searching for books and dissertations. Computer searching saves much time and effort and is more effective than manual searching. A researcher should consult a search analyst in the library for information on this service.

Interlibrary loan service can also be very helpful. If researchers find references to books or other materials that are not available in the library they are using, they may be able to borrow those materials from other libraries through their library's interlibrary loan service. They may also inquire about the resources of other libraries in the area and the possibility of using these libraries and borrowing materials from them directly.

Although this and similar guides are designed to help students or researchers work independently, they should not overlook the value of the services of reference librarians and other members of a library staff. They are well-trained, experienced professionals whose purpose is to give assistance when needed.

I. BOOKS

References to books can be found through the card catalog of the library the student is using, through the catalogs in book form of
large and specialized libraries, through trade bibliographies, and
through subject bibliographies.

A. Card Catalog

The first source that should be used to find books is the
card catalog of the library. Books are listed by author, title, and
subject. In some libraries all three types of cards are interfiled
in one alphabet. In some libraries author and title cards are filed
together in one catalog, and subject cards in a separate catalog.
Students looking for a particular book should look under the
author or title. If they are looking for a book or books on a particular subject and do not know specific authors or titles, their approach must be by subject. Under each subject heading cards are
filed alphabetically by authors' names. It is sometimes difficult to
determine the proper heading for the subject of interest. Most
card catalogs provide "see cards" from headings not used to headings under which books are listed, and "see also cards," which refer
to related subjects. (See illustrations below.) Students may also
look for appropriate headings in Library of Congress Subject Headings, 8th ed. (Washington, D. C.: Library of Congress, 1975).
This list shows the headings used in card catalogs, refers from
headings not used to those used, and refers to related headings. If
the students are unable to find any books listed on their subject in
the card catalog, they may consult a reference librarian for assistance.
Catalog cards give full bibliographic information on books, including the author's full name, the complete title, place of publication, publisher, date of publication, and total paging. Other information may include an editor's name, an edition number, a series
title, and the number of volumes. The tracings at the bottom of
the card indicate the subject or subjects treated in the book. This
information is sometimes helpful in providing subject headings under

3

which additional references can be found.   The number in the upper left corner of the card indicates the subject classification and the location on the shelves in the library.
Illustrated below are the types of cards included in a card catalog.

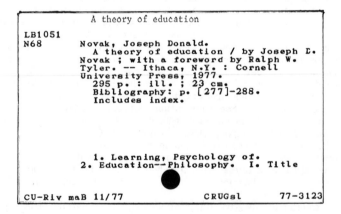

LB1051
N68
Novak, Joseph Donald.
A theory of education / by Joseph D. Novak ; with a foreword by Ralph W. Tyler. -- Ithaca, N.Y. : Cornell University Press, 1977.
295 p. : ill. ; 23 cm.
Bibliography: p. [277]-288.
Includes index.

1. Learning, Psychology of.
2. Education--Philosophy.   I. Title

Author card

A theory of education

LB1051
N68
Novak, Joseph Donald.
A theory of education / by Joseph D. Novak ; with a foreword by Ralph W. Tyler. -- Ithaca, N.Y. : Cornell University Press, 1977.
295 p. : ill. ; 23 cm.
Bibliography: p. [277]-288.
Includes index.

1. Learning, Psychology of.
2. Education--Philosophy.   I. Title

CU-Riv maB 11/77   CRUGsl   77-3123

Title card

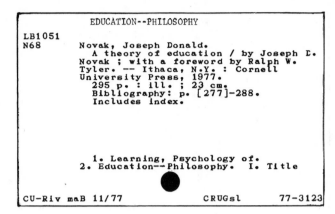

EDUCATION--PHILOSOPHY

LB1051
N68

Novak, Joseph Donald.
A theory of education / by Joseph D.
Novak ; with a foreword by Ralph W.
Tyler. -- Ithaca, N.Y. : Cornell
University Press, 1977.
295 p. : ill. ; 23 cm.
Bibliography: p. [277]-288.
Includes index.

1. Learning, Psychology of.
2. Education--Philosophy.   I. Title

CU-Riv maB 11/77   CRUGsl   77-3123

Subject card

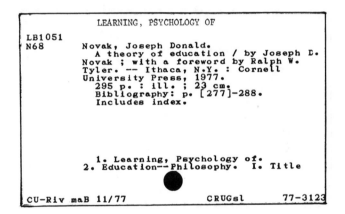

LEARNING, PSYCHOLOGY OF

LB1051
N68

Novak, Joseph Donald.
A theory of education / by Joseph D.
Novak ; with a foreword by Ralph W.
Tyler. -- Ithaca, N.Y. : Cornell
University Press, 1977.
295 p. : ill. ; 23 cm.
Bibliography: p. [277]-288.
Includes index.

1. Learning, Psychology of.
2. Education--Philosophy.   I. Title

CU-Riv maB 11/77   CRUGsl   77-3123

Subject card

```
Psychology of learning

        see

Learning, Psychology of
```

"See" Reference Card

```
Learning, Psychology of

        see also

Concept learning
```

"See also" Reference Card

Some libraries classify books by the Dewey Decimal Classification System; others use the Library of Congress scheme.

The schedules below illustrate the divisions of these two systems.

DEWEY DECIMAL CLASSIFICATION

370 EDUCATION

370. 1   Philosophy, Theories, Principles
  . 11   Aims, objectives, value

.15   Educational psychology
.19   Education and society
.193   Educational sociology
.194   Fundamental education
.195   Comparative education
.196   Intercultural education

.7   Study and teaching of education—
.71   Professional education of teachers
.712   For specific grades or levels
.72   Teachers' conferences, institutes, workshops
.76   Professional education of administrators
.78   Educational research ⌐

371   The School
.1   Teaching and teaching personnel
.2   Educational administration
.3   Methods of instruction and study ⌐
.4   Guidance and counseling
.5   School discipline
.6   Physical plant
.7   School health and safety
.8   The student
.9   Special education

372   Elementary Education
.1   The elementary school
.2   Levels of elementary education
.3   Science and health
.4   Reading
.5   Creative and manual arts
.6   Language arts
.7   Mathematics
.8   Other studies
.9   Historical and geographical treatment of elementary educa-
       tion and schools

373   Secondary Education
.1   The secondary school
.2   Types and levels of secondary education and schools
.3 - .9   Secondary education and schools by continent, country,
       locality

374   Adult Education
.1   Self-education
.2   Group education
.4   Correspondence schools and instruction
.8   Continuation schools
.9   Historical and geographical treatment

375   Curriculums
.01 - .99   Courses of study in specific subjects

376   Education of Women
- . 5   Convent education
- . 6   Education of women by level
- . 7   Coeducation versus separate education for women
- . 8   Colleges for women
- . 9   Historical and geographical treatment

377   Schools and Religion
- . 1   Religious instruction and exercises in nonsectarian schools
- . 2   Moral, ethical, character education
- . 3   Monastic schools
- . 6   Mission schools
- . 8   Schools supported by Christian groups
- . 9   Schools supported by other groups

378   Higher Education
- . 1   Institutions of higher education
- . 2   Academic degrees
- . 3   Student finances
- . 4 - . 9   Higher education and institutions by continent, country, locality in the modern world

379   Education and State
- . 1   State financial support, control, supervision of public education
- . 2   Public education
- . 3   Relation of state to private education
- . 4 - . 9   Public education by continent, country, locality in the modern world

LIBRARY OF CONGRESS CLASSIFICATION

L

EDUCATION

L		Education (General)
		For periodicals, congresses, directories, etc.
LA		History of education
LB		Theory and practice of education
	51-885	Systems of individual educators and writers
	1025-1050	Teaching (Principles and practice)
		Including programmed instruction, remedial teaching, non-graded schools, audiovisual education, methods of study, reading (General)
	1051-1091	Educational psychology
	1101-1139	Child study. Psychical development
	1140	Preschool education
	1141-1489	Kindergarten

	1501-1547	Primary education
	1555-1602	Elementary or public school education
	1603-1695	Secondary education. High schools
	1705-2286	Education and training of teachers
	2300-2411	Higher education
	2801-3095	School administration and organization
	3205-3325	School architecture and equipment
	3401-3498	School hygiene
	3525-3640	Special days. School life. Student customs
LC		Special aspects of education
	8-63	Forms of education
		Including self, home, and private school education
	65-245	Social aspects of education
		Including education and the state, religious instruction in public schools, compulsory education, illiteracy, educational sociology, community and the school, endowments
	251-951	Moral and religious education. Education under church control
	1001-1091	Types of education
		Including humanistic, vocational, and professional education
	1390-5153	Education of special classes of persons
		Including women, Negroes, gifted and handicapped children, orphans, middle class
	5201-6691	Adult education. Education extension
		Individual institutions: universities, colleges, and schools
LD		United States
LE		America, except United States
LF		Europe
LG		Asia. Africa. Oceania
LH		College and school magazines and papers
LJ		Student fraternities and societies, United States
		For other countries, see LA, LE-LG
LT		Textbooks
		For textbooks covering several subjects. For textbooks on particular subjects, see those subjects in B-Z

B.   Library Catalogs in Book Form

The card catalogs of some large, specialized libraries have been photographically reproduced in book form. They may be consulted for references not found in the college or university library the student is using.

Listed below are the catalogs of comprehensive collections in the field of Education.

1   Columbia University. Teachers College. Library. Diction-
     ary Catalog of the Teachers College Library. 36 vols.
     Boston: G. K. Hall, 1970. First Supplement. 5 vols.
     1971. Second Supplement. 2 vols. 1973. Third Supple-
     ment. 10 vols. 1977.
A photoreproduction of the card catalog of a collection of more than
400, 000 books and periodicals. The Library includes reference
sources dealing with 200 educational systems of the world; 1, 800
periodicals; a comprehensive collection of publications on American
elementary and secondary education, including original documents,
historical and contemporary textbooks, early histories of academies
and schools, courses of study, surveys, and administrative reports
of school systems of all the states and many major cities; and the
most extensive collection in the United States of educational periodicals published in the USSR. Supplemented by Bibliographic Guide
to Education, 1978-. Annual. (See No. 11.)

2   U. S. Department of Health, Education and Welfare. Catalogs
     of the Department Library. Author-Title Catalog, 29 vols. ;
     Subject Catalog, 20 vols. Boston: G. K. Hall, 1965-66.
     Author-Title Catalog. First Supplement. 7 vols. 1973.
     Subject Catalog. First Supplement. 4 vols. 1973.
A photoreproduction of the card catalog of a collection of 500, 000
volumes, especially strong in education and the social sciences. In
education special strengths include historical materials on all levels,
textbooks in all subject fields and grade levels through secondary
school, and foreign titles. Legislative histories trace legislation
from earliest hearings to final disposition of bills.

     The author and subject catalogs of the Library of Congress,
covering all fields, may also be used to find references to education
books.

3   U. S. Library of Congress. Catalog of Books Represented by
     Library of Congress Printed Cards Issued to July 31, 1942.
     167 vols. Ann Arbor, Mich. : J. W. Edwards, 1942-46.
     Supplement: Cards Issued August 1, 1942-December 31,
     1947. 42 vols. 1948. Author Catalog, 1948-1952. 24
     vols. 1953.
An author and main entry catalog of books in the Library of Congress and other libraries for which Library of Congress cards have
been printed. Continued by National Union Catalog, 1958-.

4   U. S. Library of Congress. National Union Catalog. Washing-
     ton, D. C. : Library of Congress, 1958-. Monthly with
     cumulations.
A cumulative author list representing Library of Congress printed
cards and titles reported by other American libraries, 1953 to date.

5   U. S. Library of Congress. Library of Congress Catalog . . .
     Books: Subjects. Ann Arbor, Mich. : J. W. Edwards,
     1950-. Quarterly with annual and five-year cumulations.
"A continuing and cumulative subject bibliography of works currently

received and cataloged by the Library of Congress and other American libraries participating in its cooperative cataloging program. " -- Introduction.

C.   Trade Bibliographies

6   Publishers Weekly. New York: R. R. Bowker: Weekly.
A weekly listing by author of new books, with a monthly title index. Also includes advance announcements.   Special numbers in Spring, Summer, and Fall.

7   Cumulative Book Index. New York: H. W. Wilson, 1933-.
Monthly with cumulations.
A comprehensive list of books in English in dictionary form with entries under author, title, and subject.   Entries give author, short title, edition, publisher, price, date, and paging.   Preceded by United States Catalog, 4th ed. , 1928, covering books in print in 1928.

8   Books in Print. 4 vols. New York: R. R. Bowker.   Annual.
Consists of two 2-volume indexes, the first by author and editor, the second by title and series.   Lists all types of books, covering all subjects, published or exclusively distributed in the United States, and available for purchase.   Excludes government publications, audio-visual materials, microform, and pamphlets.   The 1978-79 edition lists 496, 288 titles from 6, 900 publishers.   Entries in both the author index and the title index give complete bibliographical information and price.   Vol. 4 includes a directory of publishers and a key to publishers' and distributors' abbreviations.

9   Subject Guide to Books in Print. 2 vols. New York: R. R. Bowker.   Annual.
A subject listing of books from Books in Print.   Lists all in-print titles, except fiction, poetry, and drama by one author, under 62, 000 Library of Congress subject headings.   Entries give the same information as in Books in Print.   Includes a key to publishers' and distributors' abbreviations.

10   Books in Print Supplement. New York: R. R. Bowker.
Annual.
A mid-year updating service listing new and forthcoming books, price changes, and out-of-print titles.   Separate listings for authors, titles, and subjects in one volume.   Information in entries is the same as in Books in Print and the Subject Guide.   Includes a key to publishers' and distributors' abbreviations.

D.   Subject Bibliographies

General bibliographies covering the entire field of education may be located through the card catalog or catalogs in book form under the heading Education - Bibliography.   Bibliographies on specific areas within the field of education may be found under the subject and the subheading, Bibliography. (Example: Learning, Psychology of - Bibliography.) Following is an annotated list of bibliographies of general education and bibliographies of special subjects. Many bibliographies include other types of publications and materials in addition to books, such as periodical articles, government publications, pamphlets, theses, and dissertations.

General Education

11   Bibliographic Guide to Education. Boston: G. K. Hall, 1979-.
      Annual.
The 1979 volume is the first in an annual series that supplements the Dictionary Catalog of the Teachers College Library (see No. 1). Includes materials added to Teachers College Library during the past year, with additional entries from the New York Public Library. Covers all aspects of education, including American elementary and secondary education, higher education, adult education, early childhood education, history and philosophy of education, applied pedagogy, international and comparative education, educational administration, education of the culturally disadvantaged and physically handicapped, education of minorities and women, and administrative reports of departments of education in the United States and abroad.

12   Education Abstracts. Paris: UNESCO, 1949-1965.
An annotated guide to publications of interest to educators. Each monthly issue contains a bibliographical essay devoted to selected works on a particular aspect of education. International in coverage.

13   Education Book List. Washington, D. C.: Phi Lambda Theta,
      1926-1975. Annual.
A comprehensive, classified list of approximately 700 books of the year, followed by an annotated list of outstanding books of the year. Published separately 1967-1975. Published in School and Society, 1926-1946; in Phi Delta Kappan, 1947-1952; in Educational Horizons, 1953-1966.

14   Educational Documentation and Information. Geneva: UNESCO,
      International Bureau of Education, 1926-. Quarterly.
Former title: International Bureau of Education Bulletin, 1926-1970. Describes institutions of educational documentation and research and recent reference works in education. Each issue contains an annotated bibliography on a specific theme. Recent themes include development education, bibliographical sources, environmental education, counseling and information services, and sources of educational statistics. Published in English and in French.

15   Harvard University. Library. Education and Education Peri-
      odicals. Widener Library Shelflist, 16-17. 2 vols. Cam-
      bridge, Mass.: Harvard University Library, 1968.
Vol. 1 includes a classified listing of books and a separate classified listing of periodicals. Vol 2 includes an alphabetical listing of books by author and journals by title, and a chronological list of books from 1503 through 1967.

16   International Bureau of Education.   Annual Educational Bibliog-
        raphy.   Geneva: The Bureau, 1955-1970.
A cumulation of the annotated bibliographies from the International
Bureau of Education Bulletin.   A bibliography of the books added to
the library of the Bureau during the year.   International in scope
and covers all aspects of education.   In a classified arrangement
with an author index.

17   International Guide to Educational Documentation, 1955-1960.
        Paris: UNESCO, 1963.
The first section contains an annotated list of basic reference works
and a listing of international organizations and their publications on
education.   The major section contains chapters on countries of the
world arranged alphabetically, giving for each: a national documentation center,   and annotated references listed under reference works,
legislative and policy documentation,   administration of the educational
system,   structure and organization,   educational studies and research,
textbooks, associations, journals, statistics, biography, libraries
and museums, and interavailability of educational resources.   Also
contains an annotated list of 76 references on foreign education.
Index of authors, titles, and organizations.

18   International Guide to Educational Documentation, 1960-1965.
        Vol. 2.   Paris: UNESCO, 1971.
The second volume has a similar arrangement and includes annotated
bibliographies of publications that appeared 1960-1965, for 95 countries and territories.   Index of countries.   Trilingual edition.

19   Marks, Barbara S. , ed.   New York University List of Books
        in Education.   New York: Citation Press, 1968.
A comprehensive, annotated bibliography of 2, 857 books in a classified arrangement.   Subjects are arranged alphabetically.   Books
are listed alphabetically by author under each subject.

20   Monroe, Walter S. , and Louis Shores.   Bibliographies and
        Summaries in Education to July 1, 1935.   New York: H.
        W. Wilson, 1936.
Lists bibliographies published since 1910, giving for each: period
covered, number of references, degree of completeness, types of
materials, arrangement, kinds of annotations, and general character
of summaries.

21   Monroe, Will S.   Bibliography of Education.   New York: D.
        Appleton and Co. , 1897.   Reprint ed.   Detroit: Gale
        Research, 1968.
A classified list of 3, 200 books and pamphlets.   Subject and author
index.   Includes separate sections listing major American and
English educational journals, and the contents of the reports of the
U. S. Commissioner of Education, Horace Mann's state reports, and
the St. Louis reports of William T. Harris.

22   Richmond, William K.   The Literature of Education: A Criti-
        cal Bibliography, 1945-1970.   London: Methuen, 1972.

In ten chapters on philosophy, theory, curriculum, psychology, history, sociology, administration, comparative education, economics, and technology.   Each chapter consists of a bibliographic essay followed by a briefly annotated bibliography.

Adult Education

23   Aker, George F.   Adult Education Procedures, Methods and
        Techniques: A Classified and Annotated Bibliography, 1953-
        1963.   Compiled for the University of Chicago Program of
        Studies and Training in Continuing Education.   Syracuse,
        N. Y.:   The Library of Continuing Education at Syracuse
        University and University College of Syracuse University,
        1965.
A bibliography of research studies, descriptions of practices, and problems of adult education methodology covering 1953-1963, with some earlier works included.   In five parts: I, General References; II, Residential Centers for Continuing Education; III, Methods (Individual); IV, Methods (Group); V, Techniques of Adult Education. Each major section and subdivision is divided into four categories: (1) description, interpretation, and practice; (2) theoretical formulations; (3) research, (4) bibliographies.   Author index.

24   Kelly, Thomas, ed.   A European Bibliography of Adult Educa-
        tion.   London: National Institute of Adult Education, 1975.
A bibliography of the works of European scholars on adult education, in English, French, and German.   Arranged by broad subject headings and chronologically by date of publication under each heading. Includes general background material, history and organization of adult education in various European countries, and material on the teaching situation, with sections on the adult student, psychology of adult learning, teaching methods, and evaluation and training of adult educators.   Includes lists of bibliographies and periodicals. Author index.

25   Kelly, Thomas.   Select Bibliography of Adult Education in
        Great Britain Including Works Published to the End of the
        Year 1961.   London: National Institute of Adult Education,
        1962.   Supplements.
A briefly annotated bibliography of books, pamphlets, and articles in a classified arrangement.   Major sections are: General; Social and Educational Background; History and Organization; Theory and Method. Author and subject indexes.   Supplements are published in the Year Book of the National Institute of Adult Education.

26   Mezirow, Jack D. , and David Epley.   Adult Education in
        Developing Countries: A Bibliography.   Pittsburgh: Inter-
        national Clearinghouse of the International and Development
        Program, School of Education, University of Pittsburgh,
        1965.
A comprehensive bibliography arranged by geographical areas (Africa, Near East, South and Southeast Asia, Far East and Oceania, and

Latin America), each subdivided by country.   Includes references on
76 countries.   Also contains separate sections for references that
are principally topical (general and comparative, community development, literacy, health education, agricultural extension education,
vocational education, workers' education, out-of-school youth programs, women's programs, and liberal adult education).   Each entry
is coded for cross-referencing.   Includes references to journal
articles, books, articles in yearbooks, reports, and UNESCO publications.   Most of the references are to material in English, but some
references in French, Spanish, Portuguese, Chinese, and Japanese
are included.

27   Mezirow, Jack D. , and Dorothea Berry.   The Literature of
      Liberal Adult Education, 1945-1957.   Compiled for the
      Center for the Study of Liberal Education for Adults.   New
      York: Scarecrow Press, 1960.
A comprehensive guide to 1, 027 books, dissertations, journal articles,
government publications, and pamphlets published in major segments
of the field 1945-1957, in the United States, Great Britain, and
Canada.   Major sections are: I, Direction Finding: Philosophy and
Trends; II, Research and Bibliography; III, The Roles of Universities
and Colleges; IV, The Roles of Other Agencies; V, Courses and
Curricula.   Entries in Sections I-III are annotated or abstracted.
Some references in Sections IV and V are annotated in other sections.
Author and title index; subject index.

Anthropology and Education

28   Rosenstiel, Annette.   Education and Anthropology: An Annotated
      Bibliography.   New York: Garland Publishing, 1977.
"Designed as a single source reflecting (1) historical influences, (2)
current trends, (3) theoretical concerns, and (4) practical methodology
at the interfaces of these disciplines. "--Introd.   Contains 3, 435
annotated entries from education, anthropology, and relevant items
in psychology, sociology, literature, philosophy, and international
development.   Includes material in English, French, Spanish, German,
Italian, and Portuguese, with foreign titles in original language and
in English translation.   Includes books, articles, papers, and dissertations covering 1689 to 1976.   Arranged alphabetically by author
with topical index and regional index.

Bilingual Education

29   Cahir, Stephen, Rosa Montes, and Brad Jeffries.   A Selected
      Bibliography on Mexican American and Native American
      Bilingual Education in the Southwest.   Cal. ERIC/CLL Series
      on Languages and Linguistics, No. 6.   Arlington, Va.:
      ERIC Clearinghouse on Languages and Linguistics, Center
      for Applied Linguistics; Las Cruces, N. M.:   ERIC Clearing-
      house on Rural Education and Small Schools, New Mexico
      State University, 1975.
Contains 263 entries compiled from abstracts that appeared in Re-

search in Education, January, 1971-June, 1974. In three sections:
(1) an analysis of individual entries in terms of their sociolinguistic
significance; (2) ERIC abstracts in numerical order; (3) subject
index. Emphasizes biculturalism, bilingualism, content analysis,
English as a second language, program evaluation, and Spanish.
Includes research reports, program descriptions and evaluations,
and resource materials.

30   Trueba, Henry T. , comp. With the assistance of Juan Moran
      and others. Bilingual Bicultural Education for the Spanish
      Speaking in the United States: A Preliminary Bibliography.
      Champaign, Ill.: Stipes Publishing, 1977.
An unannotated bibliography of references on fundamental issues in
bilingual/bicultural education and on interdisciplinary approaches to
this field. Part I lists six sections or index categories: Bibliographies, Bilingual/Bicultural Education, Bilingualism, Education,
Language, and Sociocultural Perspectives. Part II is a topical index
with authors listed alphabetically in each category. Part III, the
main section, lists 1, 021 entries alphabetically by author, with index
numbers. Includes books, articles, reports, and government publications.

Comparative and International Education

31   Bibliography: Reports from the International Conference on
      Education, 1975. Paris: UNESCO, 1977.
A bibliography of 137 documents from 52 countries on major trends
in education and the changing role of the teacher. Entries include
abstracts. A source of information on national, international, and
comparative education. Subject index in English and French.

32   Bristow, Thelma, and Brian Holmes. Comparative Education
      through the Literature: A Bibliographic Guide. London:
      Archon Books, 1968.
A selective, annotated bibliography of works in English, with emphasis
on British publications. Major sections are: Teaching Comparative
Education; Imaginative Writing and Comparative Education; National
Area Studies in Comparative Education; Cross-Cultural and Case
Studies; and Library Tools and Research in Comparative Education.
Personal-name and title index, and an analytical subject index.

33   London. University. Institute of Education. Catalogue of the
      Comparative Education Library. 6 vols. Boston: G. K.
      Hall, 1971. First Supplement, 1974. Second supplement in
      preparation.
Contains more than 150, 000 photolithographed cards. The merger of
the Catalogue of the Collection of Education in Tropical Areas with
the collection of the Institute of Education's Department of Comparative Education resulted in a library of materials on education and
related fields that are worldwide in scope. There is extensive
coverage on both tropical and nontropical areas, with emphasis on
the Americas, Europe, Australia, and India. In three sections:

Author-Title; Country; and Subject.   Entries in the country section
are subdivided by subjects.   Entries in the subject section are subdivided by country.   Contains many references to periodical articles
and collections.

34   Tysse, Agnes M.   International Education: The American
        Experience: A Bibliography.   3 vols.   Metuchen, N. J. :
        Scarecrow Press, 1974-.
A comprehensive bibliography in three volumes covering all aspects
of foreign student study in the United States and educational activities
of Americans abroad.   Vol. I, Dissertations and Theses, published
in 1974, includes 553 doctoral dissertations and 139 masters' theses,
arranged alphabetically by author in separate sections.   Dissertations
are annotated, and references are given to Dissertation Abstracts
International.   Masters' theses are not annotated.   Includes a subject
index.   Vol. 2, Periodical Articles, published in 1977, contains more
than 10, 500 references from 700 periodicals.   Part I covers general
material on international education, international cooperation, educational and cultural exchange, brain drain, foreign students in the
United States, Americans abroad, medical education for foreigners,
and technical assistance and development abroad.   Part II contains
geographically oriented references arranged by continent, area, and
country.   Entries are briefly annotated.   Subject index and personal
name index.   Vol. 3, Books, Essays, Government Documents, is
in preparation.

35   Von Klemperer, Lily.   International Education: A Directory of
        Resource Materials on Comparative Education and Study in
        Another Country.   Garrett Park, Md. :   Garrett Park Press,
        1973.
A selective, annotated bibliography of 1, 371 references arranged in
two main parts.   Part I, Description and Comparison of Education
Systems of the World, is divided into sections on Worldwide, Conti-
nents and Regions, and Individual Countries.   Part II, International
Exchange of Persons, is divided into sections on General, Brain
Drain, Crosscultural Studies, and Evaluation of U. S. Sponsored
Study Programs Abroad.   Entries include bibliographic information,
price, and brief annotation.   Appendix A, Periodicals Dealing with
International Education.   Appendix B, Organizations: Their Acro-
nyms, Full Names, and Addresses.   Author and subject indexes.

Individual Countries

36   Apanasewicz, Nellie.   Education in the U. S. S. R. :   An Annotated
        Bibliography of English Language Materials, 1965-1973.
        Washington, D. C. :   Government Printing Office, 1974.
An annotated bibliography of 347 books, journal articles, government
publications, and reports, arranged alphabetically by 224 subject
categories.   Numerous cross-references are given to other subjects
covered.   Emphasis is given to subjects of current interest in
American education.   Author index.

37   Baron, George. A Bibliographical Guide to the English Educa-
          tional System.   3d ed.   London: University of London,
          Athlone Press, 1965.
Contains 19 bibliographical essays on reference books; periodicals;
general, primary, secondary, and higher education; youth clubs;
types of schools; agricultural education; teacher training institutions,
etc.

38   Brown, Cecily, comp.   Bibliography of Australian Education
          from Colonial Times to 1972.   Hawthorn, Victoria: Austral-
          ian Council for Educational Research, 1973.
An unannotated bibliography of 1, 702 books about Australian education.
Excludes articles, texts, government publications, and theses.   Arrangement is by broad subject headings, with works listed chronologically under subjects.   Contents are listed for some titles.   Section
A, 19th Century Views of Australian Education, has subsections for
publications 1831 to 1899, and 20th century views of 19th century
education.   Section B, Australian Education of the 20th Century, has
subsections on educational aims and policies; education in practice;
process of education; students; schools.

39   Craigie, James.   A Bibliography of Scottish Education, 1872-
          1972.   London: University of London Press, 1974.
An unannotated bibliography of printed and published material, including books, journal articles, reports, and transactions.   Covers
reference works, periodicals, acts of Parliament, biography, different types and levels of education, educational reform, educational
research, educational statistics, finance, historical studies, schools,
teachers, universities.   Index of authors, subjects, and places.

40   Fraser, Stewart E. , and Kiang-liang Hsu.   Chinese Education
          and Society: A Bibliographic Guide; The Cultural Revolution
          and Its Aftermath.   White Plains, N. Y. : International Arts
          and Sciences Press, 1972.
Items included are from English- and Chinese-language sources, with
some from Japanese, French, German, and Italian publications, most
of which are available in English translation.   In 14 sections, including bibliography and reference; general survey and background;
primary, secondary, higher, and teacher education; rural education;
student affairs; international relations in education; ideology and
education; educational development and the Great Proletarian Cultural
Revolution (1966-68); and Mao Tse-Tung's educational thought.

41   Fraser, Stewart E. , and Barbara J. Fraser.   Scandinavian
          Education: A Bibliography of English Language Materials.
          White Plains, N. Y. :   International Arts and Sciences Press,
          1973.
A briefly annotated bibliography of books and articles published 1960-
1973.   Major sections are: Scandinavia; Denmark; Norway; Sweden.
Subdivisions of these sections include general education; educational
research; preschool, primary, secondary, and higher education;
teacher education; adult education; vocational education; sex education;
administration; guidance; educational media; international studies;

bibliography. Introductory material includes "Notes on Principal Bibliographic Sources" and "Selected List of Official Sources. "

42 Passin, Herbert. Japanese Education: A Bibliography of Materials in the English Language. New York: Teachers College Press, Columbia University, 1970.
Lists 1, 500 items, including translations of Japanese works as well as those written in English, grouped under eight headings: General, Historical, American Occupation, Moral Education, Students, Teachers, Women, and Specialized. Also includes lists of serial publications, serial publications of the Japanese Ministry of Education, and journals published outside the United States. General index.

See also:

Altbach, P. G. Comparative Higher Education Abroad (No. 54).
Altbach, P. G. Higher Education in Developing Countries (No. 55).
Altbach, P. G. , and D. H. Kelly. Higher Education in Developing Nations (No. 56).
McCarthy, J. M. International List of Articles on the History of Education (No. 70).
Mezirow, J. D. , and D. Epley. Adult Education in Developing Countries (No. 26).
Paulston, R. G. Non-Formal Education (No. 84).

Culturally Disadvantaged

43 Culturally Disadvantaged: A Bibliography and Keyword-Out-of-Context (KWOC) Index. Detroit: Wayne State University Press, 1967.
The first section is a subject index arranged alphabetically by keywords. The second section is a bibliography of 1, 400 books, monographs, reports, and periodical articles, arranged alphabetically by an author code.

44 Educator's Complete ERIC Handbook. Phase One: Educational Research Information Center Researches on the Education of Disadvantaged Children. Englewood Cliffs, N. J. : Prentice-Hall, 1967.
Abstracts of 1, 700 research reports on the education of culturally deprived or otherwise disadvantaged children. Part I consists of 23 chapters, each of which is devoted to a pioneering educational project. Part II presents a number of other programs developed simultaneously, including documents on civil rights, curriculum guides for the gifted, mentally retarded, migrants, etc.

45 Quay, Richard H. , comp. In Pursuit of Equality of Educational Opportunity: A Selective Bibliography and Guide to the Research Literature. New York: Garland Publishing, 1977.

An unannotated bibliography of books, parts of books, journal articles, ERIC documents, and other materials, most of which were published in the 1960s and 1970s.   Arrangement is alphabetical by author or main entry.   Also includes a bibliography of bibliographies, a list of sources consulted, and a subject index.

46   U. S. Educational Research Information Center.   Catalog of
          Selected Documents on the Disadvantaged.   2 vols.   Washing-
          ton, D. C.:   Government Printing Office, 1966.
Vol. 1, Number and Author Index, lists 1, 740 documents on the educational needs of the disadvantaged.   Citations are in numerical sequence.   Vol. 2 is a subject index.

47   Weinberg, Meyer.   The Education of the Minority Child: A
          Comprehensive Bibliography of 10, 000 Selected Entries.
          Chicago: Integrated Education Associates, 1970.
Includes selected references to books, reports, articles, dissertations, and government publications on the education of minority children in the United States and elsewhere.   Emphasis is on the education of black children, but references are also included on Mexican Ameri-can, Puerto Rican, Indian American, Oriental, poor white, Jewish, and European immigrant children.   Most of the references are to literature of the past 70 years, but for black and Indian American children references go back to the colonial period.   In addition to sections on specific ethnic groups, some other sections are: Chil-dren: Problems and Change; The American Scene, with entries ar-ranged by state; School Organization; The Teacher in the Classroom; Educational Deprivation; Innovative Approaches; Student Movements; Law and Government; Social Conditions; Community; Church; The World Scene, divided by country; a list of 500 periodicals with ad-dresses; and a list of 250 bibliographies.   Author index.

Curriculum

48   Tyler, Louise L.   A Selected Guide to Curriculum Literature:
          An Annotated Bibliography.   Washington, D. C.:   National
          Education Association, Center for the Study of Instruction, 1970.
Includes references to 67 books and articles, organized "according to a stated conceptualization of curriculum"--Foreword.   Gives for each book bibliographic information, analysis of structure, interpre-tation of contents, and criticism.   Author and title indexes.

Economics of Education

49   Blaug, Mark.   Economics of Education: A Selected Annotated
          Bibliography.   3d ed.   New York: Pergamon Press, 1978.
An annotated, classified bibliography of 2, 000 references to published literature in English, French, and German, including books, journal articles, government publications, and UNESCO publications.   Also includes a number of unpublished papers available from national institutions and international agencies.   In two major divisions: A,

Developed Countries, with subdivisions for general surveys, the
economic contribution of education, the economic aspects of education, educational planning, brain drain and international trade, social
mobility and reserves of talent, the politics of education, and the
economics of health; B, Developing Countries, with subdivisions for
general surveys, economic contribution of education, economic
aspects of education, and educational planning.   Most of the subdivisions are further subdivided.   Within each section items are
arranged chronologically by date of publication.   Each section is
introduced by a bibliographic essay reviewing the literature in that
area and pointing out main lines of advance in research.   Section
C is a bibliography of bibliographies.   Section D contains 65 items
received too late to be classified.   Index of Authors and Index of
Countries.

Educational Technology

50   Aa, H. J. van der, and others, eds.   Computers and Educa-
        tion: An International Bibliography on Computer Education.
        New York   Science Associates International, 1970.
An annotated bibliography of 1,788 references to books and articles.
In sections on computers in primary schools, computers in secondary
schools, computers in colleges and universities, educational technology, courses in universities and other schools, training for automation, and professions in the field of automation.

51   Cantwell, Zita M., and Hortense A. Doyle.   Instructional
        Technology: An Annotated Bibliography.   Metuchen, N. J. :
        Scarecrow Press, 1974.
An annotated bibliography of 958 journal articles, research reports,
and government publications, most of which were published in
English between 1960 and 1972.   Emphasis is on studies of actual
use of an aspect of instructional technology in a learning situation.
Covers nine types of technology: general audiovisual media; videotape; instructional television; radio; programmed instruction; language laboratory; computer-assisted instruction; dial access; simulation and games.   Entries are arranged alphabetically by author and
numbered.   Entries give bibliographic information, an annotation, a
code to indicate category of technology, and educational level.   Also
includes listings by category of technology, and a subject index.

52   Razik, Taher A., ed.   Bibliography of Programmed Instruction
        and Computer Assisted Instruction.   Englewood Cliffs, N. J. :
        Educational Technology Publications, 1971.
Includes references to books, doctoral dissertations, ERIC publications, reports, and journal articles published between 1954 and 1970.
Also contains selected references to unpublished papers, speeches,
and memoranda.   The section on programmed instruction is subdivided into sections on general, characteristics, program types,
program forms, type of response, subject audience, content subject,
and research.   The section on computer-assisted instruction is not
subdivided since the body of literature is smaller.

53   Taggart, Dorothy T.   A Guide to Sources in Educational Media
          and Technology.   Metuchen, N. J.:   Scarecrow Press, 1975.
Contains 310 annotated references to books and periodicals.   Includes
sections on the history of the audiovisual movement; selection of
media materials; facility planning; instructional films and television;
programmed instruction; computer-assisted instruction; design and
production of instructional materials; pre-service and in-service
training of teachers; administration of educational media; media in
curriculum design; instructional systems analysis, design, and
development; system evaluation; learning theory; media research;
aspects of change.   Also includes a select bibliography of periodicals
on educational media; a list of professional organizations with
descriptive notes including titles of their publications; an annotated
list of 16 indexes to media; a directory of publishers; and author
and title indexes.

Higher Education

54   Altbach, Philip G. , ed.   Comparative Higher Education Abroad:
          Bibliography and Analysis.   New York: Praeger Publishers.
          1976.
Part I is a comprehensive bibliography of 1, 732 books, articles, and
dissertations on higher education in all countries except the United
States, most of which were published in 1973 and 1974.   Arrangement is by region and country.   References are in English, French,
Spanish, and German.   A subject cross-reference index follows the
bibliography.   Part II, Book Notes, is a listing of significant books
published in 1973 and 1974 on comparative higher education, with a
descriptive review of each.   Part III contains two bibliographical
essays, "Economics of Higher Education, " and "Japanese Higher
Education, " each consisting of a critical review of the literature and
a selected bibliography.   Appendix A is a list of international and
regional agencies concerned with research and publication on higher
education.   Appendix B is a list of publications of the International
Council for Educational Development.

55   Altbach, Philip G.   Higher Education in Developing Countries:
          A Select Bibliography.   With the assistance of Bradley
          Nystrom.   Occasional Papers in International Affairs, No.
          24.   Cambridge, Mass.:   Center for International Affairs,
          Harvard University, 1970.
An unannotated bibliography of books, journal articles, official
documents, and reports arranged by region, subdivided by geographical area or country.   Emphasis is on material published 1960-1970.
Includes references in English, French, Spanish, and Portuguese.
The main section is preceded by a general section divided into
Bibliographies, Developing Countries, and Theoretical Perspectives
in Higher Education.   Also includes an introductory essay on higher
education in developing countries.   No index.

56   Altbach, Philip G. , and David H. Kelly.   Higher Education in
          Developing Nations: A Selected Bibliography, 1969-1974.
          New York: Praeger Publishers, 1975.

An unannotated list of 2, 438 books, journal articles, dissertations, publications of public and private agencies, government and international agencies. References are in English, French, Spanish, and German. Covers all the countries of Africa, Latin America, and Asia, except Japan. The main section is arranged by region and country. The second section is a cross-reference index according to major analytical categories with numbers referring to the main section. Also includes an introductory essay on higher education in developing countries, and a list of journals. An appendix lists international and regional agencies concerned with research and publication on higher education.

57   Beach, Mark. A Bibliographic Guide to American Colleges
      and Universities from Colonial Times to the Present.
      Westport, Conn.: Greenwood Press, 1975.
An unannotated list of 2, 806 books, articles, and dissertations relating to the history of specific institutions of higher learning. Arrangement is by state, and alphabetical by names of institutions under each state. Index of institutions and personal names as subjects.

58   Chambers, Fredrick, comp. Black Higher Education in the
      United States: A Selected Bibliography on Negro Higher
      Education and Historically Black Colleges and Universities.
      Westport, Conn.: Greenwood Press, 1978.
A selective, unannotated bibliography of 3, 700 references arranged by type of publication in six chapters: Doctoral Dissertations, 1918-1976; Institutional Histories, 1867-1976; Periodical Literature, 1857-1976; Masters' Theses, 1922-1974; Selected Books and General References; Miscellaneous (autobiographies, biographies, proceedings, reports, government publications). Entries in each chapter are arranged alphabetically by author, except in Chapter 2, in which the arrangement is first by state, then by institution, and alphabetical by author under each institution. Includes an introduction on black higher education by James P. Louis. Index of subjects including names of institutions and personal names as subjects.

59   Dressel, Paul L. , and Sally B. Pratt. World of Higher Educa-
      tion: An Annotated Guide to the Major Literature. San
      Francisco: Jossey-Bass Publishers, 1971.
A selected, annotated bibliography of 700 references to books, articles, reports, unpublished dissertations, and government publications. Includes major sections on institutional research as a field of activity; governance, administration, management; students; faculty and staff; curriculum and instruction; research methodology; and related bibliographies and other reference materials. Index of authors and titles.

60   Harris, Robin S. , and Arthur Tremblay. A Bibliography of
      Higher Education in Canada. Toronto: University of
      Toronto Press, 1960. Supplement, 1965. Supplement, 1971.
The first volume is an unannotated list of 4, 000 books, pamphlets, theses, dissertations, and periodical articles in a classified arrange-

ment.   Part I, Background, contains sections on Canadian culture
and Canadian education.   Part II, Higher Education in Canada, includes sections on history and organization, curriculum and teaching,
the professor, and the student.   Entries are arranged chronologically
in each section.   Includes references in English and French.   Each
of the supplements contains almost 4,000 entries.

61   Mayhew, Lewis B.   The Literature of Higher Education.   San
        Francisco: Jossey-Bass Publishers, 1972.
Includes reviews of 200 books in a classified arrangement.   Sections
are: Trends; Administration, Organization, and Governance; Student
Protest; Students and Their Affairs; Curricular and Instructional
Concerns; Educational Opinion and Policy; Types of Institutions;
Faculty and Their Affairs; History, More or Less; Bibliographies.
Reviews are about one page in length.   Index of titles and authors.

62   Powell, John P.   Universities and University Education: A
        Select Bibliography.   2 vols.   London: National Foundation
        for Educational Research in England and Wales, 1966-1971.
Vol. 1 is a list of 1,189 references to journal articles, books,
pamphlets, reports, and proceedings published to the end of 1964.
Arranged in sections on General; American Universities; British
Universities; University History, General; History, Institutions; Aims
and Functions; Curriculum; Teaching Methods; Teaching Aids;
Teaching Methods, Special Fields; Examinations; Libraries; Academic
Profession; Students; Study Methods.   Brief annotations are given for
some entries.   Author index.   Vol. 2, in a similar arrangement,
contains 2,301 references to material published 1965-1970.   Primarily
a guide to higher education in Britain, but American and Australian
as well as British sources are included for coverage of certain fields.

63   Quay, Richard H.   Research in Higher Education: A Guide to
        Source Bibliographies.   New York: College Entrance Exami-
        nation Board, 1976.
A bibliography of bibliographies and reviews of literature, published
1960-1975, on all levels of higher education from the junior college
through graduate education.   Includes 572 references, arranged
alphabetically by author, with a subject classification scheme.   Some
entries are briefly annotated.

64   Silver, Harold, and S. John Teague.   The History of British
        Universities, 1800-1969, Excluding Oxford and Cambridge:
        A Bibliography.   London: Society for Research into Higher
        Education, 1970.
An unannotated bibliography in sections on general histories and
histories of individual institutions.   The first part contains lists of
books, pamphlets, reports, theses, and periodical articles on the
general history of British universities, general histories of education,
histories of relevant further education, academic disciplines, university administration, and academic biographies.   The remainder
of the bibliography lists works about individual universities, arranged
alphabetically by name of university.   Materials on each institution
include source material, histories, periodical publications, and report literature.   Index of personal names.

65   Willingham, Warren W.   The Source Book for Higher Education:
     A Critical Guide to Literature and Information on Access to
     Higher Education.   New York: College Entrance Examination
     Board,   1973.
A selective, annotated bibliography of more than 1, 500 books, journal
articles, reports, and government publications in five sections: I,
Access Processes (student guidance, financing education, admissions,
educational process, educational evaluation, manpower utilization);
II, The System (organization and administration, structure of the
system); III, The Students (distribution of talent, educational opportunity, selected student groups); IV, Access Agents (organizations,
programs); V, Sources of Information (periodicals, special resources).
Author and subject indexes.

History and Philosophy of Education

66   Broudy, Harry S. , and others.   Philosophy of Education: An
     Organization of Topics and Selected Sources.   Urbana:
     University of Illinois Press, 1967.   Supplement, 1969.
A briefly annotated bibliography of books, articles, parts of books,
and dissertations in a classified arrangement.   Sections are: Philo-
sophical Background; Nature and Aims of Education; Curriculum
Design and Validation; Organization and Policy; Teaching-Learning;
Educational Research and the "Science of Education"; Philosophy of
Education as a Subject; Index of Topics; History of Educational
Thought.   The supplement, by Christiana M. Smith and Harry S.
Broudy, adds more than 500 items from the literature published
since 1967.   Organized by the same scheme as the first volume.
Author index.

67   Cordasco, Francesco, and William W. Brickman.   A Bibliog-
     raphy of American Educational History: An Annotated and
     Classified Guide.   New York: AMS Press, 1975.
A briefly annotated list of 3, 000 books and articles with primary
focus on the history of American education.   Part I includes sections
on general bibliographies and encyclopedic works, collections of
source materials, historiography of American education, and comprehensive histories of American education.   Part II contains sections
on elementary education; secondary education; vocational education;
education in individual states; higher education; school books, children's literature, and ethnic bias in instructional materials; the
teaching profession; church, state, and education; federal government and education; education of women; biographies of educators;
foreign influences on American education; and contemporary issues.
Part III is a listing by period from the colonial period to and including the 20th century.

68   Herbst, Jurgen.   The History of American Education.   North-
     brook, Ill.:   AHM Publishing, 1973.
An unannotated bibliography of books and journal articles.   Part I,
General Works (bibliography; historiography; texts; anthologies;
special subjects; transatlantic relations; religious education; church,

state, and education; government, courts, and education; education of
minorities; education of women; education in individual states; vocational, secondary, and higher education).   Part II, The Colonial
Period (European background; general works; The South; Middle
Colonies; New England; higher education; the professions, science,
and learning).   Part III, From Revolution to Reconstruction (general
works; the founding fathers and national leaders; geographic regions;
higher education; scientific, technical, and professional education;
black Americans).   Part IV, America in the Urban Age (general
works; response to immigration; response to industrial civilization;
progressive education; education as a discipline; the schools; higher
education).   Author index.

69   Higson, C. W. J.   Sources for the History of Education.
        London: Library Association, 1967.   Supplement, 1976.
An unannotated list of books and pamphlets in the libraries of the
institutes and schools of education of several British universities.
Both the first volume and the supplement contain listings of books
published from the 15th century to 1870, textbooks and children's
books published 1801-1870, and government publications up to and
including 1918.   The first volume contains more than 5,500 entries.
The 1976 supplement contains approximately 5,000 entries for
material added to the libraries of the institutes and schools of education from 1965 to 1974.   Both volumes include a subject index,
and an author index to government publications.

70   McCarthy, Joseph M.   An International List of Articles on the
        History of Education, Published in Non-Educational Journals,
        1965-1974.   New York: Garland Publishing, 1977.
An unannotated list of references from 500 journals, including publications in several languages.   Arranged by regions, subdivided by
countries.   Major sections are: I, Europe; II, Africa and the Near
East; III, Far East; IV, Oceania including Australia and New Zealand;
V, Central and South America; VI, North America.   Entries are
listed alphabetically by author in each section.   Also includes a list
of journal abbreviations and an index of names and authors.

71   Park, Joe.   The Rise of American Education: An Annotated
        Bibliography.   Evanston, Ill.:   Northwestern University
        Press, 1965.
"An annotated bibliography of the most important books in the
history of American education and of many related Early American
Imprints."--Introd.   Major sections are: I, Textbooks; II, European
Backgrounds; III, Studies in the Development of American Education;
IV, Histories in Higher Education; V, Elementary and Secondary
Education; VI, Higher Education; VII, Biographies, Fiction, and
Journals; VIII, Contemporary Issues and Movements in American
Education; IX, American Antiquarian Society Microprints; X, Doctoral
Dissertations on Microfilm; XI, Guides to Sources in History and
Education.   Section X is not annotated.   Includes a list of publishers.
No index.

72   Powell, John P.   Philosophy of Education: A Select Bibliog-
        raphy. 2d ed. Manchester, Eng.: Manchester University
        Press, 1970.
An unannotated list of 707 references to books and journal articles
in a classified arrangement. Includes brief sections on bibliographies,
anthologies, books, general works on philosophy, nature of philosophy
of education, philosophy of education and teacher training, education
as a discipline, nature of educational theory, concept of education,
indoctrination, moral education, aesthetic education, teaching,
learning, psychological concepts, creativity, knowledge, curriculum,
equality, freedom and authority, punishment, educational institutions,
educational theories, miscellaneous. Also includes a list of periodicals cited and an author index.

73   Winick, Mariann P.   The Progressive Education Movement: An
        Annotated Bibliography.   New York: Garland Publishing,
        1978.
A bibliography of 509 references to books, journal articles, and
government publications, arranged in categories on history, philosophy,
theory, comparative, criticism, curriculum, teacher training, evaluation and record-keeping, experimental schools, administration, parent
involvement, and journals.   The comparative section includes materials on the movement in other countries.   Author index.

        See also:

        Beach, Mark.   A Bibliographic Guide to American Colleges and
            Universities from Colonial Times to the Present (No. 57).
        Chambers, Fredrick. Black Higher Education in the United
            States (No. 58).
        Silver, Harold, and S. J. Teague.   History of British Univer-
            sities (No. 64).

Labor Education

74   Dwyer, Richard E.   Labor Education in the U.S.: An Annotated
        Bibliography.   Metuchen, N.J.: Scarecrow Press, 1977.
An extensive bibliography of more than 1, 900 books, periodical
articles, ERIC documents, archival collections, and oral-history
collections, tracing the historical development of labor education in
the United States.   In three major sections: Workers' Education,
Labor Education, and Labor Studies.   Each section is divided into
five subsections: philosophy and goals; curriculum and methods;
individual organizations; general, historical, and descriptive studies;
and miscellaneous.   Entries are briefly annotated.   Separate sections
for archival collections and oral histories are arranged by institution
or organization.   An introductory essay provides an overview of the
history of the workers' education movement from its beginning around
1900 to the present.   Includes a list of more than 80 journals
searched, a subject index, and an author index.

Language Teaching

75   Allen, Virginia F., and Sidney Forman. English as a Second
        Language: A Comprehensive Bibliography. New York:
        Teachers College Press, Columbia University, 1967.
An unannotated bibliography of books and other materials in a classified arrangement. Major sections are: Linguistics; Language
Culture Area; Language Learning; Texts; and Reference. Each section is further subdivided. Includes author and title indexes and a
list of publishers.

76   Centre for Information on Language Teaching. A Language
        Teaching Bibliography. 2d ed. Cambridge, Eng.: University
        Press, 1972.
A selective, annotated bibliography of books on the theory and practice
of foreign-language teaching. Section 1, Language, covers aspects
of linguistics applicable to the teaching of any language. Section 2,
Language Teaching, covers the contributions of psychology, and the
methodology and techniques of classroom teaching applicable to
language teaching in general. Section 3, Particular Languages,
covers the teaching of English, French, German, Italian, Russian,
and Spanish. Author index.

77   Frey, Herschel J. Teaching Spanish: A Critical Bibliographic
        Survey. Rowley, Mass.: Newbury House Publishers, 1974.
A selective bibliography of Spanish applied linguistics and teaching
methodology. Includes 119 books and articles. Excludes unpublished
dissertations and papers and other materials not readily available.
Entries give a lengthy (one page or more) description and critique.
Book reviews are cited for some of the longer studies. In 12
sections: I, General Studies; II, Teaching Phonology; III, Teaching
Grammar; IV, Listening and Speaking; V, Reading and Writing; VI,
Drills and Drilling; VII, Methodology and Method Evaluation; VIII,
Material Evaluation; IX, The Language Laboratory; X, Programed
Instruction; XI, Testing; XII, Miscellaneous. The appendix includes
a list of bibliographies, and a list of selected works on Spanish
phonology and Spanish grammar. Also includes an index to books
and articles reviewed, arranged by author under the topic headings
of the bibliography, giving author, title, and publication date for
each entry.

78   McConnell, Ruth E., and H. P. Wakefield. Teaching English
        as an Additional Language: Annotated Bibliography. Van-
        couver: University of British Columbia, Extension Depart-
        ment, 1970.
A bibliography of books and articles in 15 sections: I, Methodology;
II, Materials; III, Addresses for Additional Information and Materials;
IV, General Texts; V, Phonology; VI, Contrastive Studies and Bi-
lingualism; VII, Grammars, Traditional; VIII, Grammars, Structural;
IX, Grammars, Transformational, Generative; X, History of the
English Language; XI, Journal Articles; XII, Related Fields; XIII,
Reference Books; XIV, Periodicals; XV, Bibliographies. Appendix:
Phonemic System of Canadian English.

79 Robinson, Janet O. An Annotated Bibliography of Modern
      Language Teaching: Books and Articles, 1946-1967. New
      York: Oxford University Press, 1969.
Following a general modern-language section, there are sections on
individual languages (French, German, Italian, Russian, and Spanish).
Each section includes references on curriculum planning, policy and
administration, training and qualifications of teachers, planning and
conducting the lesson, examinations, teaching methods principles,
teaching of special skills, teaching of literature, teaching of the
language for vocational purposes, teaching different age groups,
teaching exceptional students, and teaching aids.

Learning Disabilities

80 Chicorel Index to Learning Disorders. Edited by Marietta
      Chicorel. Chicorel Index Series, Vols. 18 and 18A. New
      York: Chicorel Library Publishing, 1975.
A comprehensive listing of more than 2, 500 publications under 42
subjects.   Listing under each subject is alphabetical by author.
Entries include bibliographic information, price, and abstract.

81 Chicorel Index to Reading Disabilities: An Annotated Guide.
      Edited by Marietta Chicorel. Chicorel Index Series, Vol.
      14. New York: Chicorel Library Publishing, 1974.
Annotates and evaluates more than 600 books and articles dealing
with various aspects of reading disabilities.   Each entry includes
bibliographic data, scope, level of use, and rating of usefulness.
Arrangement is alphabetical by author.   The Subject Index is a
listing of books under 32 subjects.

Multicultural Education

82 Bengelsdorf, Winnie. Assisted by Susan Norwitch and Louise
      Vrande. Ethnic Studies in Higher Education: State of the
      Art and Bibliography. Washington, D. C.: American
      Association of State Colleges and Universities, 1972.
The first section, State of the Art, contains views of experts on
ethnicity, population figures on ethnic groups, federal impact,
society factors influencing ethnic studies, the state scene,
conferences, foundation effort, role of higher education in ethnic
studies, and summary of survey findings.   The bibliography is in
sections for ethnic groups: Asian-American Studies; Black Studies;
Chicano Studies; Indian Studies; Puerto Rican and Other Spanish-
Speaking American Studies; White Ethnic Studies; Multi-Ethnic Studies;
and Teacher Training.   Each section is subdivided by surveys and
research, pending research, general information, history and sociology sources, reference sources, periodicals, bibliography, and an
institutional list.   Also includes sections on minority enrollment and
minority opportunities.   Entries are annotated.   Some have ERIC
numbers.   Author and title indexes.

83   Gollnick, Donna M. , Frank H. Klassen, and Joost Yff. Multi-
      cultural Education and Ethnic Studies in the United States:
      An Analysis and Annotated Bibliography of Selected ERIC
      Documents. Washington, D. C. : American Association of
      Colleges for Teacher Education and ERIC Clearinghouse on
      Teacher Education, 1976.
A selective, annotated bibliography of about 300 ERIC documents
relating to multicultural education and ethnic studies in the United
States.   Arranged in five major divisions: concept materials
(teacher education, general reports, surveys); classroom materials
(teacher education, junior high/high school); curriculum materials
(preschool/elementary, junior high/high school, college, general);
program materials (teacher education, college, general); and other
materials (bibliographies, directories).   Information on each document includes author, title, institution or publisher, date of publication, number of pages, ERIC index number, indication of availability,
ethnic identification code, and annotation.   The bibliography is followed by a chapter on analysis of the bibliography including an
explanation of ERIC indexing, ERIC searching, limitations, observa-
tions, implications and recommendations.   An introductory chapter
is "Multicultural Education - A Literature Review. " Appendix A
lists libraries that have ERIC microfiche collections.   Appendix B
is a glossary of ERIC terms.   No index.

Nonformal Education

84   Paulston, Rolland G. , ed.   Non-Formal Education: An Anno-
      tated International Bibliography.   New York: Praeger
      Publishers, 1972.
A selected, annotated bibliography of 875 items, including scholarly
and popular publications and unpublished materials in English,
Spanish, and French.   Covers theory and practice in nonformal
education in developed and underdeveloped countries.   Main sections
are: Orientation and Basic Issues; Area Studies; Organizations
Conducting Programs; Target Learner Populations; Program Content;
Instructional Methodologies and Materials; Reference Materials and
Publications.   Area index and author index.

Politics and Education

85   Harman, G. S.   Politics of Education: A Bibliographical
      Guide.   New York: Crane, Russak, 1974.
A comprehensive, partially annotated bibliography on education and
politics.   International in coverage with emphasis on Australia,
United States, Britain, and Canada.   Covers alternative patterns of
control of education, influence of pressure groups and political
parties, conflicts between educational and governmental institutions
and agencies, student unrest, political functions of schools and their
contribution to political institutions and processes.   Index.

Private Schools

86   Zeidner, Nancy I.   Private Elementary and Secondary Educa-
        tion: A Bibliography of Selected Publications (1950-1974).
        Washington, D. C.:   Council for American Private Education,
        1976.
An annotated bibliography of 500 books and pamphlets published in
the United States and England.   In sections covering the status of
private education, its relation to church and government, characteristics of church-related education, nontraditional approaches to
private education, issues for administrators, teaching methods and
materials, and religious instruction.   Index.

Schools-Desegregation

87   Jones, Leon.   From Brown to Boston: Desegregation in Edu-
        cation, 1954-1974.   2 vols.   Metuchen, N. J.:   Scarecrow
        Press,   1979.
Reviews the literature of desegregation in education in America from
the Brown decision of 1954 to 1974.   Includes more than 5, 000 abstracts
of books, articles, and legal cases.   Also includes a lengthy introduction;
a foreword by Roy Wilkins; an author-title index; and a subject index.

88   U. S. National Institute of Education.   The Desegregation Liter-
        ature: A Critical Appraisal.   Washington, D. C.:   National
        Institute of Education, 1976.
A bibliography of books, articles, reports, papers and other materials on school desegregation and educational equality, the process of
interracial schooling, and research on desegregation in school and
classroom situations.

89   Weinberg, Meyer.   School Integration: A Comprehensive
        Classified Bibliography.   Chicago: Integrated Education
        Associates, 1967.
An unannotated bibliography of 3, 100 books, periodical articles, parts
of books, government publications, and unpublished reports.   In 15
sections, including Effects on Children; Places and Practices; New
Approaches; Law and Government; Strategy and Tactics; School and
Work; Historical; Deprivation; Role of the Church; Community;
Spanish-Americans; American Indians; General; Foreign; New Periodicals.   Arranged alphabetically by author within sections.   Also includes a list of periodicals used and an author index.

Sociology of Education

90   Hartnett, Anthony.   Sociology of Education: An Introductory
        Guide to the Literature.   University of Liverpool, School of
        Education, Library Publication No. 3.   Liverpool, Eng.:
        University of Liverpool, 1975.
Part One, Introduction to Sociology, and Introduction to the Sociology
of Education; Part Two, Bibliographies of Selected Topics: Educa-

tion and the Economic System; Education and Politics; Education and
Family Life; Education and the Local Community; Education, Social
Class and Achievement; The Sociological Study of Educational Organizations; The Teaching Profession; Sociological Approaches to Educational Documents and to Official Publications Concerning Education;
Innovation and Education; Methods of Empirical Research in the
Sociology of Education.   Part Three, Searching for the Literature,
additional sources of information.   Some references are briefly
annotated.   No index.

Special Education

91   Edgington, Ruth, and Sam D. Clements.   Indexed Bibliography
        on the Educational Management of Children with Learning
        Disabilities (Minimal Brain Dysfunction).   Chicago: Argus
        Communications, 1967.
A selective, unannotated bibliography of 370 books and periodical
articles, arranged alphabetically by author.   A number key in
table form for 19 subject areas precedes the bibliography.   Subject
areas are: general concepts of education for children with learning
disabilities; perception; cerebral dominance; conceptualization--think-
ing disorders; behavior disorders; language disorders; speech disorders; team approach in diagnosis and treatment; counseling with
parents; types of programs; ancillary services; basic tool subjects;
classroom management; educational supplies and devices; outlook
for the child's future; vocational guidance; teacher characteristics;
teacher training; public relations.

92   Goldberg, I. Ignacy.   Selected Bibliography of Special Educa-
        tion.   New York: Teachers College, Columbia University,
        1967.
An unannotated bibliography of books and journal articles arranged in
sections on the physically handicapped, mentally retarded, gifted,
emotionally and socially handicapped, multiply handicapped, and
habilitation of the mentally retarded.   Each section is subdivided.
Entries are arranged alphabetically by author in each subdivision.
Author index.

93   Laubenfels, Jean.   The Gifted Student: An Annotated Bibliogra-
        phy.   Contemporary Problems of Childhood, No. 1.   West-
        port, Conn.:   Greenwood Press, 1977.
A bibliography of 1, 329 selected references to journal articles, books,
chapters in books, conference reports, government documents, pamphlets, and dissertations.   References are grouped in ten major
categories: General Introductory Material; Causal Factors; Characteristics of the Gifted; Identification Techniques; Programming for
the Gifted; Special Problems of the Gifted; Longitudinal Studies; Related Research; Bibliographies; and Miscellaneous.   Brief annotations
are given for all entries except dissertations.   In entries for dissertations, references are given to Dissertation Abstracts International.
All publications included are in English.   Covers primarily material
published since 1961, but some earlier publications of importance are

included for background material.   Appendixes: A, Some Individuals
and Organizations Concerned with the Gifted; B, List of Instruments
Useful in Identifying the Gifted; C, Audiovisual Materials for Professional Use; D, Media Aids for Student Use; E, Basic Bibliographic
Tools.   Author Index and Selective Key Word Index.

94   Thomas, D. J.   A Guide to the Literature of Special Education.
     Liverpool University Education Library Publication No. 2.
     Liverpool, Eng.:   Liverpool University Press, 1968.
A classified list of references to works published 1959-1966 on
handicapped children (general), slow-learning children, children with
communication difficulties, children with impaired hearing and
visual defects, the physically handicapped, cerebral palsied children,
children with neurological handicaps, and emotionally disturbed children.   Also includes a list of British societies and organizations
concerned with handicapped children, and a list of journals dealing
with aspects of special education.   Author index.

95   U. S. Maternal and Child Health Service.   Bibliography on
     Speech, Hearing and Language in Relation to Mental Re-
     tardation, 1900-1968.   By Maryann Peins.   Washington,
     D. C.:   Government Printing Office, 1970.
A comprehensive list of references in seven categories: Speech and
Language Behavior; Assessment of Speech and Language of the Mentally
Retarded; Hearing: Assessment, Hearing Problems, Rehabilitation,
Research, and Related Facets; Habilitation Procedures: Speech,
Language, and Oral Communication; Research: Needs and Trends;
Books, Chapters, and Research Projects; Dissertations, Theses, and
Unpublished Materials.

Students

96   Altbach, Philip G. , and David H. Kelly.   American Students:
     A Selected Bibliography on Student Activism and Related
     Topics.   Lexington, Mass.:   Lexington Books, 1973.
A comprehensive bibliography of materials on student activism in
American higher education, and a more selective guide to the litera-
ture on other aspects of American students and student life.   Major
divisions are: Students and Student Activism; Minority Students in
American Higher Education; and Students and Student Life in Ameri-
ca.   Also includes a 60-page introductory essay by P. G. Altbach,
"Student Activism and Academic Research: Action and Reaction. "
Student Activism outside the United States is covered in P. G. Altbach,
Select Bibliography on Students, Politics, and Higher Education
(Cambridge, Mass.:   Harvard Center for International Affairs, 1970).

Urban Education

97   Spear, George E. , and Donald W. Mocker.   Urban Education:
     A Guide to Information Sources.   Detroit: Gale Research,
     1978.
A selective bibliography of books, parts of books, journal articles,

and research reports.   In three parts: (1) preschool, elementary,
and secondary education; (2) urban higher education; (3) adult education.   The first part includes sections on changing population patterns in urban areas, improvement of instruction in urban schools,
training and recruitment of teachers, community control, and
prospects of urban education.   The second part contains sections on
nontraditional programs, citizen involvement, programs for minorities, and staff training.   The third section covers finances, partici-
pation and recruitment, curriculum development, and synergy among
institutions and organizations.   In each section entries are arranged
alphabetically by author.   Most entries are briefly annotated.   Some
include ERIC numbers.   Author, title, and subject indexes.

Vocational Education

98   Cordasco, Francesco.   A Bibliography of Vocational Education:
        An Annotated Guide.   New York: AMS Press, 1977.
Lists 3, 000 books, articles, dissertations, and reports on vocational,
industrial, manual, trade, and career education, with brief annotations.   Arranged by types of material.   Subject and author indexes.

99   Goodman, Leonard H.   Current Career and Occupational Litera-
        ture: 1973-1977.   New York: H. W. Wilson, 1978.
The first volume in a series to be published every two years.   Part
I lists 40 vocational series from 28 publishers.   Part II lists 2, 400
books and pamphlets under 450 occupational headings.   Entries include descriptive annotations and age levels, kindergarten through
adult.

100   U. S. National Institute of Education.   Key Resources in Career
        Education: An Annotated Guide.   By David V. Tiedeman,
        Marilyn Schreiber, and Tyrus R. Wessell, Jr.   Washing-
        ton, D. C. : Government Printing Office, 1976.
A classified bibliography of books, pamphlets, reports, and ERIC
documents.   Arranged in sections on concepts of career education,
factors in implementing career education, model and program
construction, resource guides, and organizational resources.   Entries give author, title, date, number of pages, availability, subject,
intended audience, purpose, and summary of contents.

Women's Education

101   Astin, Helen S. , Nancy Suniewich, and Susan Dweck.   Women:
        A Bibliography on Their Education and Careers.   Washing-
        ton, D. C. : Human Service Press, 1971.
An annotated bibliography of 352 books, articles, papers, and
doctoral dissertations.   Arranged in seven main categories: De-
terminants of Career Choice; Marital and Familial Status of Working
Women; Women in the World of Work; Developmental Studies; History and Economics of Women at Work; Commentaries and Policy
Papers; Continuing Education of Women.   Most publications included

are based on empirical research.   Historical accounts, policy papers, and articles are also included.   Author and subject indexes.

102   U. S. Office of Education.   Resources in Women's Educational
        Equity.   Washington, D. C. :   Government Printing Office,
        1977.
Contains résumés of documents and journal articles relating to educational opportunities for women, from nine machine-readable data bases.   Arrangement is by data base.   Subject and author indexes.

103   Westervelt, Esther M. , and Deborah A. Fixter.   With the
        assistance of Margaret Comstock.   Women's Higher and
        Continuing Education: An Annotated Bibliography with
        Selected References on Related Aspects of Women's Lives.
        New York: College Entrance Examination Board, 1971.
A classified, annotated bibliography of books, journal articles, and government publications.   Sections are: Statements, Studies, and Documents Pertaining to Women's Status; Statements on the Education of Women; Basic Research Relevant to Women's Education (Theories and Research on Women's Social and Cultural Roles, on Feminine Psychology and Development, and on Sex Differences in Intellectual Characteristics and Academic Performance); Educational Behavior and Aspirations of High School Students; Educational Behavior and Aspirations of College Students; Educational Behavior and Aspirations of Graduate Students; Educational Behavior and Aspirations of the Mature Woman; Women and Employment; Bibliographies on Related Topics: A, On the Education and Continuing Education of Women; B, On Women in the Labor Force; C, General, Multifaceted, or Specialized.   No index.

II. PERIODICALS

A. Directories of Periodicals

Periodical Directories Covering All Fields

104 Katz, William, and Berry G. Richards. Magazines for Libraries: For the General Reader and School, Junior College, College, University, and Public Libraries. 3d ed. New York: R. R. Bowker, 1978.
A directory of 6, 500 American, Canadian, and foreign periodicals recommended for libraries. Arranged by subject and alphabetically by title under each subject. At the beginning of each subject section there are cross-references to related subjects; a list of basic periodicals and basic abstracts and indexes for that subject field; and an introduction explaining inclusion of titles. Entries include title, date of first issue, frequency, price, editor, publisher, address; indication of indexes, illustrations, and book reviews; circulation figures; availability of microform; month when volume ends; where indexed or abstracted; availability of sample copies; indication of appropriate audience or type of library; and a descriptive and critical annotation. Includes a detailed table of contents, and an index of titles and subjects.

105 Standard Periodical Directory. New York: Oxbridge Communications. Biennial.
The 6th edition, 1979-1980, contains information on 68, 720 U. S. and Canadian periodicals, arranged in 230 subject categories. Includes periodicals with a frequency of at least once every two years. Includes sections on Education and related subjects. Entries give title, previous titles, publisher's name, address, and telephone number, name of editor, name of advertising director, description of editorial content, indexing and abstracting information, year established, frequency, subscription rate, price of single copy, circulation, distribution of readership, cost of advertising, size of the publication, method of printing, average number of pages per issue, use of color, and catalog number of government publications. Index of titles. Also includes a cross-index to subjects preceding the main listing.

106   Ulrich's International Periodicals Directory: A Classified Guide
        to Current Periodicals, Foreign and Domestic.   New York:
        R. R. Bowker.   Biennial.
Includes periodicals currently in print, issued more frequently than
once a year, and published at regular intervals over an indefinite
period of time.   The 17th edition, 1977-1978, lists 60, 000 periodicals arranged under 250 subject headings, and alphabetically by title
under each subject.   Information on entries includes year of first
issue, frequency, price, publisher, place of publication, editor,
circulation figures, inclusion of book reviews, illustrations and
charts, where indexed, availability of back issues, and availability
of microform.   Other sections are: Abbreviations (general, abstracting and indexing services, money symbols, micropublishers,
and country of publication codes); Scope Notes; Key to Subjects;
Cross-Index to Subjects; Cessations; Index to Publications of International Organizations; Title Index.   Kept up to date between biennial
editions by Ulrich's Quarterly, which provides information on new
serial titles, title changes, and cessations.

107   Irregular Serials and Annuals: An International Directory.
        New York: R. R. Bowker.   Biennial.
The 5th edition, 1978, is a classified list of 32, 500 currently published serials issued less frequently than twice a year, such as
proceedings, transactions, advances, progresses, reports, yearbooks,
handbooks, annual reviews, and monographic series, arranged under
256 subject headings.   Information on entries includes title, language
if other than English, year of first issue, frequency, price, publisher, address, editor, country of publication code, Dewey Decimal
classification number, notes on availability of back issues, availability of microform, where indexed, supplements and special issues,
inclusion of book reviews or media reviews, bibliography, abstracts,
illustrations, and charts.   Other sections are: Abbreviations; International Standard Serial Numbers; Scope Notes; list of subject headings
in English, French, German, and Spanish; Cross Index to Subjects;
Cessations; Index to Publications of International Organizations;
ISSN Index; and Title Index.

108   Sources of Serials: An International Publisher and Corporate
        Author Directory.   New York: R. R. Bowker, 1977.
Lists all titles in Ulrich's International Periodical Directory, Irregular Serials and Annuals, and Ulrich's Quarterly.   The first
edition, 1977, lists 90, 000 serial titles by 181 countries, alphabetically by name of country, and under each country by publisher
or corporate author.   Information on entries includes publisher or
corporate author, address, titles of publications, frequency of issue,
ISSN number, and co-publisher and distributor where applicable.
Also includes a List of Countries and Country Codes, and an International Index, which is an alphabetical list of the 63, 000 publishers
and corporate authors, with country code for each one.

109   Union List of Serials in Libraries of the United States and
        Canada.   3d ed.   5 vols.   New York: H. W. Wilson,
        1965.

An alphabetical list of 156, 449 titles.   Entries give title, publisher, place of publication, volume numbers and beginning and ending dates, variations in title, and location in libraries.   Excludes newspapers. Supplemented by New Serial Titles.

110   New Serial Titles: A Union List of Serials Commencing Publi-
      cation after December 31, 1949; 1950-1970 Cumulative.
      4 vols.   Washington, D. C.:   Library of Congress; New York:
      R. R. Bowker, 1973.   Monthly and quarterly supplements
      with annual cumulations.   1971-1975 Cumulation.   2 vols.
      Washington, D. C.:   Government Printing Office, 1976.
An alphabetical list of 220, 000 serials issued throughout the world, with information on holdings in 800 United States and Canadian libraries.   Entries include title, publisher, place of publication, beginning and ending dates, location in libraries, Dewey Decimal classification number, ISSN, and country code.   The monthly and quarterly issues give frequency, address of publisher, and sub-scription price.   New Serial Titles - Classed Subject Arrangement is published monthly without cumulation.

111   New Serial Titles, 1950-1970.   Subject Guide.   2 vols.   New
      York: R. R. Bowker, 1975.
A comprehensive subject and country index to 220, 000 titles in 800 United States and Canadian libraries.   Arranged under 255 Dewey-derived subject headings.   Arrangement under each subject is by country and title.   Includes 1, 200 cross-references.   Publications from 200 countries and international sources are included.   Entries give title, corporate author or publisher, place of publication, begin-ning date, frequency, ISSN, and Dewey classification number.

Directories of Education Periodicals

112   America's Education Press: A Classified List of Educational
      Publications Issued in the U. S. and Canada.   Glassboro,
      N. J.:   Educational Press Association of America.   Biennial.
Lists more than 2, 000 national, state, regional, and local educational periodicals issued in the United States and Canada.   Information for each includes the number of issues per year, subscription price, pub-lisher, editor, address, year founded, circulation, indication of inclusion of advertising and book reviews.

113   Arnold, Darlene B. , and Kenneth O. Doyle, Jr.   Education/
      Psychology Journals: A Scholar's Guide.   Metuchen, N. J.:
      Scarecrow Press, 1975.
An alphabetical list of 122 journals, with focus on the interface of education and psychology.   Information for each entry includes title, former title, year founded, editor's name and address, publisher and copyright holder, subscription data, description of typical content of articles (purpose, emphasis, scope), typical disciplines and profes-sional specialties of readers and contributors, intended audience, special features of journal content, acceptance/rejection criteria and procedures, manuscript disposition, style requirements, payment or

page charges, availability and cost of reprints. Also includes a list
of style manuals, a list of indexes and abstracts, and a subject
index.

114 Camp, William L. , and Bryan L. Schwark. Guide to Periodi-
      cals in Education and Its Academic Disciplines. 2d ed.
      Metuchen, N. J.: Scarecrow Press, 1975.
A directory of 602 education and education-related periodicals issued
in the United States, covering all aspects of education. Arranged
alphabetically by subject. Each entry contains subscription data,
editorial address, statement of editorial policy, information on
manuscript preparation and manuscript disposition, and copyright.
Also includes a list of style manuals, Master List of Subject Headings, subject index, and title index.

115 Krepel, Wayne J. , and Charles R. Duvall. Education and
      Education-Related Serials: A Directory. Littleton, Colo.:
      Libraries Unlimited, 1977.
An alphabetical listing of 501 journals and newsletters, U. S. and
Canadian, including for each title: beginning date, publisher, circulation, frequency, subscription price, annual index, editor's name
and address, book review editor's name and address, where indexed,
journal description, and information for submitting manuscripts. An
appendix lists agencies that index or abstract journals contained in
the directory.

B. Periodical Indexes

Periodical indexes list articles, giving in each reference the
title and author of the article, title of the periodical, volume number,
paging, and date. Most periodical indexes list articles by subject.
Some also include author entries or separate author listings.
The most useful periodical indexes in the field of Education
are the Education Index and the Current Index to Journals in Education.

116 Education Index. New York: H. W. Wilson, 1932-. Monthly
      with cumulations.
A cumulative index to more than 400 educational periodicals, covering
the entire field of education. Also includes yearbooks and monographs. Volumes for July 1961-June 1969 are subject indexes only.
Other volumes include author and subject entries and references to
book reviews.

117 Current Index to Journals in Education. New York: Macmillan
      Information, 1969-. Publisher changed to Oryx Press in
      1979. Monthly with cumulations.
Indexes articles in more than 700 education and education-related
journals. In four sections: Main Entry Section; Subject Index;
Author Index; and Journal Contents Index. The Main Entry Section
gives complete references to articles, subject descriptors, and
annotations. It is arranged by subject categories (descriptor groups)

in EJ (ERIC Journal) accession number sequence.   Entries in other
sections refer to the Main Entry Section by EJ numbers.   ERIC
clearinghouses review and index the articles listed in CIJE.

Other Indexes to Education Periodicals

118   Australian Education Index.   Hawthorn, Victoria: Australian
        Council for Educational Research, 1957-.   Bimonthly.
Author and subject index to periodical articles, books, and pamphlets
published in Australia.

119   British Education Index.   London: Library Association, 1960-.
        3 issues per year with cumulations.
Indexes more than 70 periodicals.   In a subject arrangement with
author index.   Vol. 1, covering 1954-1958, published 1960; Vol. 2,
1958-1961, published 1963.   Beginning with Vol. 3, each cumulative
volume covers two years.

120   Canadian Education Index.   Toronto: Canadian Education As-
        sociation, 1965-.   5 issues per year.
A subject index to 160 Canadian periodicals and newspapers in the
field of education and related fields.   Also includes a checklist of
monographs.

121   State Education Journal Index.   Westminster, Colo., 1963-.
        Semiannual.
A subject index to more than 50 state and association publications.

Indexes to All the Social Science Fields Including Education

122   Current Contents in Social and Behavioral Sciences.   Philadel-
        phia: Institute for Scientific Information, 1969-.   Weekly.
Reproduces the tables of contents of more than 1,100 journals in the
social sciences, including education.   Arranged by subject.   Author
index and journal title index.

123   Index to U.S. Government Periodicals.   Chicago: Infordata
        International, 1974-.   Quarterly with annual cumulations.
A subject and author index to more than 150 periodicals issued by
more than 100 government agencies.   Periodicals are selected for
articles of research and reference value.

124   Public Affairs Information Service Bulletin.   New York: Public
        Affairs Information Service, 1915-.   Weekly with cumula-
        tions.
A subject index to current books, government publications, pamphlets,
and periodical articles in the social sciences.   Includes material on
several aspects of education.

125   Social Sciences Citation Index: An International Multidisciplinary
        Index to the Literature of the Social, Behavioral, and Related

Sciences.   Philadelphia: Institute for Scientific Information, 1967-.   Annual.
Provides comprehensive coverage of more than 1, 500 important social science journals in 26 disciplines, including education, educational research, and other areas related to education.   Also provides selective coverage of many journals from the natural, physical, and biomedical sciences for articles on the social sciences.   SSCI is made up of three separate but related indexes, the Citation Index, the Source Index, and the Permuterm Subject Index.

126   Social Sciences Index.   New York: H. W. Wilson, 1974-.
Quarterly with cumulations.
An author and subject index to English-language periodicals in all the social science fields.   Contains a separate author listing of citations to book reviews.   Includes entries for several aspects of education, mostly from noneducation journals.   Preceded by Social Sciences and Humanities Index, 1965-1974.

Indexes for Special Subject Fields

Periodical indexes in special subject areas are also of interest to teachers and education students, particularly for references on teaching specific subjects, and for the relationship of other fields to education.

Social Sciences

127   Advance Bibliography of Contents: Political Science and Government.   Santa Barbara, Calif. :   American Bibliographical Center, Clio Press, 1969-.   5 issues per year.

128   Anthropological Index to Current Periodicals in the Library of the Royal Anthropological Institute.   London: Royal Anthropological Institute, 1963-.   Quarterly.

129   Business Periodicals Index.   New York: H. W. Wilson, 1958-.   Monthly with cumulations.

130   Contents of Current Legal Periodicals.   Wilmington, Del. :   Corporation Service, 1972-.   Monthly.

131   Contents of Recent Economic Journals.   London: Department of Trade, HMSO, 1971-.   Weekly.

132   Ethnic Studies Bibliography.   Pittsburgh: University Center for International Studies, University of Pittsburgh, 1975-.   Annual.

133   Guide to Social Science and Religion in Periodical Literature.   Flint, Mich. :   National Library of Religious Periodicals, 1964-.   Quarterly.

134   Index of Economic Articles in Journals and Collective Volumes.
      Nashville, Tenn.:   American Economic Association, 1969-.
      Annual.   Preceded by Index to Economic Journals, 1961-
      1967.

135   Index to Legal Periodicals.   New York: H. W. Wilson, 1909-.
      Monthly with cumulations.

136   Index to Literature on the American Indian.   San Francisco:
      Indian Historian Press, 1971-.   Annual.

137   Index to Periodical Articles by and about Blacks.   Boston:
      G. K. Hall, 1973-.   Annual.

138   Index to Periodical Articles Related to Law.   Dobbs Ferry,
      N. Y.:   Glanville Publishers, 1959-.   Quarterly.

139   International Bibliography of Economics.   Chicago: Aldine
      Publishing, 1952-.   Annual.

140   International Bibliography of Political Science.   Chicago:
      Aldine Publishing, 1952-.   Annual.

141   International Bibliography of Social and Cultural Anthropology.
      Chicago: Aldine Publishing, 1955-.   Annual.

142   International Bibliography of Sociology.   Chicago: Aldine
      Publishing, 1951-.   Annual.

                              Humanities

143   American Humanities Index.   Troy, N. Y.:   Whitston Publishing,
      1975-.   Quarterly.

144   Annual Bibliography of English Language and Literature.   Lon-
      don: Modern Humanities Research Association, 1920-.
      Annual.

145   Architectural Periodicals Index.   London: British Architectural
      Library, 1972-.   Quarterly.

146   Art Index.   New York: H. W. Wilson, 1929-.   Quarterly with
      cumulations.

147   Arts and Humanities Citation Index.   Philadelphia: Institute
      for Scientific Information, 1977-.   Annual.

148   Avery Index to Architectural Periodicals.   2d ed.   15 vols.
      Boston: G. K. Hall, 1973.   First Supplement.   1 vol.
      1975.   Second Supplement.   1 vol.   1977.

149   British Humanities Index. London: Library Association, 1963-.
      Quarterly with cumulations.

150   Catholic Periodical and Literature Index.   Haverford, Pa.:
      Catholic Library Association, 1967-.   Bimonthly.

151   Humanities Index.   New York: H. W. Wilson, 1974-.   Quar-
      terly with cumulations.   Preceded by Social Sciences and
      Humanities Index, 1965-1974.

152   International Guide to Classical Studies: A Continuous Index
      to Periodical Literature.   Darien, Conn.:   American
      Bibliographic Service, 1961-.   Quarterly.

153   International Guide to Medieval Studies: A Continuous Index
      to Periodical Literature.   Darien, Conn.:   American
      Bibliographic Service, 1961-.   Quarterly.

154   MLA International Bibliography of Books and Articles on
      Modern Languages and Literatures.   New York: Modern
      Language Association of America, 1922-.   3 vols. per
      year.

155   Music Article Guide.   Philadelphia: Information Services Inc.,
      1965-.   Quarterly.

156   Music Index.   Detroit: Information Coordinators, 1949-.
      Monthly with annual cumulations.

157   Philosopher's Index.   Bowling Green, Ohio: Bowling Green
      University, 1967-.   Monthly with cumulations.

158   Popular Music Periodicals Index.   Metuchen, N. J.:   Scare-
      crow Press, 1974-.   Annual.

159   Recently Published Articles.   Washington, D. C.:   American
      Historical Association, 1976-.   3 issues per year.

160   Religion Index One.   Periodicals.   Chicago: American Theo-
      logical Library Association, 1977-.   Semiannual.   Preceded
      by Index to Religious Periodical Literature, 1953-1977.

General Science

161   Applied Science and Technology Index.   New York: H. W.
      Wilson, 1958-.   Monthly with cumulations.

162   British Technology Index.   London: British Library Associa-
      tion, 1962-.   Monthly with cumulations.

163   General Science Index.   New York: H. W. Wilson, 1978-.
      Monthly.

164   Science Citation Index.   Philadelphia: Institute for Scientific
        Information, 1961-.   Quarterly with annual cumulations.

Biological Sciences

165   Bibliography of Agriculture.   Phoenix: Oryx Press, 1942-.
        Monthly.

166   Biological and Agricultural Index.   New York: H. W. Wilson,
        1964-.   Monthly with cumulations.

167   Bioresearch Index.   Philadelphia: BioSciences Information
        Service of Biological Abstracts, 1967-.   Monthly.

168   Current Contents: Agriculture, Biology, and Environmental
        Sciences.   Philadelphia: Institute for Scientific Information,
        1970-.   Weekly.

169   Current Contents: Life Sciences.   Philadelphia: Institute for
        Scientific Information, 1958-.   Weekly.

170   Environment Index.   New York: Environment Information
        Center, 1971-.   Annual.

171   Index Medicus.   Washington, D. C.:   National Library of
        Medicine, 1960-.   Monthly with cumulations.

Physical Sciences and Mathematics

172   Bibliography and Index of Geology.   Boulder, Colo.:   Geological
        Society of America, 1934-.   Monthly.

173   Chemical Titles.   Washington, D. C.:   American Chemical
        Society, 1961-.   Biweekly.

174   Current Contents: Engineering, Technology and Applied
        Sciences.   Philadelphia: Institute for Scientific Information,
        1970-.   Weekly.

175   Current Contents: Physical and Chemical Sciences.   Philadel-
        phia: Institute for Scientific Information, 1961-.   Weekly.

176   Current Index to Statistics: Applications, Methods and Theory.
        Washington, D. C.:   American Statistical Association and the
        Institute of Mathematical Statistics, 1975-.   Annual.

177   Current Mathematical Publications.   Providence, R. I.:   Ameri-
        can Mathematical Society, 1969-.   Biweekly.

178   Current Physics Index.   New York: American Institute of
        Physics, 1975-.   Quarterly.

179   Engineering Index. New York: Engineering Index, 1906-.
         Monthly with cumulations.

180   Geotitles Weekly. London: Geosystems, 1969-. Weekly.

Physical Education and Sports

181   Physical Education Index. Cape Girardeau, Mo.: Ben Oak
         Publishing, 1978-. Quarterly with annual cumulations.

182   Physical Education/Sports Index. Albany, N.Y.: Marathon
         Press, 1978-. Quarterly with annual cumulations.

C.   Abstract Journals

Abstract journals also list periodical articles by subject. In
addition to the reference to an article, they give an abstract or
summary of the contents of each article listed. Some abstract journals list books and other materials as well as periodical articles.

Abstract Journals in Education

183   Capsules: A Review of Higher Education Research. Moore-
         head, Minn.: Concordia College, 1972-. Monthly.
A looseleaf service providing abstracts from 200 journals and books
on research in higher education. Covers journals not indexed by
Education Index and Current Index to Journals in Education. Annual
subject-author-title index.

184   Chicorel Abstracts to Reading and Learning Disabilities.
         Chicorel Index Series, Vol. 19. New York: Chicorel
         Library Publishing, 1976-. Annual.
An annual series covering the journal literature of the previous year
on reading and learning disabilities. The 1976 volume includes
abstracts for 1,200 articles from 130 journals. Arranged by subject,
with cross-referencing. Each entry gives bibliographic data and an
abstract covering scope, level of language, methodology of research,
intended audience, and conclusions. Covers all levels, kindergarten
through college. Includes author and title indexes and a list of
journals surveyed.

185   Child Development Abstracts and Bibliography. Washington,
         D.C.: National Research Council, Committee on Child
         Development, 1927-. 3 issues per year.
Subject arrangement with author index in each issue. Each issue
also contains a book review section. Annual cumulative author and
subject index.

186   Children's Literature Abstracts. Birmingham, Eng.: Inter-
         national Federation of Library Associations, 1973-. Quarterly.

Abstracts of articles on children's literature from professional library periodicals published in the United States, England, and Australia.

187 College Student Personnel Abstracts. Claremont, Calif.: College Student Personnel Institute, 1965-. Quarterly.
A compilation of abstracts from journals, conference proceedings, and research reports pertaining to college students and college student services. In a classified arrangement with author and subject indexes.

188 DSH Abstracts. Washington, D. C.: Deafness, Speech and Hearing Publications, 1960-. Quarterly.
Noncritical abstracts of literature pertinent to deafness, speech, and hearing, published in all major languages. Major sections are: Hearing; Hearing Disorders; Speech; Speech Disorders; and General. Each section is subdivided by subject. Author index in each issue. The last issue of each volume contains annual author and subject indexes, and a list of more than 300 journals covered.

189 Developmental Disabilities Abstracts. Washington, D. C.: U. S. Department of Health, Education and Welfare, Office of Human Development, Developmental Disabilities Office, 1964-. Quarterly.
Former titles: Mental Retardation Abstracts (1964-1973); Mental Retardation and Developmental Disabilities Abstracts (1974-1976). Abstracts of journal articles, books, reports, and government publications. Arranged in sections on: Broad Aspects of Developmental Disabilities; Medical Aspects; Developmental Aspects; Treatment and Training Aspects; Programmatic Aspects; Family; Personnel. Author and subject indexes in each issue.

190 Education Abstracts. Bloomington, Ind.: Phi Delta Kappa, 1937-1944. 10 issues per year.
Each issue contains more than 100 abstracts. Includes foreign literature; subject and author indexes for each volume.

191 Educational Administration Abstracts. Columbus, Ohio: University Council for Educational Administration, 1966-. 3 issues per year.
Abstracts of articles from about 100 journals in education and related fields. In a classified arrangement. Major sections are: Tasks of Administration; Administrative Processes and Organizational Variables; Societal Factors Influencing Education; and Programs for Educational Administrators. Author index and journal index in each issue.

192 Exceptional Child Education Resources. Reston, Va.: Council for Exceptional Children, 1969-. Quarterly.
Former title: Exceptional Child Education Abstracts (1969-1977). Comprehensive coverage of publications in all aspects of special education. Covers more than 200 journals, as well as books, research reports, curriculum guides, administrative surveys, papers, texts, and ERIC documents. Cumulative subject, author, topic-classification, and keyword indexes.

193   Language Teaching and Linguistics: Abstracts. London:
        Cambridge University Press, 1968-. Quarterly.
Former title: Language Teaching Abstracts (1968-1974); preceded by
English Teaching Abstracts (1961-1967). Abstracts of articles from
more than 400 international periodicals on teaching modern languages,
including English as a second language. Also covers relevant works
in psychology, linguistics, language studies, teaching methodology
and technology, and experimental teaching. In a classified arrangement, with an annual cumulative subject index.

194   Sociology of Education Abstracts. Liverpool, Eng.: Sociology
        of Education Abstracts Service, 1965-. Quarterly.
Each issue contains about 150 abstracts, principally of journal
articles, with some abstracts of books, reports of research, conference reports, critiques, reviews of research, and bibliographies.
Arrangement is alphabetical by author. Each issue contains five
indexes: Theories Index, Methods of Research Index, Empirical
Situations Index, Data Index, and Form of Document Index.

195   Technical Education Abstracts from British Sources.... Liver-
        pool, Eng.: Information for Education Limited, School of
        Education, University of Liverpool, 1961-. Quarterly.
Abstracts of periodical articles and separately published works concerned with science, technical, and further education including education and training for industry and commerce. Cumulative subject
and author indexes.

Abstract Journals in Special Subject Fields

Social Sciences

196   Abstracts in Anthropology. Westport, Conn.: Greenwood
        Periodicals, 1970-. Quarterly.

197   Abstracts on Criminology and Penology. Deventer, Nether-
        lands: Kluwer B. V., 1969-. 6 issues per year. Preceded
        by Excerpta Criminologica, 1961-1968.

198   Criminal Justice Abstracts. Hackensack, N. J.: National
        Council on Crime and Delinquency, 1970-. Quarterly.

199   International Political Science Abstracts. Oxford, Eng.:
        Basil Blackwell, 1951-. Quarterly.

200   Key to Economic Science. The Hague: Martinus Nijhoff, 1953-.
        Bimonthly. Former title: Economic Abstracts (1953-
        1975).

201   Psychological Abstracts. Lancaster, Pa.: American Psycho-
        logical Association, 1927-. Monthly.

202   Sage Urban Studies Abstracts. Beverly Hills, Calif.: Sage Publi-
        cations, 1973-. Quarterly.

203   Social Work Research and Abstracts.   Washington, D. C. :
        National Association of Social Workers, 1977-.   Quarterly.
        Preceded by Abstracts for Social Workers, 1965-1977.

204   Sociological Abstracts.   New York: Sociological Abstracts,
        1953-.   8 issues per year.

205   Women Studies Abstracts.   Rush, N. Y. :   Rush Publishing,
        1972-.   Quarterly.

206   Work Related Abstracts.   Detroit: Information Coordinators,
        1973-.   Monthly.   Preceded by Employment Relations
        Abstracts, 1967-1972.

                              Humanities

207   Abstracts of English Studies.   Champaign, Ill. :   National
        Council of Teachers of English, 1958-.   Monthly.

208   Abstracts of New World Archaeology.   Salt Lake City: Society
        for American Archaeology, 1959-.   Annual.

209   America: History and Life.   Santa Barbara, Calif. :   Clio
        Press, 1964-.   3 issues per year.

210   American Literature Abstracts.   San Jose, Calif. :   Burbank
        Press, 1967-.   Semiannual.

211   Graphic Arts Abstracts.   Rochester, N. Y. :   Rochester Institute
        of Technology, Graphic Arts Research Center, 1947-.
        Monthly.

212   Historical Abstracts.   Part A: Modern History Abstracts,
        1775-1914; Part B: Twentieth Century Abstracts, 1914-.
        Santa Barbara, Calif. :   Clio Press, 1955-.   Quarterly.

213   Language and Language Behavior Abstracts.   Ann Arbor:
        University of Michigan, Center for Research on Language
        and Language Behavior, 1967-.   Quarterly.

214   MLA Abstracts of Articles in Scholarly Journals.   New York:
        Modern Language Association of America, 1971-1977.   3
        vols. per year.

215   New Testament Abstracts.   Cambridge, Mass. :   Weston School
        of Theology, 1956-.   3 issues per year.

216   Religious and Theological Abstracts.   Myerstown, Pa. :   Reli-
        gious and Theological Abstracts, 1958-.   Quarterly.

217   RILM Abstracts of Music Literature.   Flushing, N. Y. :   Inter-
        national RILM Center, City University of New York, 1967-.
        Quarterly.

218 Speech Communication Abstracts. Pleasant Hill, Calif.: Thea-
     tre, Drama and Speech Information Center, 1974-. 3 issues
     per year.

219 Theatre/Drama Abstracts. Pleasant Hill, Calif.: Theatre,
     Drama and Speech Information Center, 1974-. 3 issues
     per year.

Biological Sciences

220 Abstracts of Health Effects of Environmental Pollution. Phila-
     delphia: BioSciences Information Service of Biological
     Abstracts, 1972-. Monthly.

221 Applied Ecology Abstracts. Arlington, Va.: Information Re-
     trieval, 1975-. Monthly.

222 Biological Abstracts. Philadelphia: BioSciences Information
     Service of Biological Abstracts, 1926-. Biweekly.

223 Bioengineering Abstracts. New York: Engineering Index,
     1974-. Monthly.

224 Ecological Abstracts. Norwich, Eng.: GeoAbstracts, Univer-
     sity of East Anglia, 1974-. Bimonthly.

225 Environment Abstracts. New York: Environment Information
     Center, 1971-. Monthly.

226 Excerpta Medica: The International Medical Abstracting Service.
     Amsterdam: Excerpta Medica, 1947-. Monthly.

227 Oceanography Abstracts and Oceanographic Bibliography. Elms-
     ford, N.Y.: Pergamon Press, 1977-. Monthly.

Physical Sciences and Mathematics

228 Astronomy and Astrophysics Abstracts. Berlin: Springer
     Verlag, 1969-. Semiannual.

229 Chemical Abstracts. Easton, Pa.: American Chemical Society,
     1907-. Semimonthly.

230 Current Abstracts of Chemistry and Index Chemicus. Phila-
     delphia: Institute for Scientific Information, 1970-. Weekly.
     Continues Index Chemicus, 1960-1969.

231 Energy Abstracts. New York: Engineering Index, 1974-.
     Monthly.

232 Energy Information Abstracts. New York: Environment Infor-
     mation Center, 1976-. Bimonthly.

233   Energy Research Abstracts.   Washington, D. C.:   U. S. Depart-
        ment of Energy, Technical Information Center, 1976-.
        Semimonthly.

234   GeoAbstracts.   Norwich, Eng.:   GeoAbstracts, University of
        East Anglia, 1972-.   6 issues per year.   (In 7 parts)
        Preceded by Geographical Abstracts, 1960-1971.

235   Geophysical Abstracts.   Norwich, Eng.:   GeoAbstracts, Uni-
        versity of East Anglia, 1977-.   6 issues per year.

236   International Aerospace Abstracts.   New York: American
        Institute of Aeronautics and Astronautics, Technical Infor-
        mation Service, 1961-.   Semimonthly.

237   Mathematical Reviews.   Providence, R. I.:   American Mathe-
        matical Society, 1940-.   Monthly.

238   Meteorological and Geoastrophysical Abstracts.   Boston:
        American Meteorological Society, 1950-.   Monthly.

239   Nuclear Science Abstracts.   Washington, D. C.:   U. S. Energy
        Research and Development Administration, 1975-.   Semi-
        monthly.   Continues U. S. Atomic Energy Commission,
        Nuclear Science Abstracts, 1947-1975.

240   Renewable Energy Bulletin.   London: Multi-Science Publishing,
        1974-.   Quarterly.

241   Science Abstracts.   London: Institution of Electrical Engineers.
        Section A: Physics Abstracts, 1898-.   Biweekly.   Section
        B: Electrical and Electronics Abstracts, 1898-.   Monthly.
        Section C: Computer and Control Abstracts, 1966-.   Month-
        ly.

242   U. S. Geological Survey.   Abstracts of North American Geology.
        Washington, D. C.:   Government Printing Office, 1966-.
        Monthly.

D.   Indexes to Book Reviews

The indexes listed below are helpful in locating reviews of
books in the field of education.

243   Education Index.   New York: H. W. Wilson, 1932-.   Monthly
        with cumulations.
A source of references to book reviews in professional journals,
except the volumes for July, 1961-June, 1969.   Reviews are listed
alphabetically by author under the heading "Book Reviews."   Beginning with Vol. 26, July, 1975, book reviews are listed in a separate
section at the back of each issue and cumulative volume.

244 Book Review Digest. New York: H. W. Wilson, 1905-.
      Monthly with cumulations.
A digest and index of selected book reviews in American and English
periodicals. Arranged alphabetically by author of book reviewed,
with title and subject index. Each entry gives bibliographic information, price, a brief descriptive note, quotations from selected reviews with references to the periodicals in which the reviews appear,
and the number of words in each review.

245 Book Review Index. Detroit: Gale Research, 1965-. Monthly
      with cumulations.
An index to book reviews in general and specialized periodicals,
particularly in the fields of the social sciences and humanities. Arranged alphabetically by author with title index.

246 Current Book Review Citations. New York: H. W. Wilson,
      1977-. Monthly with cumulations.
An author and title index to book reviews in more than 1,300 periodicals. Includes fiction and nonfiction, foreign-language titles, and
new editions. Reviews of books for children and young adults are
included. Part I of each issue is the Author Index, which lists reviews alphabetically under author of book and gives title of book,
date of publication, and citations to reviews in periodicals including
name of the reviewer. Part II, Title Index, is an alphabetical
listing of titles of books, with name of the author for each book.
Also included is a list of periodicals cited. Each issue is a cumulation of all reviews indexed in other Wilson indexes plus reviews in
periodicals not indexed by other Wilson services.

    If no reviews are listed for a book in these indexes, it is
sometimes possible to find them in the book review sections of
periodicals covering the subject of the book. For example, a review of a book on reading might be found in the Journal of Reading
or in the Reading Teacher. A book on educational psychology might
be reviewed in the Journal of Educational Psychology or in Psychology of Learning and Motivation. The annual indexes of periodicals
are helpful in locating book reviews.

III. RESEARCH STUDIES

In this section are listed bibliographies, abstracts, and indexes of ERIC documents, theses and dissertations, and other types of research studies.

A.   ERIC Documents

A very important source of information on research reports and other educational materials is the Educational Resources Information Center (ERIC).   It is a national information system sponsored and supported by the National Institute of Education.   It consists of a coordinating staff (Central ERIC) in Washington, D.C., and 16 clearinghouses established at universities and headquarters of professional organizations throughout the United States.   Each clearinghouse is concerned with a specific area of education, and collects, processes, and disseminates documents in its specific field.

The 16 areas covered by the clearinghouses are: career education; counseling and personnel services; elementary and early childhood education; educational management; handicapped and gifted children; higher education; information resources; junior colleges; languages and linguistics; reading and communication skills; rural education and small schools; science, mathematics, and environmental education; social studies/social science education; teacher education; tests, measurement, and evaluation; and urban education.

The ERIC material includes reports from all projects supported by the U.S. Office of Education and other federal agencies concerned with academic research, reports from the National Education Association, state departments of education, foundations, universities, professional organizations, and individuals.   Documents selected are abstracted and indexed, and are listed in Resources in Education (see No. 248).

ERIC documents can be obtained in microfiche or hard copy, except copyrighted material available from publishers.   Many college and university libraries have complete files of ERIC documents on microfiche.   Hard copy or microfiche may be ordered from the ERIC Document Reproduction Service.   Order information is given in each issue of Resources in Education.

Other ERIC publications are: Thesaurus of ERIC Descriptors, a listing of terms for indexing and searching (see No. 598); Directory of Eric Microfiche Collections, a listing by state and city of all institutions and organizations with sizable ERIC microfiche collections; and Directory of ERIC Search Services, a listing by state and city of organizations that provide computerized searches of the ERIC data base.   The ERIC data base covers the documents listed in Resources in Education, 1966 to date, and journal articles listed in Current Index to Journals in Education, 1969 to date.

Manual searching for ERIC materials is carried out by use of the Thesaurus, Resources in Education, and Current Index to Journals in Education.   Computer searching service is available in many libraries.   The ERIC data base is the most comprehensive in the field of education, though others in related areas, such as Exceptional Child Education Resources, Language and Language Behavior Abstracts, and Psychological Abstracts, may also be used.   The student or researcher discusses with a search analyst the specific subject and terminology for the search.   The analyst chooses the descriptors that index the concepts involved, and conducts the search by means of the computer.   The computer searching service provides the user with a list of citations printed in the same form as used in RIE and CIJE.   Computer searching is more complete and more effective than manual searching.   The charge for this service varies from one library to another.   If computer searching is not available locally, the researcher may request bibliographies directly from an ERIC clearinghouse.

An explanation of ERIC publications and services is given in How to Use ERIC, a pamphlet issued by the National Institute of Education.   It is free on request.

ERIC documents and earlier research reports of the Office of Education are listed in the following publications.

247   U. S. Educational Research Information Center.   Office of Education Research Reports, 1956-65.   2 vols.   Washington, D. C. : Government Printing Office, 1967.
Vol. 1 lists, with abstracts, research reports produced on projects sponsored by the Bureau of Research, Office of Education, for the years 1956-1965.   Vol. 2 contains indexes by authors, institutions, subjects, and report numbers.   Continued by Research in Education (ERIC), 1966-.

248   U. S. Educational Resources Information Center.   Resources in Education.   Washington, D. C. : Government Printing Office, 1966-.   Monthly.
Former title: Research in Education (1966-1975).   The main section is Document Résumés, listing recent research studies available from ERIC and other agencies in a classified arrangement with bibliographic information and abstract for each.   Other sections are: Subject Index; Author Index; Institution Index; Accession Number Cross Reference Index; and New Thesaurus Terms.

249   Complete Guide and Index to ERIC Reports Through December 1969.   Englewood Cliffs, N. J. :   Prentice-Hall, 1970.

Lists more than 24, 500 documents in a classified arrangement under
the 4, 252 descriptor terms from the Thesaurus of ERIC Descriptors,
2d ed.   Indexes the reports by subject, author, number, and clearinghouse that coordinated the research.

250   ERIC Educational Documents Abstracts.   New York Macmillan
         Information, 1972-.
An annual cumulation of the report résumés from the monthly issues
of Resources in Education.   Availability of the original document is
indicated with each abstract.   Subject and author indexes.

251   ERIC Educational Documents Index.   New York Macmillan
         Information, 1972-.
Brings together references to all research documents in the ERIC
collection, including the ERIC Catalog of Selected Documents on the
Disadvantaged; Office of Education Research Reports, 1956-1965; and
Research in Education, 1966 through 1971.   Two volumes cover
1966-1969.   A third volume covers 1970-1971.   Annual volumes since
1972.   Subject and author indexes list complete titles and ERIC
accession numbers, which refer to abstracts in ERIC Educational
Documents Abstracts, to microfiche of the documents, and to the
original documents.

B.   Theses and Dissertations

252   American Doctoral Dissertations.   Ann Arbor, Mich.:   Xerox
         University Microfilms, 1957-.   Annual.
An annual listing of doctoral dissertations arranged by subject, and
by university under each subject.   Each volume contains a section
on education.   Author index.   Former title: Index to American
Doctoral Dissertations, 1955/1956 - 1962/1963.   Preceded by Doctoral
Dissertations Accepted by American Universities, 1934-1955; and
U. S. Library of Congress, List of American Doctoral Dissertations
Printed from 1912-1938.

253   Dissertation Abstracts International.   Ann Arbor, Mich.:   Xerox
         University Microfilms, 1952-.   Monthly.
Abstracts of doctoral dissertations available in complete form on
microfilm.   Beginning with Vol. 27, No. 1, July, 1966, published
in two sections: A: Humanities and Social Sciences; B: The
Sciences and Engineering.   Each issue of Section A contains a section
on education with subdivisions for major areas.   Since July, 1969,
abstracts of dissertations from some European universities are included.   Keyword, title and author indexes.   Retrospective Index for
Education, 1970, in two parts, covers Vols. 1-24.

254   Comprehensive Dissertation Index, 1861-1972.   37 vols.   Ann
         Arbor, Mich.:   Xerox University Microfilms, 1973.   Annual
         supplements.
A keyword index to all dissertations accepted for academic doctoral
degrees by U. S. educational institutions, and some by foreign universities, for the period covered.   A total of more than 417, 000 are

listed by academic disciplines, and by subject divisions within some disciplines, in 32 volumes. Entries include title, author, degree, date, university, number of pages, code for source of citation, and order number. Vols. 33-37 list dissertations by authors' names, with complete bibliographic information on each entry. Annual supplements list all doctoral dissertations accepted in the preceding year.

255   Directory of Education Studies in Canada. Toronto: Canadian
        Education Association, 1969-. Annual.
A classified list of theses and dissertations and other research studies. Arranged by subject with an author index. Entries include abstracts. In English and French.

256   Masters' Theses in Education. Cedar Falls, Iowa: Research
        Publications, 1952-. Annual.
An annual listing of theses in a classified arrangement, giving author, title, and institution for each entry. Institutional Index, Author Index, and Subject Index.

257   Phi Delta Kappa. Research Studies in Education. Bloomington,
        Ind.: Phi Delta Kappa, 1953-1970.
A compilation from the Social Sciences-Education section of Doctoral Dissertations Accepted by American Universities 1941/42 - 1950/51, published 1953, is arranged in more than 30 subject categories and alphabetically by author within each category. Information for each entry includes author's name, title of the study, institution granting the degree, and date of the degree. A second compilation, Research Studies in Education, 1953-1963: A Cumulative Subject and Author Index of Doctoral Dissertations, Reports, and Field Studies for an Eleven Year Period, published 1965, is a cumulation of annual supplements to the 1941-1951 compilation. Arrangement is the same as in the earlier volume. An annual, Research Studies in Education: A Subject-Author Index and Research Methods Bibliography, was published 1964-1970.

258   Monroe, Walter S. Ten Years of Educational Research, 1918-
        27. University of Illinois, College of Education, Bureau of
        Educational Research Bulletin No. 42. Urbana: University
        of Illinois Press, 1928.
A listing by author of 3,650 research studies, with topical index. Also lists Doctors of Philosophy in Education by Institution, 1918-1927.

259   Reynolds, Michael M. A Guide to Theses and Dissertations:
        An Annotated, International Bibliography of Bibliographies.
        Detroit: Gale Research, 1975.
An annotated, international listing of 2,000 bibliographies of theses and dissertations produced through 1973. Arranged by broad subjects and subdivided into more specific subjects and institutional listings. The section on Education is subdivided into General, Individual Institutions, Places (countries and regions), Special and Racial Groups, and Special Subjects. The volume has an index of institutions, an index of names and titles, and a subject index.

260   U. S. Office of Education.   Bibliography of Research Studies in
       Education.   Washington, D. C. :   Government Printing Office,
       1926-1940.
A classified list of doctors' dissertations, masters' theses, and
faculty research studies covering all aspects of education.   Entries
give author, title, degree, date of completion, name of institution,
number of pages, and a brief descriptive note.   Author and subject
index.   Issued annually in the Bulletin series.   Republished in 4
vols. by Gale Research Company in 1974.

Bibliographies of Dissertations and Theses on Specific Aspects of
the Field of Education

261   Cordasco, Francesco, and Leonard Covello.   Educational
       Sociology: A Subject Index of Doctoral Dissertations
       Completed at American Universities, 1941-1963.   New
       York: Scarecrow Press, 1965.
A classified list of 2, 146 titles under 14 headings.   Information for
each entry includes author's name, title of dissertation, university,
and date.

262   De Crow, Roger, and Nehume Loague.   Adult Education Dis-
       sertation Abstracts, 1963-1967.   Syracuse, N. Y. :   ERIC
       Clearinghouse on Adult Education, 1971.
A classified listing of 505 dissertations on the education and training
of adults.   Entries include abstracts.   Author, institution, and
methodological indexes.

263   Eells, Walter C.   American Dissertations on Foreign Educa-
       tion: Doctor's Dissertations and Master's Theses Written
       at American Universities and Colleges Concerning Educa-
       tion and Educators in Foreign Countries and Education of
       Groups of Foreign Birth or Ancestry in the United States,
       1884-1958.   Washington, D. C. :   National Education Associa-
       tion, Committee on International Relations, 1959.
Lists 5, 716 dissertations and theses.   Arranged by continent, then
by country.   Entries include bibliographic information and indication
of availability on microfilm.   Author and subject indexes.

264   Gross, Richard E. , and Leonardo De La Cruz.   Social Studies
       Dissertations, 1963-1969.   Boulder, Colo. :   ERIC Clearing-
       house for Social Studies/Social Science Education, 1971.
Lists 216 American dissertations with abstracts, in sections on
curriculum, instruction, cognition and learning, teacher education
and teacher evaluation, and general.   Each section is subdivided by
elementary, secondary, higher, and general.   Author and subject
indexes.

265   Kniefel, David, and Tanya S. Kniefel.   Annotated Bibliography
       and Descriptive Summary of Dissertations and Theses on
       Rurality and Small Schools.   University Park, N. M. :   New
       Mexico State University, ERIC Clearinghouse on Rural Edu-
       cation and Small Schools, 1970.

Lists 76 American dissertations completed 1963-1968, with abstracts.
Arranged alphabetically by author, with subject index.

266   Little, Lawrence C.   Bibliography of Doctoral Dissertations on
        Adults and Adult Education.   Rev. ed.   Pittsburgh: Univer-
        sity of Pittsburgh Press, 1963.
Lists by author more than 2,500 dissertations on all aspects of adult
education.   Information for each entry includes title, institution,
year, paging, and reference to an abstract.

267   Parker, Franklin, ed.   American Dissertations on Foreign
        Education: A Bibliography with Abstracts.   Troy, N. Y. :
        Whitston Publishing, 1971-.
A series that includes volumes on Canada, India, Japan, Africa,
Scandinavia, China, Korea, Mexico, Central America, and South
America.   Future volumes will cover the USSR, Israel, and other
countries.   Each volume is arranged alphabetically by author.
References include author, title of dissertation, institution, and date.
Abstracts are quoted in full from Dissertation Abstracts International
and from abstracts published by individual institutions.   Subject
index in each volume.   Includes some Canadian dissertations.

268   Parker, Franklin, and Anne Bailey.   Junior and Community
        College: A Bibliography of Doctoral Dissertations, 1918-
        1963.   Washington, D. C. :   American Association of Junior
        Colleges, 1965.
A classified listing with an author index.   Information on each
dissertation includes author's name, title, institution, and date.
Includes a list of references.

C.   Other Research Studies

269   Encyclopedia of Educational Research.   Edited by R. L. Ebel.
        4th ed.   New York   Macmillan, 1969.
A critical evaluation, synthesis, and interpretation of the literature
of educational research.   Particularly useful for its long, selective
bibliographies.   The Review of Educational Research and the Review
of Research in Education serve as supplements.

270   Review of Educational Research.   Washington, D. C. :   American
        Educational Research Association, 1931-.   Quarterly.
"Contains integrative reviews and interpretations and educational research literature on both substantive and methodological issues. "
From Vol. 1, 1931 through Vol. 40, No. 2, April, 1970, each issue
reviewed the literature of research in one particular area.   Since
that date, each issue is made up of reviews of research in several
areas.   All articles include lists of references.

271   Review of Research in Education.   Edited by Fred N. Kerling-
        er.   A publication of the American Educational Research
        Association.   Itasca, Ill. :   F. E. Peacock Publishers,
        1973-.   Annual.

An annual series that reviews research in education through critical
and synthesizing essays.   Each volume contains several chapters
organized into parts covering particular areas, such as history of
education, learning and instruction, research methodology.   Each
part is made up of essays by various authors.   Each essay contains
a bibliography.   The more important areas are reviewed periodically.

272   Travers, Robert M. W. , ed.   Second Handbook of Research on
      Teaching.   A project of the American Educational Research
      Association.   Chicago: Rand McNally, 1973.
Contains 42 chapters, written by specialists, that review the research in specific areas.   Grouped in four parts: Part I, Introduction; Part II, Methods and Techniques of Research and Development;
Part III, Research on Special Problems of Teaching; Part IV, Research on the Teaching of School Subjects.   Each chapter includes a
list of references.   Name and subject indexes.

273   Monson, Dianne L. , and Bette J. Peltola.   Research in Chil-
      dren's Literature: An Annotated Bibliography.   Newark,
      Del. :   International Reading Association, 1976.
Includes 332 research studies completed or reported 1960-1974.
Part 1 contains abstracts of 177 dissertations and ERIC documents
dealing with literature for children and adolescents.   Summaries include information about subjects, instrumentation, findings, and type
of study.   University Microfilm order numbers and ERIC numbers
are included.   Part 2 is an unannotated bibliography of 107 reports
of research in children's literature published in journals 1965-1974.
Part 3, Related Subjects, is an unannotated list of 48 entries including books and monographs, ERIC documents, dissertations,
bibliographies, and unpublished library school masters' theses.
Entries in all sections are arranged alphabetically by author.   Part
4 is an index by general subject of the research, instruments used,
and type of study.

274   U. S.   Educational Resources Information Center.   Clearinghouse
      on Early Childhood Education.   Research Relating to Chil-
      dren.   Washington, D. C. :   Government Printing Office,
      1950-.   Irregular.
Issued by U. S. Children's Bureau, Clearinghouse for Research in
Child Life, 1950-1970.   An inventory of studies in progress or
research recently completed, giving for each: title, purpose,
subjects, methods, findings, duration, publication plans, principal
investigator, and cooperating group.   In a classified arrangement
with indexes of organizations, investigators, and subjects.

IV. GOVERNMENT PUBLICATIONS

Local, state, federal, and international agencies publish valuable
material in the field of Education. Of special interest are the publications of the U. S. Office of Education, the U. S. National Center for
Educational Statistics, state Departments of Education, and UNESCO.

A. U. S. Government Publications

The U. S. Office of Education publishes material on general
education; adult, vocational, and technical education; compensatory
education; education of the handicapped; educational research and
development; educational television; elementary, secondary, and
higher education; equal educational opportunity; financial assistance;
international programs, studies, and services; libraries; and teaching
various subjects. The National Center for Educational Statistics
collects, analyzes, and disseminates statistical and other data on
various aspects of education. The publications of these and other
federal agencies on education and education-related subjects are
listed in the following catalogs and indexes.

275 U. S. Office of Education. List of Publications. Washington,
D. C.: Government Printing Office, 1910-.
In the Bulletin series. Bulletin 1910, No. 3, lists publications,
1867-1910; Bulletin 1937, No. 22, 1910-1936; Bulletin 1960, No. 3,
1937-1959; Bulletin 1961, No. 7, 1960-1961. Annual since 1962.

276 U. S. Office of Education. Publications of the Office of Education. Washington, D. C.: Government Printing Office,
1960-. Issued irregularly.
A catalog listing all Office of Education publications currently available. In a classified arrangement with subject and title indexes.

277 U. S. Superintendent of Documents. Monthly Catalog of United
States Government Publications. Washington, D. C.:
Government Printing Office, 1895-.
A current listing of publications issued by all branches of the federal
government. Publications are listed by agency with full title, date,
paging, and price for each. Subject index.

278   U. S. Superintendent of Documents.   Subject Bibliography Index.
       Washington, D. C.:   Government Printing Office, 1975-.
This series, which began in 1975, replaces the former Price Lists.
It consists of bibliographies of government publications on particular
subjects or areas of interest.   The bibliographies in the field of
education cover adult education, educational statistics, school administration, financial aid to students, educational model programs,
foreign education, elementary education, reading, secondary education, higher education, vocational and career education, and libraries.
Entries give bibliographic information and annotations.

B.   State Publications

The publications of state agencies are listed in:

279   U. S. Library of Congress.   Exchange and Gift Division.
       Monthly Checklist of State Publications.   Washington,
       D. C.:   Government Printing Office, 1910-.
Includes publications of state departments of education and publications of other state agencies on education and education-related
subjects.   Monographs are listed by state and issuing agency.   Publications of associations of state officials and of regional organizations,
and library surveys, studies, manuals, and statistical reports are
listed separately.   Periodicals are listed semiannually in the June
and December issues.   The December list is a cumulation for the
year.   Bibliographic information is given for each entry.   Price is
given for some items.   Annual index.

C.   UNESCO Publications

UNESCO publishes directories; statistical sources; books
on teaching aids, curricula and methods, including teaching of
specific subjects, technical education, education for international
understanding, teaching staff, educational planning, administration,
adult and youth education; and periodicals.   Other UNESCO publications are in fields related to education, such as mass communication, science, social science, libraries, art, and literature.
UNESCO publications are listed in the following catalogs and lists.

280   General Catalogue of UNESCO Publications and UNESCO Spon-
       sored Publications, 1946-1959.   Paris: UNESCO, 1962.
       Supplement, 1960-1963.   1964.   Second Supplement, 1964-
       1967.   1969.
Lists all works produced throughout the world with the Organization's assistance, whether by UNESCO itself, by some other body
under contract, or under UNESCO auspices.   The main volume
contains 2, 500 entries in a classified arrangement.   Also includes
a list of filmstrips and art slides listed alphabetically by title; an
index of authors, titles, and series titles; a list of publishers; and
a list of national distributors.   The supplements are also in a
classified arrangement, and include a cumulative list of UNESCO

periodicals, a general index, a list of publishers, and a list of national distributors.   The first supplement lists more than 1, 300 publications; the second, more than 1, 700.   Since 1970 the Catalogue includes only books and periodicals published directly by UNESCO.

281   UNESCO List of Documents and Publications.   Paris: UNESCO, 1973-.   6 issues per year.
Covers all General Conference Executive Board, main series and working series, and field project reports.   Cumulative author-title-series listings.

Annotated catalogs of UNESCO publications currently available for purchase are issued annually.   Lists of UNESCO publications are occasionally issued on separate subjects including Education and related areas.

D.   Other Bibliographies of Government Publications

282   Government Reference Books: A Biennial Guide to U. S. Government Publications.   Littleton, Colo.:   Libraries Unlimited, 1970-.
The 5th edition, 1978, includes 1, 608 entries in four parts: Part One, General Reference; Part Two, Social Sciences; Part Three, Science and Technology; Part Four, Humanities.   All parts are divided and subdivided.   The section on Education in Part Two is subdivided into general works, comparative education, elementary and secondary education, equal educational opportunities and minority groups, higher education, libraries, and occupational education. Entries give full bibliographic information, price, Superintendent of Documents classification number, and a descriptive annotation. Author-Title-Subject Index, and Corporate Author (agency) Index.

283   Lu, Joseph K.   U. S. Government Publications Relating to the Social Sciences: A Selected Annotated Guide.   Beverly Hills, Calif.:   Sage Publications, 1975.
In 12 chapters.   Chapter VI, Education, is divided into nine sections: education in general; educational research and development; federal aid; adult, vocational, and technical education; comparative education; early childhood education; elementary and secondary education; higher education; and special education.   These sections are subdivided into bibliographies, directories, statistics, and miscellaneous. In each subdivision entries are arranged by title in the order of date of publication.   Entries include bibliographic information, Superintendent of Documents classification number, and annotation.   Appendixes: A, Background Readings; B, General Guides; C, General Ordering Information; D, List of Depositories.   Personal name index, and title index.

284   New York. Public Library.   Research Libraries.   Economics Division.   Catalog of Government Publications.   40 vols. Boston: G. K. Hall, 1972.   Supplement, 1974.   2 vols. 1976.

This collection comprises the fundamental documents of all national and colonial governments that have been published and are obtainable. Emphasis is on the United States, Great Britain, Scandinavian countries, and Western Europe.   References are entered under political units, subdivided by agencies.   Listings for each agency are in two groups, alphabetical for serial publications, and a dated listing of monographic publications.   Supplemented by Bibliographic Guide to Government Publications: U.S., 1975-.   Annual; and by Bibliographic Guide to Government Publications: Foreign, 1975-.   Annual (see Nos. 285 and 286).

285   Bibliographic Guide to Government Publications: U.S.   Boston: G. K. Hall, 1975-.   Annual.

286   Bibliographic Guide to Government Publications: Foreign. Boston: G. K. Hall, 1975-.   Annual.
Annual supplements to Catalog of Government Publications (see No. 284).   Lists materials cataloged during the past year by the Research Libraries of New York Public Library, with additional entries from Library of Congress.   Includes department reports, censuses, statistical annuals and reports, journals and monographs relating to government agencies, publications of international and regional agencies, and state and provincial government publications.

287   Parish, David W.   State Government Reference Publications: An Annotated Bibliography.   Littleton, Colo.:   Libraries Unlimited, 1974.
A selected list of more than 800 publications of state and territorial agencies.   Includes bibliographies, handbooks, directories, reports, and other reference books.   Arranged alphabetically by state, and by main entry within each state.   Entries include bibliographic information and an annotation covering contents and purpose of the publication.   Also includes a bibliography of writings about state documents, a directory of agencies, an author-title index, and a subject index.

See also:

Index to U.S. Government Periodicals (No. 123).

[Note: The U.S. Department of Education was created by legislation passed by Congress in September, 1979 and signed by the President on October 17.   Shirley M. Hufstedler was sworn in as the first Secretary of Education December 6, 1979.   The Department officially came into existence May 4, 1980, with a staff of 17,000 employees and an annual budget of $14 billion.   The former Department of Health, Education and Welfare is now the Department of Health and Human Services.]

A. Literature for Children and Young Adults

Bibliographies of Books About Children's Literature

288 Haviland, Virginia. Children's Literature: A Guide to
    Reference Sources. Washington, D. C. : U. S. Library of
    Congress, 1966. First Supplement, 1972. Second Supple-
    ment, 1977.
The basic volume is an extensive, annotated bibliography of 1, 073
books, articles, and pamphlets. Major sections are: History and
Criticism; Authorship; Illustration; Bibliography; Books and Children;
The Library and Children's Books; International Studies; National
Studies. The first supplement covers 746 publications issued 1966-
1969. It contains two new subsections: The Publishing and Promo-
tion of Children's Books, and The Teaching of Children's Literature.
The second supplement includes 929 publications issued 1970-1974.
New subsections are Selection of Nonprint Material, Research in
Children's Literature, Translation, and French Canada.

289 Meacham, Mary. Information Sources in Children's Literature:
    A Practical Reference Guide for Children's Librarians,
    Elementary School Teachers, and Students of Children's
    Literature. Westport, Conn. : Greenwood Press, 1978.
A guide to reference and information sources, including listings of
trade books; periodical reviewing sources; selection aids and reference tools for specific subjects and types of publications; reference
books about authors, illustrators, and awards; guides for using books
with children; and guides for ordering and cataloging. Lengthy
evaluative annotations are given, with photoreproductions of sample
pages from the sources. Appendices include a list of titles about
media centers, an evaluation guide, and references for further
reading.

290 Pellowski, Anne. World of Children's Literature. New York
    R. R. Bowker, 1968.
A comprehensive, annotated bibliography of more than 4, 400 books,
parts of books, articles, and complete periodicals related to the

history and criticism of children's literature;   subjects related to
children's literature, such as storytelling and folklore; library work
with children; book clubs; reading interests of children; writing and
illustrating children's books; national bibliographies and special ex-
hibitions of children's books; lists of recommended books for children; biographical dictionaries of children's authors and illustrators;
and indexes for locating children's literature.   Arranged by large
geographical areas, subdivided by countries.   Brief surveys of the
development of children's literature and libraries are given at the
beginning of each section and country.

Bibliographies of Books for Children and Young Adults

Catalogs

291   Children's Catalog.   13th ed.   New York: H. W. Wilson,
          1976.   Annual supplements.
Lists 5, 415 titles and 13, 375 analytical entries appropriate for preschool through 6th grade.   Also includes professional books for
librarians, journals, and reviewing media.   Part I, Classified Catalog, lists nonfiction titles according to Dewey Decimal classification,
and fiction titles and short story collections alphabetically by author
in separate sections.   Each entry gives bibliographic information,
price, grade level, subject headings, and annotation.   Part 2 is an
author, title, subject, and analytical index.   Part 3 is a directory
of publishers and distributors.   A new edition is issued every five
years.   Each annual supplement adds more than 500 new titles.

292   Junior High School Library Catalog.   3d ed. New York: H.
          W. Wilson, 1975.   Annual supplements.
Includes 3, 791 titles and 10, 673 analytical entries appropriate for
grades 7 through 9.   Part 1, Classified Catalog, lists nonfiction
according to Dewey Decimal classification, and fiction titles and
short story collections alphabetically by author in separate sections.
Each entry gives bibliographic information, price, subject headings,
and annotation.   Part 2 is an author, title, subject, and analytical
index.   Included are subject analytics to parts of books and author-
title analytics to collections.   Part 3 is a directory of publishers
and distributors.   A new edition is issued every five years.   Each
annual supplement adds more than 500 new titles.

293   Senior High School Library Catalog.   11th ed.   New York:
          H. W. Wilson, 1977.   Annual supplements.
Lists 5, 281 books and 17, 587 analytical entries appropriate for
grades 10 through 12.   Part 1, Classified Catalog, lists nonfiction
titles according to Dewey Decimal classification, followed by
separate listings of fiction and short story collections arranged
alphabetically by author.   Each entry gives bibliographic information,
price, subject headings, and an annotation.   Part 2 is an author,
title, subject, and analytical index to Part 1.   Part 3 is a directory
of publishers and distributors.   A new edition is issued every five
years.   Each annual supplement adds more than 500 new titles.

Annual Listings of All Children's Books in Print

294   Children's Books in Print.   New York: R. R. Bowker, 1969-.
        Annual.
An index of children's books currently available for purchase.   In
three parts: Author Index, Title Index, and Illustrator Index.   In
each part bibliographic information, price, and grade level are given
for each book listed.   Also includes a directory of publishers.   The
11th edition, 1978-79, includes 38, 700 titles from 940 U. S. publishers.   Excludes textbooks and workbooks.

295   Subject Guide to Children's Books in Print.   New York: R. R.
        Bowker, 1970-.   Annual.
A cross-referenced subject arrangement of the books listed in Children's Books in Print.   The 1978-79 edition lists 38, 700 titles under
7, 800 subject categories.   All entries include bibliographic information, price, and grade level.   Includes a key to publishers' and
distributors' abbreviations.

General Bibliographies

296   American Library Association.   Children's Services Division.
        Notable Children's Books, 1940-1970.   Chicago: American
        Library Association, 1977.
A selection of the notable children's books from annual lists published in the Booklist.   Criteria for selection include: (1) literary
quality, (2) originality of text and illustrations, (3) clarity and style
of language, (4) excellence of illustration, (5) excellence of design
and format, (6) timelessness, (7) subject matter of interest to children, (8) acceptance by children.   Arranged alphabetically by author.
Bibliographic information and brief annotation are given for each
book.   Includes a title index and a list of illustrators.

297   Arbuthnot, May H. , and others.   Children's Books Too Good
        to Miss.   Rev. and enl. ed.   Cleveland: The Press of
        Case Western Reserve University, 1971.
An annotated list of 230 titles arranged by age level and type.   The
section "The Artist and Children's Books" contains black-and-white
reproductions of illustrations from 18 books, with comments on each
illustrator.   Title Index and Price List, and Author-Illustrator Index.

298   Best Books for Children, Preschool Through the Middle Grades.
        Edited by John T. Gillespie and Christine B. Gilbert.   New
        York: R. R. Bowker, 1978.
The 15th edition, 1978, is a briefly annotated list of 5, 500 recommended books for K-6 levels, published through 1977.   This list was
published annually from 1959 to 1972.   The 1978 edition is the first
since 1972.   Arranged by subject.   Grade level and sources of recommendation are indicated for each book.   Title index and author-
illustrator index.

299   Best of the Best: Picture, Children's and Youth Books from
        110 Countries or Languages.   2d enl. ed.   Edited by Walter

Scherf.   Munich: Verlag Dokumentation; distributed by R.
R. Bowker, 1976.
An unannotated listing of 4,000 titles representing 67 languages,
selected by librarians and children's literature specialists from
several countries.   Entries are arranged alphabetically by country.
Each section is subdivided by age group (3-6, 7-9, 10-12, and
13-18), with entries arranged by author within each age group.
Entries include name of author, title in the original language and
in German and English, publication date, name and location of
publisher.

300   Books for College Libraries: A Core Collection of 40,000
       Titles.   2d ed.   A project of the Association of College
       and Research Libraries.   6 vols.   Chicago: American
       Library Association, 1975.
Vol. I, Humanities (General, Philosophy, Religion, Music, Fine
Arts); Vol. II, Language and Literature; Vol. III, History; Vol. IV,
Social Sciences; Vol. V, Psychology, Science, Technology, Bibliography; Vol. VI, Indexes (Author, Title, Subject).   Limited to books,
including some monographic series and some annual reviews.   Entries are Library of Congress cards in run-on style, giving full
bibliographic information.   In each volume arrangement is by Library
of Congress classification.

301   Books for Junior College Libraries: A Selected List of Ap-
       proximately 19,700 Titles.   Compiled by James W. Pirie.
       Chicago: American Library Association, 1969.
Arranged by academic subject areas and alphabetically by author
within each area.   Entries give author, title, edition, publisher,
date, price, paging, and Library of Congress card number.   Author
and subject indexes.

302   Child Study Association of America.   The Children's Bookshelf:
       A Guide to Books for and About Children.   New rev. ed.
       New York: Bantam Books, 1965.
A selected, annotated list of more than 2,000 titles arranged by age
group, from preschool age through 14, and by subject within each
group.   Also includes introductory chapters on children's literature,
and chapters on parents' reading on several subjects.   Supplemented
by Children's Books of the Year (see No. 339).

303   Eakin, Mary K.   Good Books for Children: A Selection of
       Outstanding Children's Books Published 1950-65.   3d ed.
       Chicago: University of Chicago Press, 1966.
An annotated list of 1,391 titles selected mainly from the books
recommended in Chicago, University, Center for Children's Books,
Bulletin (see No. 338).   Annotations are both descriptive and evaluative.   Grade level is indicated for each title.   Listed alphabetically
by author with subject and title index.

304   Elementary School Library Collection.   11th ed.   Edited by
       Phyllis Van Orden and Lois Winkel.   Newark, N. J.:   Bro-
       Dart Foundation, 1977.

A list of approximately 10, 000 books, periodicals, and media items arranged by the Dewey Decimal classification.   Includes children's books, reference books, and professional books for teachers and school librarians.   Media items include films, filmstrips, sound tapes, cassettes, games, and multimedia kits.   Recommendations for first, second, and third purchase are given.   Information on each entry includes a brief annotation.   Author, title, and subject indexes.

305   Gillespie, John T. , and Diana Lembo.   Introducing Books: A Guide for the Middle Grades.   New York: R. R. Bowker, 1970.
A bibliography of 80 books designed for teachers and librarians who give reading guidance and book talks to children age 9-14.   Titles are arranged according to developmental goals of childhood.   Entries include bibliographic information, price, reading or interest level, a lengthy plot summary, thematic material, book talk material, and references to other titles with similar theme.   Author-title index and subject index.

306   Gillespie, John T. , and Diana Lembo.   Juniorplots: A Book Talk Manual for Teachers and Librarians.   New York: R. R. Bowker, 1967.
A bibliography of 80 books for teachers and librarians who give reading guidance and book talks to children age 9-16.   Titles are arranged by important goals of adolescent reading.   Information on each book includes plot analysis, thematic material, book talk material, and additional titles with similar theme.   Indexes by authors, titles, and subjects.

307   Gillespie, John T.   More Juniorplots: A Guide for Teachers and Librarians.   New York: R. R. Bowker, 1977.
A bibliography of 72 books appropriate for ages 11 to 16, arranged under nine developmental goals associated with adolescence.   Entries give bibliographic information, reading level, a lengthy plot summary, thematic material, book talk material, additional titles with similar theme, and a reference to biographical material about the author. Author-title index and subject index.

308   Greene, Ellin, and Madalynne Schoenfeld, comps. and eds. A Multimedia Approach to Children's Literature: A Selec- tive List of Films, Filmstrips, and Recordings Based on Children's Books.   2d ed.   Chicago: American Library Association, 1977.
An annotated list of 544 books, each followed by separately annotated listings of films, filmstrips, and recordings based on the book.   A total of 225 16mm films, 300 filmstrips, and 375 disc and tape- recordings are listed.   Includes picture books, folk literature, fiction, drama, poetry, and songs.   Arranged alphabetically by book title. For preschool to 6th grade level.   Entries for books give bibliogra- phic information, price, grade level, and description of contents. For nonbook materials, information includes length, color, price or rental fee, grade level, and descriptive comment.   All book titles

are in English, but Spanish editions of nonbook materials are listed
if available.   A special section on authors and illustrators lists
biographical material in multimedia form.   Also includes an annotated
listing of resources, including related readings, selection aids, program aids, and realia; and a directory of publishers.   Author,
subject, and media indexes.

309   Hinman, Dorothy, and Ruth Zimmerman.   Reading for Young
         People: The Midwest.   Chicago: American Library Asso-
         ciation,   1979.
An annotated bibliography of fiction, history, and biography pertaining
to Ohio, Indiana, Illinois, and Missouri, for grades 4-10.   Each annotation indicates the state or states covered, evaluates the strengths
and weaknesses of the book, and indicates grades for which it is
appropriate.   Subject index.

310   Jacob, Gale S.   Independent Reading Grades One Through
         Three: An Annotated Bibliography with Reading Levels.
         Williamsport, Pa.:   Bro-Dart Foundation, 1975.
An annotated bibliography of 849 books arranged in 29 subject areas,
such as animals, crafts, family relationships, nature study, sports.
Titles selected were examined for appeal of content and format,
literary quality, accuracy, and the Spache reading level formula.
Entries include bibliographic information, price, reading level, and
annotation.   Reading level index, and author-title index.

311   Kujoth, Jean S.   Best-Selling Children's Books.   Metuchen,
         N. J.:   Scarecrow Press, 1973.
A list of 958 books that have sold 100,000 copies or more since
original publication.   Books are listed by author, title, illustrator,
year of publication, number of copies sold, type of book, subject
category, and age level.   Full bibliographic information and a brief
summary of contents are given in the author entries.

312   Larrick, Nancy.   Parent's Guide to Children's Reading.   4th
         ed.   New York: Doubleday, 1975.
Includes a bibliography of more than 700 children's books arranged
by subject; a separate list of recordings, films, and filmstrips based
on children's books; and chapters on the parent's role in developing
children's reading interests, the audiovisual bridge to reading,
building a home library, paperbacks, magazines, and television and
children.

313   Laughlin, Mildred, ed.   Reading for Young People: The Great
         Plains.   Chicago: American Library Association, 1979.
An annotated list of 368 books on the cultural heritage and social
influences of the area, including books on the culture of the Plains
Indians, pioneer life, and heroes of fact and fiction.   Includes fiction,
folktales, poetry, music, drama, biography, and other informational
books for K-12 grade levels.   Each annotation includes a short quote
to identify style, theme, or general mood of the book, and a brief
description of contents, scope, and grade level.   Author, title, and
subject index.

314   National Association of Independent Schools.   Library Commit-
       tee.   Books for Secondary School Libraries.   5th ed.   New
       York: R. R. Bowker, 1976.
A classified list of books selected for college preparatory students in
senior high school.   The 5th edition includes 6, 291 nonfiction titles
ranging from the basic subjects to topics of current concern.   Arranged by Dewey Decimal classification system.   Includes a directory
of publishers and an author-title-subject index.

315   National Council of Teachers of English.   Adventuring with
       Books: A Booklist for Pre-K--Grade 8.   New ed.   Edited
       by Patricia J. Cianciolo.   Urbana, Ill.:   National Council
       of Teachers of English, 1977.
Lists more than 2, 500 titles published since 1970 in 13 categories,
including stories for primary children, novels and short stories,
biography, biological sciences, social studies, crafts and hobbies,
and "just for fun. "   Entries include information about plot or factual
content, style, illustrations, suggested age level, and awards won.
Many of the books included have won national awards.   An introductory section, Children's Literature in the Seventies, discusses
current trends in subject, style, and illustration of books for children.   Author and title indexes.

316   National Council of Teachers of English.   Books for You: A
       Booklist for Senior High Students.   New ed.   Edited by
       Kenneth Donelson.   Urbana, Ill.:   National Council of
       Teachers of English, 1976.
A classified, annotated list of more than 2, 500 titles, including fiction
and nonfiction, most of which were published after 1971.   Arranged
in more than 50 subject categories.   Title and author indexes.

317   National Council of Teachers of English.   Picture Books for
       Children.   Edited by Patricia J. Cianciolo.   Chicago:
       American Library Association, 1973.
An annotated list of 393 titles for preschool through junior high
school age.   Arranged in broad categories with an index of authors,
illustrators, and titles.   Entries include publishing data, price, suggested age level, comments on story theme and style of art.   Includes 35 full-page illustrations.   An introduction defines criteria
for evaluation and selection of picture books.

318   National Council of Teachers of English.   Your Reading: A
       Booklist for Junior High Students.   5th ed.   Edited by
       Jerry L. Walker.   Urbana, Ill.:   National Council of
       Teachers of English, 1975.
A classified, annotated list of more than 1, 600 titles of fiction and
nonfiction, most of which were published after 1970.   Many are
national award winners.   Arranged under more than 40 subject
headings.   Annotations for fiction titles include a summary of the
plot and introduction of the characters.   Annotations for nonfiction
include the scope and purpose.   Includes a directory of publishers,
and title and author indexes.

319   O'Neal, Robert, ed.   Teachers' Guide to World Literature for
       the High School. Urbana, Ill.:   National Council of Teachers
       of English, 1966.
Includes reviews of more than 200 world classics in translation.
Emphasis is on European, British, and American literature, but
well-known classics from Africa, China, Japan, India, and South
America are included.   Genres represented are epics, novels, short
stories, lyrics, comedy, and tragedy.   Reviews discuss the importance of the work, give a summary of the plot, brief information on
the author's life and other writings, and list other works for comparative reading.   Also suggests thematic units of study, and a
reference library for teachers.   Author and title indexes.

320   Owen, Betty M.   Smorgasbord of Books: Titles Junior High
       Readers Relish.   New York: Citation Press, 1974.
An annotated bibliography of approximately 300 titles for readers age
12-14.   Arranged in four categories: teen fiction, teen nonfiction,
anthologies and collections, and adult books.   Annotations give lengthy
summaries and critical comments.   Includes a directory of publishers,
and author and title indexes.

321   Paperbound Books for Young People.   New York: R. R.
       Bowker, 1979.
The first edition, 1979, lists 8, 800 in-print paperback books, in
four separate indexes: subject, author, title, and illustrator.   Full
bibliographic information, with price, is given for each title in all
the indexes.

322   Pittsburgh.   Carnegie Library.   Stories to Tell to Children:
       A Selected List.   8th ed.   Revised and edited by Laura E.
       Cathon, Marion McC. Haushalter, and Virginia A. Russell.
       Margaret Hodges, Consultant.   Pittsburgh: University of
       Pittsburgh Press, 1974.
A list of stories grouped according to interests of children of different ages: preschool children; 6 to 10 years of age; older boys
and girls.   Also includes a listing of stories for holiday programs.
Entries indicate whether story is a fable, folktale, legend, myth,
modern imaginative story, or modern realistic story; and give
author and title of the collection in which the story appears.   A list
of Books Referred To follows the list of stories.   It is arranged by
author or editor and gives title, publisher, and date of each book.
Also includes a list of aids for the storyteller, a classified list of
stories, and an alphabetical list of stories.

323   Polette, Nancy.   E Is for Everybody: A Manual for Bringing
       Fine Books into the Hands and Hearts of Children.   Metuchen,
       N.J.:   Scarecrow Press, 1976.
A selected list of 147 picture books covering a variety of subjects,
for kindergarten through junior high school level.   Titles were
chosen to stimulate independent reading, to serve as a means of
introducing concepts in areas of the curriculum, and as a spring-
board to creative activities in language arts, music, drama, and art.
Each entry includes an annotation and suggested creative classroom
or library activities.   Subject index.

324   Polette, Nancy, and Marjorie Hamlin.   Celebrating with Books.
       Metuchen, N. J. :   Scarecrow Press, 1977.
A list of 169 books on holiday themes, arranged under holidays.
Entries give bibliographic information, grade level, descriptive annotation, and suggestions for activities.   The last chapter includes
examples of how the use of holiday books can vitalize development
of study skills.

325   Quimby, Harriet B. , and Rosemary Weber.   Building a
       Children's Collection: A Suggested Basic Reference Col-
       lection for Academic Libraries and a Suggested Basic Col-
       lection of Children's Books.   Rev. ed.   Middletown, Conn. :
       Choice, 1978.
Originally appeared as two bibliographic essays in the November and
December, 1974, issues of Choice.   The first part cites and discusses reference books in the field of children's literature, including
the history of children's literature, authors, illustrators, awards,
and prizes.   The second part lists children's books for a basic collection, including fiction, picture and easy books, folklore, biography,
poetry, and nonfiction.   Includes more than 1, 000 titles with bibliographic information on each.   Author and title indexes.

326   Rosenberg, Judith K. , and Kenyon C. Rosenberg.   Young
       People's Literature in Series: Fiction: An Annotated
       Bibliographical Guide.   Littleton, Colo. :   Libraries Un-
       limited, 1972.
Lists all series published since 1955 for grade levels 3-9.   Arranged
by author with individual titles listed chronologically within the
series.   Annotations consider plot content, depth and believability of
characterization, writing style, and book format.   A total of 1, 428
titles are listed.

327   Rosenberg, Judith K. , and Kenyon C. Rosenberg.   Young
       People's Literature in Series: Publishers' and Non-Fiction
       Series: An Annotated Bibliographical Guide.   Littleton,
       Colo. :   Libraries Unlimited, 1973.
Includes all in-print series for grades 3-12 published through 1972.
Arranged alphabetically by series title, with individual volumes for
each series listed alphabetically by author.   Untitled author series
are arranged by author.   Annotations are based on quality, durability,
format, reading level, and inclusion of illustrations, indexes, and
bibliographies.   A total of 6, 023 books are listed.   Author index
and title index.

328   Rosenberg, Judith K.   Young People's Literature in Series:
       Fiction, Non-Fiction, and Publishers' Series, 1973-1975.
       Littleton, Colo. :   Libraries Unlimited, 1977.
Supplements Young People's Literature in Series: Fiction (1972)
and Young People's Literature in Series: Publishers' and Non-
Fiction Series (1973).   Contains 2, 877 individual titles.   Fiction
series included are new ones published since 1972, older series
omitted from the first volume, and continuations of series listed in
the first volume.   For grade levels 3-9.   Arrangement in the Fiction

Series section is alphabetical by author, with titles listed chronologically under each author.   Criteria for including fiction are plot,
writing quality, characterization, format, and author's reputation.
Annotations give brief description of plot and age level.   The
Publishers' and Non-Fiction Series are arranged alphabetically by
series title or author's name.   Limited to grade levels 3-12, with
some easier series included for reluctant readers.   Annotations include general quality, merits of individual titles for some series,
grade level, and indication of inclusion of illustrations, indexes, and
bibliographies.   Entries are cross-referenced to the two main volumes.   Includes a directory of publishers, fiction series title index,
author index, and title index.

329   Special Committee of the National Congress of Parents and
         Teachers and the Children's Services Division, American
         Library Association.   Let's Read Together: Books for
         Family Enjoyment.   3d ed.   Chicago: American Library
         Association, 1969.
An annotated list of 577 titles for reading aloud, for a child's own
reading, and for the home library.   Arranged by subject categories,
and by age levels within each category.   Titles range from books
for the youngest child to those for the early teens.

330   Spirt, Diana L.   Introducing More Books: A Guide for the
         Middle Grades.   New York: R. R. Bowker, 1978.
A bibliography of 72 books, mostly fiction, published since 1970, for
ages 8 to 15.   Supplements Introducing Books, 1970 (No. 305) and
Juniorplots, 1967 (No. 306).   Entries are grouped under nine developmental goals.   Each entry includes bibliographic information, price,
summary of plot, analysis of themes, suggestions for discussion,
and a list of recommended books and audiovisual materials on
similar themes.

331   Sutherland, Zena.   The Best in Children's Books: The Uni-
         versity of Chicago Guide to Children's Literature, 1966-1972.
         Chicago: University of Chicago Press, 1973.
A list of 1,400 titles selected from the Bulletin of the Center for
Children's Books.   Entries include bibliographic citation, review,
and grade level.   Arranged alphabetically by author, with indexes of
titles, developmental values, curricular use, reading levels, subjects,
and types of literature.   Includes a directory of American and
British publishers.

332   Walker, Elinor.   Book Bait: Detailed Notes on Adult Books
         Popular with Young People.   3d ed.   Chicago: American
         Library Association, 1979.
A selected list of 100 titles of easy-to-read adult fiction and nonfiction of interest to young people.   Lengthy annotations include a
summary of contents, suggestions for book talks, and titles of related works.

333   Weber, J. Sherwood, ed.   Good Reading: A Helpful Guide for
         Serious Readers.   21st ed.   New York: R. R. Bowker,
         1978.

An annotated list of more than 2,000 titles arranged in 28 subject
areas.   Major sections are: Regional and Historical Cultures, with
subdivisions for Greece, Rome, India and the Far East, Middle East
and Africa, Latin America, Middle Ages, Renaissance, 17th century,
18th century; Literary Types, with sections for the novel (19th and
20th century, continental, British and American), the short story,
poetry, drama, biography, essays, letters and criticism; Humanities,
Social Sciences, and Sciences, including sections for fine arts,
philosophy, religion, history, politics, economics, geography, anthropology and sociology, language, psychology, biological sciences,
physical sciences, and mathematics, with a supplementary list of
science fiction; and a special section for reference books.   Each
section has an introduction written by an authority.   Entries give
bibliographic information, editions, price, level of difficulty, and a
brief annotation.   Includes a "100 Best Books" section.   Author,
title, subject index.

General Bibliographies Published Periodically

334   Association for Childhood Education International.   Bibliography
        of Books for Children.   Washington, D.C.:   The Associa-
        tion, 1937-.   Biennial.
A selective, annotated list designed as a resource for selection of
children's literature and basic reference books for elementary and
junior high school libraries.   The 1978 edition includes about 1,800
fiction and nonfiction titles in four major sections: For Early
Childhood; For Middle and Older Children; For All Ages; and Reference Books.   Each section is subdivided by subject.   Age level is
indicated for each book.   Includes a directory of publishers, and
title and author indexes.

335   Booklist.   Chicago: American Library Association, 1905-.
        Semimonthly.
Each issue includes annotated lists of children's books, books for
young adults, books for easy reading, and films and filmstrips.

336   Books for Children, Preschool Through Junior High School.
        Chicago: American Library Association, 1960-.   Annual.
A compilation of reviews of books recommended in the children's
book section of Booklist.   Arranged in broad subject categories with
subdivisions.   Entries give bibliographic information, price, and
descriptive and critical annotations that summarize the contents,
point out special uses or features, and indicate grade level.

337   CCL Canadian Children's Literature: A Journal of Criticism
        and Review.   Guelph, Ontario: Canadian Children's Press
        in cooperation with the Canadian Children's Literature As-
        sociation, 1975-.   Quarterly.
Contains reviews of Canadian children's books and review articles.
Articles in English and French.

338   Chicago.   University.   Center for Children's Books.   Bulletin.
        Chicago: University of Chicago Press, 1947-.   Monthly.

A monthly listing of new books for preschool through high school, giving bibliographic information, price, descriptive and evaluative annotation, indication of grade level, and rating for each book.

339   Child Study Association of America.   Children's Book Committee.   Children's Books of the Year.   New York: The Association, 1961-.   Annual.
An annotated list of more than 600 books of outstanding quality published during the previous year, for children preschool age through age 14.   Arranged in four age level categories, subdivided by subject.   Other categories include special interests, books for parents and children, reprints and new editions, and a list of paperbacks.   Brief annotations include age level.   Title index.

340   Horn Book Magazine.   Boston: Horn Book, 1924-.   Bimonthly.
Each issue contains a booklist divided by age group.   Entries give bibliographic information and a review for each book.   Author and title index to books reviewed.   Also included in each issue are a separate review section on science books, a section on current adult books of interest to teenagers, a list of recommended paperbacks, and audiovisual reviews.   Also includes articles on children's literature.

341   Junior Bookshelf.   Huddersfield, Eng.:   Marsh Hall, 1936-.   6 issues per year.
Each issue reviews more than 100 books for preschool through 8th grade level.   Reviews are critical and descriptive.   Most books reviewed are published in the United Kingdom.   Also contains articles on children's literature.

342   New York.   Public Library.   Committee on Books for Young Adults.   Books for the Teen Age.   New York: New York Public Library, Office of Young Adult Services, 1932-.   Annual.
A selected, classified list designed primarily for leisure reading. Covers a variety of interests and reading abilities of teenagers. The 1978 edition includes 1,250 titles.

343   School Library Journal.   New York: R. R. Bowker, 1954-.   Monthly, September-May.
Each issue contains signed reviews of books for children and young adults.   Best books of their type are starred.   Semiannual features are Best Books of the Spring and Best Books of the Year.   Also includes articles on school libraries, public library service for children, and young adult library services.

344   U. S. Library of Congress.   Children's Books.   Washington, D. C.:   Government Printing Office, 1964-.   Annual.
A selected list of approximately 200 books for preschool through junior high school level.   Arranged by age group and by subject. Information on each book includes bibliographic information, brief annotation, and grade level.

345 Wilson Library Bulletin. New York: H. W. Wilson, 1914-.
Monthly, September-June.
Regular features include reviews of picture books for children; reviews of books for young adults; reviews of films; reviews of current reference books of interest to school and public librarians, including bibliographies and other reference books concerning children's literature; and brief announcements of publications concerning children and their reading and audiovisual materials. Also frequently contains articles on children's literature.

Bibliographies on Special Subjects

History

346 American History Booklist for High Schools: A Selection for Supplementary Reading. National Council for the Social Studies Bulletin 42. Edited by Ralph Brown and Marian Brown. Washington, D. C.: National Council for the Social Studies, 1969.
A list in 17 chapters, arranged alphabetically by author in each chapter. The first chapter is a basic list of books for a junior or senior high school library. The second chapter lists collections of sources and volumes of readings. Chapters 3-17 are listings of books with brief annotations, by chronological periods. Classification as source material, general nonfiction, biography, or fiction is indicated for each book. Reading level (adult, adolescent, or for slower readers) is also indicated.

347 Dickinson, A. T., Jr. American Historical Fiction. 3d ed. Metuchen, N. J.: Scarecrow Press, 1971.
Lists 2,440 novels, published 1917-1969, classified into chronological periods from colonial days to the space age. Brief annotations. Author-title index and subject index.

348 Hotchkiss, Jeanette. American Historical Fiction and Biography for Children and Young People. Metuchen, N. J.: Scarecrow Press, 1973.
An annotated bibliography of more than 1,500 titles. The first part is a chronological listing of books about the United States from early exploration to mid-twentieth century. The second part, covering North and South America, is arranged by subjects. Reading levels from elementary through young adult are indicated by symbols following the annotations. Indexes of authors, titles, and biographees.

349 Hotchkiss, Jeanette. European Historical Fiction and Biography for Children and Young People. 2d ed. Metuchen, N. J.: Scarecrow Press, 1972.
An annotated bibliography of 1,300 titles for elementary through high school level, with designation of reading and interest levels. Arranged by geographical areas and centuries. Indexes of authors, titles, and biographees.

350 Ireland, Norma O. Index to America: Life and Customs--

Seventeenth Century.   Westwood, Mass.:   F. W. Faxon,
1979.

351   Ireland, Norma O.   Index to America: Life and Customs--
       Eighteenth Century.   Westwood, Mass.:   F. W. Faxon,
       1976.
Both volumes index more than 100 books, including both adult and
juvenile titles, for content on life and customs of the period covered.
Arranged under 2,000 subject headings, which include events, places,
personal names, and other subjects relating to the life and customs
of the period.   Other volumes are planned to cover the 19th and
20th centuries.

352   Irwin, Leonard B.   Guide to Historical Fiction for the Use of
       Schools, Libraries and the General Reader.   10th ed. new
       and rev.   Brooklawn, N. J.:   McKinley Publishing, 1971.
A briefly annotated bibliography of 2,000 titles arranged in sections
on the Ancient World; Europe; Asia, Africa, and the Pacific; United
States; Canada and Latin America.   Each subdivision includes a
separate listing for juvenile books.

353   Irwin, Leonard B.   Guide to Historical Reading: Nonfiction for
       the Use of Schools, Libraries and the General Reader.   10th
       rev. ed.   Washington, D. C.:   Heldref Publications, 1976.
A selective, annotated bibliography with sections on the Ancient
World; Europe; Asia, Africa, and the Pacific; United States; Canada
and Latin America.   Each section includes a separate listing for
juvenile books.

354   McGarry, Daniel D. , and Sarah H. White.   World Historical
       Fiction Guide: An Annotated Chronological, Geographical
       and Topical List of Selected Historical Novels.   2d ed.
       Metuchen, N. J.:   Scarecrow Press, 1973.
A selective bibliography of 6,455 representative works in English
including translations from other languages.   Arranged chronologically
in three major sections: I, Antiquity (to A. D. 400); II, Middle
Ages and Early Renaissance (400-1500); III, The Modern World
(1500-1900).   All three sections are subdivided geographically.
Entries are briefly annotated and numbered.   Author-title index.

355   Metzner, Seymour.   American History in Juvenile Books: A
       Chronological Guide.   New York: H. W. Wilson, 1966.
A bibliography of more than 2,000 titles of fiction and nonfiction
for the elementary and junior high school levels.   Arranged in a
chronological sequence with topical subheadings.   Each subdivision
is divided into fiction, biography, and other nonfiction.   These
sections are arranged by reading levels.   Author, biographical subject, and title indexes.

356   Metzner, Seymour.   World History in Juvenile Books: A
       Geographical and Chronological Guide.   New York: H. W.
       Wilson, 1973.
A bibliography of more than 2,700 titles of fiction and nonfiction for

elementary and junior high school levels.   Arranged by country or
geographical area, then by historical period, with fiction and nonfiction listed separately.   Author, biographical subject, and title
indexes.

357   Sharp, Harold S.   Footnotes to American History: A Bibliog-
        raphic Source Book.   Metuchen, N. J. :   Scarecrow Press,
        1977.
Contains descriptions of 313 events from the discovery of the continent by Norsemen to the present time.   Some events are major and
some are minor but significant in terms of human interest.   Entries
include a brief description in narrative form with significant dates
and names of principal persons involved, followed by a list of readings
in which additional, in-depth information on the events can be found.
More than 4, 000 references to readings are included.   Also included
is an introductory list of general reference works of value for information on historical events.   Index of persons, places, and
subjects.

358   Sharp, Harold S.   Footnotes to World History: A Bibliographic
        Source Book.   Metuchen, N. J. :   Scarecrow Press, 1979.
Contains brief descriptions, in narrative form, of more than 300
events of world history from the legend of Atlantis to current hap-
penings.   Topics range from major events to events of less historical
importance but significant in terms of human interest.   Each description is followed by a list of readings in which additional, in-depth
information on the event can be found.   More than 4, 000 references
to readings are included.   Also included is an introductory list of
general reference works of value for information on historical events.
Index of persons, places, and subjects.

359   Sutherland, Zena.   History in Children's Books: An Annotated
        Bibliography for Schools and Libraries.   Brooklawn, N. J. :
        McKinley Publishing, 1967.
Arranged by geographical areas, and chronologically within each
area, with separate lists for grades K-5 and 6-8 under each heading.
Gives bibliographic and order information and a brief annotation for
each book listed.   Includes history, biography, and historical fiction.

360   World History Book List for High Schools: A Selection for
        Supplementary Reading.   World History Bibliography Com-
        mittee, Alice W. Spieske, Chairman.   National Council for
        the Social Studies Bulletin No. 31.   Rev. ed.   Washington,
        D. C. :   National Council for the Social Studies, 1962.
In two major sections: (1) an annotated list of 483 books arranged
alphabetically by author, giving for each entry bibliographic information, content, nature of presentation, and, where possible, indication of reading difficulty; (2) three author-title lists of the same
books, grouped by time periods, significant topics, and geographical
areas.   Title index and directory of publishers.

International and Intercultural Understanding

361   Africa: An Annotated List of Printed Materials Suitable for
      Children.   Selected and annotated by a Joint Committee of
      the American Library Association, Children's Services
      Division, and the African-American Institute, U.S. Commis-
      sion for UNICEF.   New York: Information Center on Chil-
      dren's Cultures, 1968.
An annotated list of more than 300 items published in English in nine
countries.   Arranged by regions and countries.   Includes materials
for all grade levels, preschool through junior high school.   Entries
give bibliographic information, price, grade level, and annotation
covering scope, contents, use, and evaluation.   Includes a directory
of publishers and an author, title, subject index.

362   Black World in Literature for Children: A Bibliography of
      Print and Non-Print Materials.   Edited by Joyce W. Mills.
      Atlanta: Atlanta University School of Library Service, 1975-.
      Annual.
An annotated bibliography arranged in three sections for ages 3-8,
9-12, and adult.   The first two sections are subdivided by broad
subject categories.   Within divisions entries are arranged alphabetically by title with books and audiovisual materials listed in the
same alphabet.   Includes a list of titles arranged by publisher or
distributor.   Author-title index.

363   Buttlar, Lois, and Lubomyr R. Wynar.   Building Ethnic Col-
      lections: An Annotated Guide for School Media Centers and
      Public Libraries.   Littleton, Colo.:   Libraries Unlimited,
      1977.
Part I, General Titles on Ethnicity, is divided into sections on
reference sources, teaching methodology and curriculum materials,
nonfiction, literature and fiction, and audiovisual materials.   Part
II, Individual Ethnic Groups, is divided into 41 sections on different
ethnic groups plus a section for multiethnic materials.   Individual
sections have subdivisions for reference sources, teaching methodology and curriculum materials, nonfiction, literature and fiction,
and audiovisual materials.   Entries give bibliographic information,
price, grade level, and annotation.   Also includes a directory of
producers and distributors of audiovisual materials, author index,
title index, and audiovisual index.

364   Byler, Mary G.   American Indian Authors for Young Readers:
      A Selected Bibliography.   New York: Association on Ameri-
      can Indian Affairs; distributed by Interbook, 1973.
An annotated list of 200 books written by American Indian authors.
Arranged alphabetically by author.   Tribal affiliation is given for
authors.   Includes a directory of publishers.

365   Chinese in Children's Books.   Prepared by Angela Au Long
      and others.   New York: New York Public Library, 1973.
A list of books about China and the Chinese people.   Includes books
in English and in Chinese, in sections on: Picture Books; Stories

for Younger Children; Stories for Older Children: Folk Tales;
People and Places; Arts and Culture; The Chinese in the United
States.

366   Haviland, Virginia. Children's Books of International Interest:
       A Selection from Four Decades of American Publishing.
       2d ed. Chicago: American Library Association, 1978.
A list of 350 American titles recommended for translation in other
countries. Arranged in categories by type or subject (picture books,
first reading books, fiction, folklore, biography, history, science,
and the arts). Books were chosen to present qualities of experience
that interest children throughout the world, and to show that cultural
differences are not barriers to understanding.

367   Hirschfelder, Arlene B. American Indian Authors: A Repre-
       sentative Bibliography. New York: Association on Ameri-
       can Indian Affairs, 1970.
A list of oral and written literary works by American Indians. Includes supplementary lists of anthologies and periodic publications.

368   Hotchkiss, Jeanette. African-Asian Reading Guide for Children
       and Young Adults. Metuchen, N. J.: Scarecrow Press,
       1976.
An annotated bibliography of 1, 209 books, from picture book through
adult level, concerning the past and present of Africa, Asia, Aus-
tralasia, and the South Seas. Reading and interest levels are indicated for all entries. Arranged geographically with author, title,
illustrator, and biographical indexes.

369   Irwin, Leonard B. Black Studies: A Bibliography for the Use
       of Schools, Libraries and the General Reader. Brooklawn,
       N. J.: McKinley Publishing, 1973.
An annotated bibliography for 6th grade through adult level. In five
sections: black history, biographies and autobiographies, analytical
works dealing with the racial situation, black art and culture, and
the African background.

370   Jackson, Miles M. A Bibliography of Negro History and
       Culture for Young Readers. Pittsburgh: University of
       Pittsburgh Press, 1968.
A bibliography of print and nonprint materials suitable for primary
grades through senior high school. Bibliographic information, price,
descriptive annotation, and grade level are given for each book
listed. Suggested uses are given for some books. Includes a
special section on audiovisual materials. Arranged by subject.
Title and subject index, and author index.

371   Jacobson, Angeline. Contemporary Native American Literature:
       A Selected and Partially Annotated Bibliography. Metuchen,
       N. J.: Scarecrow Press, 1977.
Lists Native American authors and gives sources of their literary
writings in collections, periodicals, and Native American newspapers. Includes publications from 1960 to 1976 and covers poetry,

biography, autobiography, fiction, humor, myth, legend, and spiritual expressions.   Includes a title and first line index of poems, and an author index.   Indicates authors' tribal affiliation.

372   Keating, Charlotte M.   Building Bridges of Understanding.
       Tucson: Palo Verde Publishing, 1967.
An annotated bibliography of books for children, arranged in six sections by American ethnic groups, and within each section by age groups (preschool and primary, upper elementary, junior high, and senior high school levels).

373   Keating, Charlotte M.   Building Bridges of Understanding
       Between Cultures.   Tucson: Palo Verde Publishing, 1971.
A companion volume to Building Bridges of Understanding.   Lists books dealing with race relations, minority groups, and social realities.   Includes sections on Black Americans; Indians and Eskimos; Spanish-speaking Americans; Asian Americans; nationality groups and religious minorities; books for bilingual/bicultural children; African; Caribbean.

374   Lass-Woodfin, Mary J.   Books on American Indians and
       Eskimos: A Selection Guide for Children and Young Adults.
       Chicago: American Library Association, 1977.
An annotated bibliography of 807 books, fiction and nonfiction, for grades K-12.   Arranged alphabetically by author.   Annotations cover the book's strengths, weaknesses, uses, accuracy of information and insight, and format, and give a summary of contents and grade level. Subject index of tribes, persons, and events.

375   McDonough, Irma.   Canadian Books for Children.   Toronto:
       University of Toronto Press, 1978.
An annotated bibliography of books by Canadian writers and other books about Canada.   Lists 1, 500 in-print books and magazines, including French-language publications, for preschool to 9th grade level.   Includes picture books, fiction, nonfiction, and government publications.   Arranged in English and French sections under 24 subject headings.   Entries give bibliographic information, descriptive annotation, and age level.   Also includes a list of sources for the books.   Author and title indexes.

376   Muir, Marcie.   Bibliography of Australian Children's Books.
       Boulder, Colo.:   Westview Press, 1971.   Vol. 2, 1976.
A bibliography of children's books relating to Australia, by Australian and other authors, from the earliest times to the 1970s.   Includes fiction, drama, poetry, and some nonfiction.   Arranged alphabetically by author.   A supplementary section lists books relating to the Southwest Pacific area.   Includes 42 full-page illustrations.

377   Porter, Dorothy B.   The Negro in the United States: A
       Selected Bibliography.   Washington, D.C.:   Library of
       Congress, 1970.
A list of 1, 827 entries grouped by subjects relating to various aspects of black life.   Brief annotations are given for some entries.

The fiction section lists novels and short stories by Negro authors. Index of names and subjects.

378   Recommended East Asian Core Collection for Children's, High School, Public, Community College, and Undergraduate College Libraries.   Compiled by the East Asian Bibliographic Group and edited by William H. O. Scott.   Seattle: University of Washington Libraries, 1974.

Includes 1, 782 books, periodicals, films, filmstrips, tapes and phonorecords, primarily in English, pertaining to China, Taiwan, Japan, Korea, Mongolia, and Tibet.   Reading levels and textbook use are designated for many elementary and high school titles. Intended as a basic buying list for libraries.

379   Reid, Virginia M.   Reading Ladders for Human Relations. 5th ed. Washington, D. C.:   American Council on Education, 1972.

An annotated bibliography of more than 1, 300 books arranged in four sections: Creating a Positive Self-Image; Living with Others; Appreciating Different Cultures; and Coping with Change.   Each section is divided into subcategories.   Within each division, books are arranged by maturity level and then alphabetically by author.   Includes author and title indexes, and a list of publishers.

380   Rollins, Charlemae H.   We Build Together: A Reader's Guide to Negro Life and Literature for Elementary and High School Use.   3d ed.   Champaign, Ill.:   National Council of Teachers of English, 1967.

A selected, annotated list of books for preschool to 9th grade level, arranged by type and subject (picture books, fiction, history, biography, poetry, folklore, music, science, and sports).   Grade level is indicated for each book listed.   An introduction provides background information and discusses problems related to stereotypes and the use of dialects.   Includes a list of sources, and a directory of publishers.   Indexes of biographies; authors, editors, illustrators; and book titles.

381   Rollock, Barbara.   The Black Experience in Children's Books. New York: New York Public Library, 1974.

An annotated bibliography of more than 800 titles for grade levels K-12.   A revised edition of the same title compiled by Augusta Baker in 1971.   Books were selected to present the wide range of thought and experience in the black community, to emphasize the similarity of peoples, and to develop an appreciation of the universality of human experience.   Arranged in four geographical areas: United States; South and Central America and the Caribbean; Africa; England.   Each section is subdivided by type (picture books, stories, folklore, poetry, etc.).   Within each subsection arrangement is alphabetical by title.   Entries give title, author, illustrator, publisher, date, price, and brief annotation.   Index of titles and authors.

382   Schmidt, Nancy.   Children's Books on Africa and Their Authors: An Annotated Bibliography.   New York: Holmes and Meier, 1975.

A bibliography of 837 books published in English in the United States, Europe, and Africa, 1880-1973.   Includes titles for young adults. Arrangement is by author.   Entries include brief biographical information about the author, a summary of contents, and an evaluation of the accuracy of African geography, history, and social customs. Illustrations, as well as content of the book, are evaluated.   Indexes by geographic area, co-author, illustrator, series, subject, title, and tribe.

383   Schmidt, Nancy.   Children's Literature and Audiovisual
           Materials in Africa.   New York: Conch Magazine (Publish-
           ers), 1977.
A special issue of Conch Review of Books containing reviews of children's books and other materials about Africa, published since 1970.   Sections are: Bibliographic Essays (Bibliographies of Children's Literature About Africa, 1970-1975, and Locating Sources About African Children and Children's Books on Africa); Audio-Visual Review Essays; Cultures of the Niger Portrayed in Films and Books; Picture Books; Enchantment of Africa Series; Visual Geography Series; History, Society, Politics, and Art; Folklore; Fiction; African Wildlife; Recent Books for South African Children; a list of Books Received.   Indexes of authors, materials reviewed, and reviewers.

384   Schon, Isabel.   A Bicultural Heritage: Themes for the Ex-
           ploration of Mexican and Mexican-American Culture in
           Books for Children and Adolescents.   Metuchen, N. J. :
           Scarecrow Press, 1978.
Arranged by five theme areas: customs, lifestyles, heroes, folklore, and key historical developments.   Each section is subdivided into three grade levels, K-2, 3-6, 7-12.   Each subsection contains a list of books, preceded by Outcomes, specific learnings that students may be expected to acquire from the readings and activities suggested, and followed by Discussions, with comments on individual books in relation to various subjects, and Evaluations and Follow-up Activities, which coincide with the Outcomes for each theme.   Appendix A, The Dilemma of Selecting Spanish-Language Books; Appendix B, A Sad Truth: The State of the Literature for Children and Adolescents of Mexico; Appendix C, A Heartfelt Plea: Notes on Books for Children and Adolescents from Spain.   Author and title indexes.

385   Schon, Isabel.   Books in Spanish for Children and Young Adults:
           An Annotated Guide.   Metuchen, N. J. :   Scarecrow Press,
           1978.
A bibliography of 450 titles by Hispanic authors from 14 countries in South and Central America and Spain.   Appropriate for preschool through high school age.   Arrangement is by geographic area subdivided by art, biography, classics, fiction, history, legends, poetry, religious books, songs, and theater.   Entries give bibliographic information in Spanish, critical and evaluative annotations in English, with indication of grade level and level of quality.   Translations and textbooks are not included.   Appendix I is a directory of book dealers

in Spanish-speaking countries.   Appendix II is a directory of U.S. book dealers.   Author, title, and subject indexes.

386   Stanford, Barbara D. , and Karima Amin.   Black Literature for High School Students.   Urbana, Ill. :   National Council of Teachers of English, 1978.
A survey of black American literature from colonial times to the present includes sketches of historical periods and commentary on more than 50 authors.   The bibliography describes 370 books, including fiction, biography, autobiography, poetry, anthologies, and literary criticism.   Also includes ten teaching units covering subjects from slave narrative to present day protest literature; supplementary activities; and special bibliographies.   Indexes.

387   Stensland, Anna Lee.   Literature by and About the American Indian.   Urbana, Ill. :   National Council of Teachers of English, 1973.
An annotated bibliography of more than 350 books for junior and senior high school students.   Includes books on myths, legends, poetry, fiction, biography, autobiography, history, the arts, and modern Indian life and problems.   Also includes aids to teachers, study guides, and suggestions for a basic classroom or resource center collection.   Introductory essays are on the suppression of Indian cultures in the United States, literary stereotypes of Indians, problems of selecting literature on Indians, and dominant themes in literature on Indians.

Science and Mathematics

388   AAAS Science Book List for Children.   3d ed.   Compiled by Hilary J. Deason.   Washington, D.C. :   American Association for the Advancement of Science, 1972.
A selected, annotated list of science and mathematics books for children of elementary school age.   Includes 1, 500 titles in a subject arrangement.   Titles are designated as K for preschool or kindergarten, E-P for primary or very simple, E-I for intermediate, and E-A for advanced.

389   AAAS Science Book List: A Selected and Annotated List of Science and Mathematics Books for Secondary School Students, College Undergraduates and Nonspecialists.   3d ed.   Compiled by Hilary J. Deason.   Washington, D.C. :   American Association for the Advancement of Science, 1970.
Includes 2, 441 titles of trade books, textbooks, and reference books in the pure and applied sciences and mathematics, arranged by subject.   Entries give bibliographic data, annotation, and level of difficulty.   Includes a directory of publishers and an index to subjects and titles.

390   Appraisal: Children's Science Books.   Cambridge, Mass. :   Children' Science Book Committee, 1967-.   3 issues per year.
Each issue covers 50 to 75 science books for elementary through high school levels.   Reviews by librarians and subject specialists include grade level and a rating code.

391   Dick, Elie M.   Current Information Sources in Mathematics:
      An Annotated Guide to Books and Periodicals, 1960-1972.
      Littleton, Colo.:   Libraries Unlimited, 1973.
A list of more than 1,600 publications on college level mathematics,
arranged in 37 chapters.   The first 33 chapters list references on
specific branches of mathematics--algebra, trigonometry, calculus,
analytical geometry, etc.   The last four chapters list periodicals,
directories, professional organizations, government agencies, and
publishers.

392   Growing Up with Science Books.   11th ed.   New York: R. R.
      Bowker, 1976.
A guide to 200 selected science books for children.   Arranged by
age group and subject.   Entries give title, author, illustrator,
publisher, price, and a brief annotation.

393   Matthias, Margaret, and Diane Thiessen.   Children's Mathe-
      matics Books.   Chicago: American Library Association,
      1979.
Lists and evaluates approximately 200 math picture books for preschool through 4th grade level.   Arrangement is by concepts that
correspond to the mathematical perception of children of this age
group, concepts such as number, time, measurement, shapes, and
angles.

394   Schaaf, William L.   The High School Mathematics Library.
      6th ed.   Reston, Va.:   National Council of Teachers of
      Mathematics, 1976.
Lists 925 titles arranged by subject including mathematical disciplines
(algebra, geometry, statistics, etc.) and such subjects as philosophy
of mathematics, logic, history, and biography.   Titles added since
the previous edition emphasize computers, data processing and programming, probability, abstract algebra, contemporary geometry,
topology, and recreational mathematics.   Includes a new section on
metrics.   Also includes professional books for teachers, and dictionaries, handbooks, and periodicals.   Includes a directory of
publishers.

395   Science Books and Films.   Washington, D.C.:   American As-
      sociation for the Advancement of Science, 1965-.   Quarterly.
Reviews trade books, textbooks, reference books, and films on pure
and applied science for all levels, primary through adult.   Arranged
by subject.   Entries include bibliographic data, grade level, and
critical annotations.

396   Science for Society: A Bibliography.   6th ed.   Prepared by
      Joseph M. Dasbach.   Washington, D.C.:   American As-
      sociation for the Advancement of Science, 1976.
An annotated list of books and periodical articles that focus on
problems that arise from the interaction between society and science
and technology.   Arranged in 11 subject categories, such as aging,
energy, and pollution.   Each section is further subdivided.   A list
of contents is given at the beginning of each section.   Includes a
section on bibliographies.

397   Wheeler, Margariete M. , and Clarence E. Hardgrove.   Mathe-
      matics Library: Elementary and Junior High School.   4th
      ed.   Reston, Va.:   National Council of Teachers of Mathe-
      matics, 1978.
An annotated bibliography of books for recreational and informational
reading, published mostly in the 1960s and 1970s.   Arranged alphabetically by author.   Entries give bibliographic information, description of contents, and grade level.   Includes a directory of publishers.

Sports

398   Harrah, Barbara K.   Sports Books for Children: An Annotated
      Bibliography.   Metuchen, N. J.:   Scarecrow Press, 1978.
A bibliography of 3, 509 sports books, published through 1976, appropriate for interests and reading abilities of students preschool
through grade 12.   Covers water, equestrian, hunting, individual and
team sports, sports flying, martial arts, and others.   Includes, in
addition to books on sports, biographies, histories, and fiction.   Arranged by broad group, and subdivided by specific sports.   Annotations describe contents and indicate interest and reading levels.

Bibliographies on Special Problems

Disadvantaged or Poor Readers

399   American Library Association.   Library Service to the Dis-
      advantaged Child Committee.   I Read, You Read, We Read;
      I See, You See, We See;   I Hear, You Hear, We Hear; I
      Learn, You Learn, We Learn.   Chicago: American Library
      Association, 1971.
Lists poems, stories, films, and records arranged by age levels,
preschool, 5-8, 8-11, and 12-14.   Information on each title includes
price, brief annotation, and suggested program aids.

400   High Interest-Easy Reading for Junior and Senior High School
      Students.   Edited by Marian E. White.   2d ed.   New York:
      Citation Press, 1972.
An annotated list arranged by such categories as adventure, careers,
history, mystery, folktales, poetry, science fiction, short stories,
war, biography.   Grade levels are indicated.   Includes a directory
of publishers and author and title indexes.

401   Palmer, Julia R.   Read for Your Life: Two Successful Ef-
      forts to Help People Read and an Annotated List of the Books
      That Made Them Want To.   Metuchen, N. J.:   Scarecrow
      Press, 1974.
Part I describes the author's experience with two literacy programs.
Also included is a section on library techniques for helping the disadvantaged.   Part II is an annotated bibliography of 1, 609 books
recommended to interest people with little experience in reading.
Arrangement is by the Dewey classification system.   Entries give bibliographic information, price, reading level, and interest level.   Also
includes a separate list of pamphlets, a directory of publishers, and a

list of book jobbers.   There are author, title, and biographical indexes, and a listing of entry numbers for books of interest to minority groups.

402   Spache, George D.   <u>Good Reading for Poor Readers.</u>   10th ed.
      Champaign, Ill.:   Garrard Publishing, 1978.
A bibliography of materials for reluctant and remedial readers.
Includes a listing of 700 trade books, arranged by subject with a
brief annotation and indication of reading level and interest level for
each book; a list of adapted and simplified materials, mostly classics written down for the poor reader; a list of 540 textbooks, workbooks and games; 90 magazines and newspapers with indication of
interest and grade levels; 190 book series, with brief annotation and
reading and interest levels; book clubs for children; indexes and
reading lists; programmed materials; auditory and visual perception
materials; and resources for teachers of the disadvantaged.   Introductory chapters on interests of young readers and ways to motivate
them, book selection, bibliotherapy, and estimating readability.   The
Spache Readability Formula is given in an appendix.   Includes
author and title indexes, and a directory of publishers.

403   Spache, George D.   <u>Good Reading for the Disadvantaged</u>
      <u>Reader: Multi-Ethnic Resources.</u>   Rev. ed.   Champaign,
      Ill.:   Garrard Publishing, 1975.
Lists multiethnic educational materials, including books and audiovisual materials, for elementary and secondary levels.   An introduction discusses the development of self-concept, and reading
instruction for the disadvantaged.   In 20 chapters covering black
Americans, American Indians, Eskimos and Alaska, inner city life,
Mexican Americans and migrant workers, Orientals, Puerto Ricans,
adult education, school drop-outs, professional reading improvement
for teachers, social sciences, science, art, music, literature, and
human relations.   Entries give bibliographic information, reading
level, and a brief annotation.   Includes a directory of publishers and
author and title indexes.

404   Withrow, Dorothy E., Helen B. Carey, and Bertha M. Hirzel.
      <u>Gateways to Readable Books: An Annotated Graded List of</u>
      <u>Books in Many Fields for Adolescents Who Are Reluctant to</u>
      <u>Read or Find Reading Difficult.</u>   5th ed.   New York: H.
      W. Wilson, 1975.
A list of more than 1,000 titles, classified by subject and covering
a wide range of interests.   Intended primarily for high school students with reading ability below the expected level of their grade.
Bibliographic information, price, level of difficulty, and brief annotation are given for each title.   Range is from the 4th grade level or
lower.   Also included are lists of reading texts and workbooks, books
in series, magazines and newspapers, simplified dictionaries, a
directory of publishers and distributors, author index, title index, and
index to grade level of reading difficulty.

Gifted Children

405   Baskin, Barbara, and Karen Harris.   <u>Books for the Gifted</u>
      <u>Child.</u>   New York: R. R. Bowker, 1979.

In four chapters: Who Is the Gifted Child?; Society and the Intellectually Able; Young Gifted Readers and Their Needs; and the main section, Books Useful to Gifted Readers, an annotated list of fiction and nonfiction books, periodicals, puzzle and picture books, alphabet and counting books, and poetry. Author-title-subject index.

Physically Handicapped

406   Baskin, Barbara, and Karen Harris. Notes from a Different Drummer: A Guide to Juvenile Fiction Portraying the Handicapped. New York: R. R. Bowker, 1977.
An annotated list of 311 titles, published 1940-1975, arranged by author. Entries give bibliographic information, reading level, indication of disability portrayed, a summary of the plot, and a critical analysis. Analyses are from both literary and special education points of view, and cover content, concept, characterization, and social and psychological perspectives in children's literature portraying the handicapped. The introduction contains four lengthy articles, each with a list of references: Society and the Handicapped; Literary Treatment of Disability; Assessing and Using Juvenile Fiction Portraying the Disabled; and Patterns and Trends in Juvenile Fiction, 1940-1975. Title and subject indexes.

407   Large Type Books in Print. 3d ed. New York: R. R. Bowker. 1978.
The 1978 edition lists more than 3,000 books reproduced in larger type than the original for easier reading by the visually handicapped. Includes adult trade books, children's books, and el-hi textbooks, arranged by subject. Entries give author, title, binding, price, type size, book size, discount to institutions, and publisher. The book itself is produced in 18-point type so it may be used by the visually handicapped. Author and title indexes.

408   U.S. Library of Congress. Division for the Blind and Physically Handicapped. Cassette Books. 2d ed. Washington, D.C.: Government Printing Office, 1974.
An annotated list of 1,200 titles in a classified arrangement. Includes titles of all cassette books issued since 1968. Includes a section on children's books, fiction and nonfiction.

409   U.S. Library of Congress. Division for the Blind and Physically Handicapped. For Younger Readers: Braille and Talking Books. Washington, D.C.: Government Printing Office. Biennial.
In two parts, one for Braille books and one for talking books. Each part has an annotated list of books classified as fiction and nonfiction, and books for very young readers.

410   U.S. Library of Congress. Division for the Blind and Physically Handicapped. I Went to the Animal Fair: A Selected List of Animal Books for Children Which Have Appeared in Talking Book Topics and Braille Book Review. Washington, D.C.: Government Printing Office, 1975.

A list of fiction and nonfiction books available on disc and cassette and in Braille.

Personal and Social Problems

411   Bernstein, Joanne E.   Books to Help Children Cope with
        Separation and Loss.   New York   R. R. Bowker, 1977.
Part I, An Overview, includes a discussion of children's concept of
and reaction to separation, and bibliotherapy as a means of helping
young people cope with separation and loss.   Part II is an annotated
bibliography of 438 books for ages 3 to 16, most of which were
published after 1970.   Three major divisions are: Learning to Face
Separation (accepting a new sibling, going to a new school, a new
neighborhood, etc.); Coping with Tragic Loss (death, divorce,
desertion, illness, war and displacement); Who Will Take Care of
Me (foster care, stepparents, adoption, homelessness).   Each entry
gives bibliographic information, price, classification as fiction or
nonfiction, interest level, reading level, and annotation.   Part III
contains two lists of readings for adults, one on separation and loss,
and one on bibliotherapy.   Author, title, subject, interest level, and
reading level indexes.

412   Dreyer, Sharon S.   The Bookfinder: A Guide to Children's
        Literature About the Needs and Problems of Youth Aged
        2-15.   Circle Pines, Minn. :   American Guidance Service,
        1977.
An annotated guide to 1, 031 titles.   In two separately paged parts
bound side by side.   The top section contains table of contents,
subject, author, and title indexes, and a publisher's directory to
the titles described in the section below.   Arrangement in the main
section is alphabetical by author.   Books listed are described and
categorized by 450 psychological, behavioral, and developmental
topics of concern to children and young adults.   Annotations include
themes and subthemes, synopsis, potential uses, reading level, and
availability in other forms including films, filmstrips, tapes, cassettes, records, paperbacks, large print, and Braille editions.
Most titles included are fiction, with some biographies and other
nonfiction.   Also includes an explanation of bibliotherapy, a list of
other subject bibliographies of children's books, and a list of professional readings on bibliotherapy.

413   Rudman, Masha K.   Children's Literature: An Issues Ap-
        proach.   Lexington, Mass. :   D. C. Heath, 1976.
Contains chapters that deal with the subjects of siblings, divorce,
death and old age, war, sex, the black, the Native American, and
the female.   Each chapter contains a discussion of the subject, suggested criteria for selection of books, a discussion of particular
children's books relating to the subject, an annotated list of references
that relate the subject to children and books, and an annotated
bibliography of children's books pertaining to the subject.   Chapters
on the black, the Native American, and the female also contain a
list of organizations and publishers.   Entries in the bibliographies
give bibliographic information, age level, and a descriptive and

critical annotation.   Also contains a chapter on using children's books in a reading program.   Appendixes: A, Publishers' Addresses; B, Selected Children's Book Awards; C, Other References for Children's Literature.   Author-illustrator index, title index, subject index.

414   Wilkin, Binnie T.   Survival Themes in Fiction for Children and
        Young People.   Metuchen, N. J.:   Scarecrow Press, 1978.
An annotated bibliography of materials that "reflect sensitivity to the individual and to societal issues."   Emphasis is on fiction but some nonfiction is included.   Some audiovisual items are also listed. Most materials were issued in the 1960s and 1970s.   The introduction includes a historical outline of developments in England and America that affected children's literature.   Main parts of the bibliography are: I, The Individual (sections on loneliness, feelings, sexuality, images); II, Pairings and Groupings (friendship, peer pressures, family); III, Views of the World (man and the environment, religion and politics, war and peace, celebration of life and death).   Entries in each section are arranged by title.   They give bibliographic information and a summary of plot or contents.   Each section is introduced by an essay discussing educational, psychological, and sociological perspectives.   Quotations from taped interviews with young people are also included.   Part IV, Sources and Notes, is an annotated bibliography of background materials, sources used, articles that offer criticism of books included, and bibliographies on the various categories.   Author-title-subject index.

Sexism, Racism

415   Adell, Judith, and Hilary D. Klein.   A Guide to Non-Sexist
        Children's Books.   Edited by Waltraud Schacher.   Introduc-
        tion by Alan Alda.   Chicago: Academy Press, 1976.
An annotated bibliography of books that "treat boys and girls as people who have the same kinds of frailties and strengths."   Divided into grade levels (preschool-3, 3-7, 7-12, all ages), and subdivided as fiction and nonfiction.   Arranged alphabetically by author within sections.   Annotations emphasize reasons for selection.   Title and author indexes.

416   Council on Interracial Books for Children.   Racism and
        Sexism Resource Center for Educators.   Human and Anti-
        Human Values in Children's Books: A Content Rating
        Instrument for Educators and Concerned Parents; Guidelines
        for the Future.   New York: The Center, 1976.
The first section identifies the "isms" in children's books that limit human potential, such as racism, sexism, ageism, elitism, escapism, materialism, individualism, and nonconformism.   The main section contains analyses of 235 children's books published in 1975, preschool through high school level, selected for their minority, feminist, or social themes.   Each book is scored on a Values Rating Checklist in the categories of racism, sexism, etc.

417   Davis, Enid.   The Liberty Cap: A Catalogue of Non-Sexist
        Materials for Children.   Chicago: Academy Press, 1977.

Part 1 consists of 15 short articles on authors of children's books.
Part 2 contains 650 reviews arranged in six chapters: picture
books; easy readers; fiction, grades 3-10; nonfiction, grades 3-10;
adult books for young adults; and nonbook materials.   Part 3 is a
listing of 121 resources for parents and professionals.   Part 4 contains five indexes (author; title; general subject; fiction, subject; and
nonfiction, subject), and a list of publishers, distributors, and
organizations.

418   Feminists on Children's Media.   Little Miss Muffet Fights
      Back: A Bibliography of Recommended Non-Sexist Books
      About Girls for Young Readers.   Rev. ed.   New York:
      Feminists on Children's Media, 1974.
A selective bibliography of 178 books that show girls and women as
vital human beings, or show understanding of social conditions that
encourage or prevent self-fulfillment.   In sections on picture books,
fiction, biography, and history and women's rights.   Entries give
author, title, publisher, date of publication, and a brief annotation.
The appendix includes information on how to encourage production,
purchase, and use of good books that portray women positively, how
to get a children's book published, and where to find articles on
sexism in children's books; and a list of articles and books on sexism
in education and on background on the women's movement.

419   Kulkin, Mary Ellen.   Her Way: Biographies of Women for
      Young People.   Chicago: American Library Association,
      1976.
A guide to biographies of approximately 800 women from all periods
of history and all parts of the world.   The first section includes
profiles of 260 women.   Each profile is followed by an annotated list
of biographies for preschool through high school level.   Annotations
indicate grade level.   The second section is an annotated list of 300
collective biographies.   An appendix classifies women by geographic
area and by area of achievement.

420   Rosenfelt, Debora S.   Strong Women: An Annotated Bibliogra-
      phy of Literature for the High School Classroom.   Old
      Westbury, N.Y.: Feminist Press, 1976.
An annotated list of 127 books that emphasize strength and achievement in women who lived at various times and in various places.
Includes anthologies, autobiographies and biographies, plays, novels,
short stories, and poetry.   Cross-topical index.

Reference Books

421   Lock, Muriel.   Reference Material for Young People.   Rev.
      and enl. ed.   Hamden, Conn.: Shoe String Press, 1971.
Arranged in sections on: Encyclopedias and Encyclopedic Guides to
Knowledge; Dictionaries and Word Books; Atlases, Maps, and Globes;
"Lifemanship," the World Scene and Current Affairs; The World of
Nature; The World of Man; Planning for the Future: Career Books;
Audiovisual Material and Equipment.   Descriptive and evaluative
comment is given for each entry.   Index of names, and index of
titles.

422   Peterson, Carolyn S.   Reference Books for Elementary and
      Junior High School Libraries.   2d ed.   Metuchen, N. J.:
      Scarecrow Press, 1975.
An annotated list of nearly 900 titles, including encyclopedias,
language dictionaries, handbooks, indexes, atlases, biographical
dictionaries, bibliographies, and special reference books covering
subject areas of the curriculum and children's interests.   Also includes sections on ethnic groups in America, review sources, and
sample basic collections for primary, intermediate, and junior high
school levels.

423   Wynar, Christine L.   Guide to Reference Books for School
      Media Centers.   Littleton, Colo.:   Libraries Unlimited,
      1973.   Biennial supplements.
The 1973 volume contains 2,575 annotated entries for reference books
suitable for grade levels K-12, covering all curricular and extra-
curricular areas.   Section 1, Media Sources, lists tools for identifying books, films, recordings, and other types of media.   Section
2, Media Selection, describes 100 selection aids for print and nonprint media.   Section 3 lists general reference sources.   In the
main body 2,300 reference books are arranged alphabetically under
50 subject headings.   Entries give bibliographic information, price,
availability of paperback editions, annotation covering scope, arrangement, purpose, reader to whom addressed, and symbols citing reviews in journals.   Author-title-subject index.   The 1974-75 supplement, published in 1976, includes 518 additional reference titles
published 1973-1975.   Biennial supplements are planned.

Periodicals

424   Dobler, Lavinia, and Muriel Fuller.   The Dobler World Direc-
      tory of Youth Periodicals.   3d enl. ed.   New York   Cita-
      tion Press, 1970.
Lists approximately 1,000 periodicals by countries.   The list for the
United States is subdivided by subjects.   Information for entries includes frequency of publication, price, editor, publisher, address,
age level, and a descriptive annotation.

      Katz, William, and Berry G. Richards.   Magazines for
      Libraries: For the General Reader and School, Junior
      College, College, University, and Public Libraries.   3d
      ed.   New York   R. R. Bowker, 1978 (see No. 104).

425   Richardson, Selma K.   Periodicals for School Media Programs.
      Chicago: American Library Association, 1978.
Lists and evaluates more than 500 periodicals appropriate for grades
K-12.   Titles were chosen to correspond with curricular demands
and students' reading levels and interests.   Includes periodicals of
interest to inner city, suburban, and rural students, and to average,
reluctant, and advanced readers.   Also includes foreign and ethnic
periodicals.   Titles are arranged alphabetically.   Information on each
periodical includes title, publisher, address, grade level, frequency,
price, evaluative annotation, source in which the periodical is in-

dexed, and cross-references to other titles covering the same subject. Earlier editions, with the title Periodicals for School Libraries, were edited by Marian H. Scott.

Indexes

Fiction

426   American Library Association.   Subject and Title Index to
        Short Stories for Children.   Chicago: American Library
        Association, 1955.
An index of 372 books for third grade through high school.   Includes a list of books indexed, which gives author, title, publisher, and grade level for each book; a subject index; and a list of stories indexed.

427   Chicorel Index to Short Stories in Anthologies and Collections.
        Edited by Marietta Chicorel.   Chicorel Index Series, Vols.
        12, 12A, 12B, 12C.   New York: Chicorel Library Pub-
        lishing, 1974.   Supplements, 1976-.
Includes 60,000 entries for short stories of all nations and throughout literary history in English or in translation, from 1,500 collections. Author, story title, and anthology title entries are in one alphabet. Author and story title entries include the title of the anthology or collection in which the story appears.   Full bibliographic information is given in each anthology or collection title entry, plus a list of contents.   Following the main section are a subject guide to the anthologies, and an alphabetical list of the anthologies analyzed.   The 1975-76 supplement includes 18,720 entries.   Following the main section are a list of anthologies, a short story title list, an author list, a translator list, and a subject guide.

428   Short Story Index.   New York: H. W. Wilson, 1953.   Supple-
        ment, 1950-1954.   1956.   Supplement, 1955-1958.   1960.
        Supplement, 1959-1963.   1965.   Supplement, 1964-1968.
        1969.   Supplement, 1969-1973.   1974.   Annual, 1974-.
An author, title, and subject index to stories in collections.   The main volume indexes 60,000 stories in 4,320 collections.   The five supplements add 47,886 stories in 3,105 collections.   The Index has been issued annually since 1974, with permanent five-year cumula-tions.   Since 1974, stories from approximately 45 periodicals in-dexed in Readers' Guide and Humanities Index have been included in addition to stories in collections.   In four parts: Part 1, Index to Short Stories, indexes stories in collections by author, title, and subject, and stories in periodicals by author and title, with refer-ences to collections or periodicals given in author entries; Part 2, List of Collections Indexed, is a list by author and title, with bib-liographic information given under author; Part 3, Directory of Publishers and Distributors; Part 4, Directory of Periodicals.   Each annual volume indexes more than 3,000 stories published during the year.   The 1974-78 cumulation indexes 11,000 stories in collections plus 2,500 from periodicals.

429   Messerli, Douglas, and Howard N. Fox.   Index to Periodical
      Fiction in English, 1965-1969.   Metuchen, N. J.:   Scare-
      crow Press, 1977.
Contains 11, 077 entries from 405 magazines published January,
1965-December, 1969.   Indexes almost all American magazines that
publish fiction and a selection of foreign periodicals published in
English.   The index is arranged alphabetically by author, except in
the first 18 entries, which are title entries for works with no author.
Entries give author, title, translator where applicable, and reference
to the periodical in which the story appears.   A list of periodicals
indexed precedes the index.   Includes a translator index and a title
index.   This volume is the first of a planned series of five-year
compilations.

430   Fiction Catalog.   9th ed.   New York   H. W. Wilson, 1976.
      Annual supplements.
Part 1 is a listing of 4, 734 titles alphabetically by author, with
bibliographic information and an annotation for each entry.   Includes
analytical entries for novelettes and composite works.   Part 2 is a
title and subject index to Part 1.   Part 3 is a directory of publishers
and distributors.   A new edition is published every five years.   Kept
up to date with annual supplements.

431   Contento, William.   Index to Science Fiction Anthologies and
      Collections.   Boston: G. K. Hall, 1978.
Covers more than 2, 000 book titles with full contents listings of
more than 1, 900 books containing 12, 000 stories by 2, 500 authors.
It attempts to include all English-language science fiction anthologies
and collections published through June, 1977.   Section I is a list of
abbreviations used for book type, publisher, story type, and original
source of story.   Section II, Checklist of Books Indexed, lists book
titles followed by author or editor, type of book, publisher, date of
publication, and notes about the book.   Section III, Author Index, is
a listing by author, giving name and notes on pseudonyms, books by
the author, stories by the author, and books containing each story.
Section IV, Story Index, is a listing of all story titles giving for
each title the author and books containing the story.   Section V, Book
Contents, lists anthologies and collections by title, with a listing of
stories and their authors contained in each book.

432   Siemon, Frederick.   Science Fiction Story Index, 1950-1968.
      Chicago: American Library Association, 1971.
Indexes 3, 400 science fiction short stories, novels, novellas, and
poems in 350 anthologies.   In three parts: Author-Title Index, a
listing of stories alphabetically by author, giving code numbers of
the anthologies in which the stories appear; Bibliography of Indexed
Anthologies, an alphabetical listing of anthologies giving complete
bibliographic information and code number for each one; and Title-
Author Index, an alphabetical listing of 3, 400 titles giving author
for each title.

433   Eastman, Mary H.   Index to Fairy Tales, Myths and Legends.
      2d ed. rev. and enl.   Boston   F. W. Faxon, 1926.   Sup-
      plement, 1937.   Second Supplement, 1952.

A title index including fairy tales, fables, stories from Greek and
Norse mythology, hero stories, and some modern stories. Includes
a list of books analyzed, with bibliographic information and price;
and a list for storytellers, geographical and racial.

434   Ireland, Norma O.   Index to Fairy Tales, 1949-1972, Including
      Folklore, Legends and Myths in Collections.   Westwood,
      Mass.:   F. W. Faxon, 1973.
An index by title and subject to fairy tales, folklore, legends, and
myths of all countries of the world.   Titles and subjects are in one
alphabet, with location in collections given in title entries.   Includes
a list of 406 collections analyzed with full bibliographic information.
Continues Eastman's Index to Fairy Tales.

Plays

435   Chicorel Theater Index to Plays for Young People in Periodi-
      cals, Anthologies and Collections.   Edited by Marietta
      Chicorel.   Chicorel Index Series, Vol. 9.   New York:
      Chicorel Library Publishing, 1974.
A guide to plays published in periodicals and books from 1900 to
recently published plays by contemporary playwrights.   Age range is
5 to 16.   The main section includes 15,000 entries arranged alphabetically.   Main entries are by periodical title or title of the anthology, collection, or record album.   Information on main entries includes subject and indication of elementary or secondary level.   Also
included in the main section are entries by titles of plays, authors,
translators, adapters, and editors.   Other sections are: Play Title
Index, Editor Index, Author Index, List of Anthologies and Collections, Adapter Index, Translator Index, and Publishers Index.   Other
play indexes in the Chicorel Index series are: Chicorel Theater
Index to Plays in Anthologies, Periodicals, Discs and Tapes, Vol. 1,
1970; Vol. 2, 1971; Vol. 3, 1972; Chicorel Theater Index to Plays
in Periodicals, Vol. 8, 1973; and Chicorel Theater Index to Plays
in Anthologies and Collections, 1970-1976, Vol. 25, 1977.

436   Drury's Guide to Best Plays.   3d ed.   By James M. Salem.
      Metuchen, N.J.:   Scarecrow Press, 1978.
Covers nonmusical plays in English from all periods and places from
Greek and Roman drama to the present day.   Includes separately
published plays and plays in collections and series.   The main section, Playwrights and Their Plays, is an alphabetical listing by
authors' names giving for each entry: full name, title of play, date
of play, publisher, translator and abridgments where applicable,
synopsis, number of acts, number of men and women in the cast,
type of set, and royalty.   Other sections are: Cast Index; Index of
Selected Subjects; Prize Plays, a list of New York Drama Critics'
Circle Award Plays, and a list of Pulitzer Prize Winning Plays;
Long Running Plays on the New York Stage, listed in the order of
number of performances; Popular Plays for High School Production,
1974-75; Frequently Produced Plays (High School Theater, 1957-
1975); Most Popular Plays for Amateur Groups; Plays Recommended
for All Groups.   Also includes addresses of play publishers repre-

sented, a list of play collections with symbols used for citing them, and an index of titles.

437 Keller, Dean H. Index to Plays in Periodicals. Rev. ed.
       Metuchen, N. J. : Scarecrow Press, 1979.
Indexes 9, 562 plays in 267 periodicals, many for their entire
runs through 1976.   Includes all types of plays, in several languages, from children's plays to classics and Broadway hits.
Entries in the author index give author's full name, dates, title
of the play, number of acts, a brief description of the play,
reference to the periodical in which it appears, names of translators, adapters, etc. , and language if other than English. Also
includes a title index.

438 Kreider, Barbara A.   Index to Children's Plays in Collections.
       2d ed.   Metuchen, N. J. : Scarecrow Press, 1977.
Indexes 1, 450 plays in collections published 1965-1974.   Includes
one-act plays, skits, monologues, and dialogues.   Plays are indexed
by author, title, and subject in one alphabet.   The author entry gives
title of the play, author or editor and title of the collection in which
it appears, and number of characters.   Also included are a cast
analysis section, a directory of publishers, and a bibliography of
collections indexed, with full bibliographic data and indication of
grade level.

439 National Council of Teachers of English.   Committee on Play-
       Lists.   Guide to Play Selection: A Selective Bibliography
       for Production and Study of Modern Plays.   3d ed.   Urbana,
       Ill. :   National Council of Teachers of English and R. R.
       Bowker, 1975.
Describes more than 800 plays suitable for high school, college, or
community theater groups.   Divided into sections on short plays,
plays by Afro-Americans, full-length plays, musical plays, and
television plays.   Arrangement is alphabetical by author in all sections.   Information on entries includes playwright's name, title of
play, translator or adapter, composer, lyricist, source from which
the play is derived, classification (comedy, tragedy, documentary,
etc.), number of acts or scenes, information on set requirements
and costumes, number and sex of players, distributor, price, any
restrictions, royalty, and a summary of the plot.   An introductory
essay discusses criteria of play selection and provides an overview
of the process of producing a play.   Appendixes are a directory of
publishers and agents, and a bibliography of more than 400 anthologies and collections with a listing of plays contained in each.   Players Index, Topical Index, Author Index, and Title Index.

440 Ottemiller's Index to Plays in Collections: An Author and Title
       Index to Plays Appearing in Collections Published Between
       1900 and Early 1975.   6th ed.   rev. and enl.   By John M.
       Connor and Billie M. Connor.   Metuchen, N. J. : Scarecrow
       Press, 1976.

Indexes 3, 686 plays by 1, 937 authors in 1, 237 collections published 1900-1975.　Covers world drama from the earliest times to the present.　Consists of an Author Index, which gives for each entry: name, birth and death dates, title of the play, date of first produc- tion, references from variant titles, and symbols for collections in which the play appears; List of Collections Analyzed and Key to Symbols, giving bibliographic information and list of plays in each collection; and Title Index, which refers to entries in the author index, and includes references from variant titles, translated titles, and subtitles.

441　Play Index.　New York: H. W. Wilson, 1953-.
The first five volumes cover plays published from 1949 to 1977. Each volume covers a five-year period and indexes approximately 4, 000 plays.　Each volume is in four parts.　Part I lists each play under author, title, and subject.　The author entry includes the title of the play, a brief synopsis of the plot, number of acts or scenes, size of the cast, number of sets needed, any required music or dances, and references to collections, or bibliographic information for separately published plays.　Plays in distinctive form, such as mysteries, one-act plays, pantomimes, plays in verse, and radio and television plays, are entered under the form also.　Plays for children and young people are so indicated by symbols.　Part II, Cast Analysis, is in six sections by type of cast (all-male, all-female, mixed, puppets, unidentified cast, and variable cast).　Within each section plays are arranged by the number of players.　Part III is a list of collections indexed.　Part IV is a directory of publishers and distributors.

Poetry

442　American Library Association.　Subject Index to Poetry for Children and Young People.　Compiled by Violet Sell and others.　Chicago: American Library Association, 1957.
An index of 157 collections for kindergarten through high school. Includes, in addition to the subject index, a list of the books indexed with bibliographic information and grade or interest level for each book.

443　American Library Association.　Subject Index to Poetry for Children and Young People, 1957-1975.　Compiled by Dorothy B. F. Smith and Eva L. Andrews.　Chicago: American Library Association, 1977.
An index to 263 anthologies.　Titles of poems are listed under more than 2, 000 subjects that reflect the range and variety of persons, places, and events that interest children.　Each entry gives title of the poem, name of author, and a code for the collection in which it can be found.　The List of Books Indexed gives bibliographic informa- tion and age level for each collection.

444　Brewton, John E. , and Sara W. Brewton.　Index to Children's Poetry.　New York: H. W. Wilson, 1942.　First Supple- ment, 1954; Second Supplement, 1965.

A title, subject, author, and first line index to poetry suitable for
preschool age through secondary school and beyond. Indexes 15,000
poems in 130 collections. The first supplement adds 7,000 poems
from 66 collections published 1938-1951. The second supplement
lists 8,000 poems from 85 collections published 1949-1963.

445 Brewton, John E., Sara W. Brewton, and G. Meredith Black-
    burn, III. Index to Poetry for Children and Young People:
    1964-1969. New York: H. W. Wilson, 1972.
An index to 11,000 poems in 117 collections. Title, subject, author,
and first line entries are in one alphabet. Fullest information is
given under title. Includes an analysis of books indexed giving in
detail the contents of each book and grade level.

446 Brewton, John E., G. Meredith Blackburn, III, and Lorraine
    A. Blackburn. Index to Poetry for Children and Young
    People: 1970-1975. New York: H. W. Wilson, 1978.
Indexes more than 10,000 poems in 109 collections published 1970-
1975. Title, first line, author, and subject entries are in one
alphabet. References to anthologies are given in title, author, and
subject entries. Fullest information is given in title entries. Also
includes a directory of publishers and distributors, and a list of all
collections indexed with an analysis of contents and indication of
grade level.

447 Chicorel Index to Poetry in Anthologies and Collections in Print.
    Edited by Marietta Chicorel. Chicorel Index Series, Vols.
    5, 5 A-C. New York: Chicorel Library Publishing, 1974.
Includes 250,000 entries in one alphabet for authors, titles of poems,
first lines, translators, adapters, editors, titles of anthologies and
collections, and titles of single author collections. Bibliographic
information and list of contents are given for all anthology and collection entries. All other types of entries refer to the anthology or
collection title. Collections of children's poetry are included. Vol.
5 C includes a subject index with titles of collections listed under
subjects; an author list; an alphabetical list of titles of collections;
a translator list; and a list of publishers.

448 Chicorel Index to Poetry in Anthologies and Collections: Retro-
    spective. Edited by Marietta Chicorel. Chicorel Index
    Series, Vols. 6, 6 A-C. New York: Chicorel Library
    Publishing, 1974.
Includes 250,000 entries in the same arrangement as Vols. 5, 5
A-C. No entries are repeated from the previous volumes. Vol. 6
C includes both a subject listing and an alphabetical listing of anthol-
ogies and collections.

449 Granger's Index to Poetry. 6th ed. rev. and enl. Edited by
    William J. Smith. New York: Columbia University Press,
    1973.
Indexes 514 anthologies published through December, 1970 by title
and first line, author, and subject. The Title and First Line Index
is the main index. Each entry gives author and symbol for anthology.

Complete information on translators, abridgments, and variant titles
are given in title entries.   The Author Index lists titles of poems
under author's names.   The Subject Index lists titles with the author
of each under subjects.   A list of anthologies with bibliographic
information and symbol for each precedes the index.

450 . Granger's Index to Poetry, 1970-1977.   Edited by William J.
        Smith.   New York: Columbia University Press, 1978.
Indexes more than 25, 000 poems in 120 anthologies published 1970-
1977.   Includes anthologies of poetry by women, by blacks, American Indians, and other ethnic groups, and anthologies of poetry for
children.   In the same arrangement as the 6th edition.

451   Index of American Periodical Verse.   Edited by Sander W.
        Zulauf and Irwin H. Weiser.   Metuchen, N. J. :   Scarecrow
        Press, 1973-.   Annual.
A guide to recent works of contemporary poets in general and
scholarly periodicals.   The first section is a list of the periodicals
indexed, giving for each: title, editor, address, subscription information, and symbols for reference to the periodical.   The main section, Index of Poets, is an alphabetical and numbered list of the
poets who have published in the periodicals indexed.   Each entry
gives name, title or first line of the poem, translator's name if the
poem is a translation, symbol of the periodical containing the poem,
and volume number, date, and page.   The first four volumes contain an index of poems that lists titles alphabetically with the poet's
number for each title.   Beginning with the 1975 volume, published
in 1977, there is no index of titles.   The 1976 and 1977 volumes,
published in 1978 and 1979, are edited by Sander W. Zulauf and
Edward M. Cifelli.

452   Marcan, Peter.   Poetry Themes: A Bibliographical Index to
        Subject Anthologies and Related Criticisms in the English
        Language, 1875-1975.   London: Clive Bingley; Hamden,
        Conn. :   Linnet Books, 1977.
A bibliographic index to 1, 964 subject anthologies that bring together
poetry on one subject or a group of related subjects.   Includes
anthologies for children or school use.   Most of the anthologies are
in English, but some are from foreign literature.   Emphasis is on
British publications.   Arranged under 21 subjects with subdivisions,
covering religion, emotional life, social life and organization, the
arts, history, geography, science, and natural history.   Entries are
numbered and give bibliographic data, notes on different editions and
reissues, and a brief annotation on type and range of material included.   Appendix lists poetry indexes and children's poetry indexes.
Author and compiler index.

Songs

453   Cushing, Helen G.   Children's Song Index: An Index to More
        than 22, 000 Songs in 189 Collections Comprising 222
        Volumes.   New York: H. W. Wilson, 1936.

Includes a list of collections indexed, a key to symbols for collections, a key to language abbreviations, and miscellaneous abbreviations.   The Index itself includes title, composer, author, subject,
and first line entries in one alphabet.   Title entries include alternate
titles, composer, author of words, language abbreviations for foreign
songs, and symbols for collections in which the song can be found.
Subject entries include symbols for collections.   Composer entries
list titles of songs under the names.   Author entries list titles of
songs and composer's names.   Entries for first lines refer to titles
of songs.   The volume includes a directory of publishers.   Most of
the collections indexed were published between 1900 and 1935.

454   Havlice, Patricia P.   Popular Song Index.   Metuchen, N. J.:
      Scarecrow Press, 1975.   First Supplement, 1978.
An index to folk songs, pop tunes, spirituals, hymns, children's
songs, sea chanteys, and blues.   Indexes 301 song books published
1940-1972.   Limited to song books with both words and music.
Part I, Bibliography, is a numbered list of song books giving author,
title, publisher, place, and date for each.   Part II is an Index of
Titles and First Lines.   Title entries include the composer's name,
first line of the song, first line of the chorus, and a number referring to the bibliography.   Entries for first lines of songs and first
lines of choruses refer to title entries.   Part III, Index of Composers and Lyricists, lists titles of songs under each name.   The
1978 supplement, in the same arrangement as the main volume,
indexes 72 song books published 1970-1975.

455   Sears, Minnie E.   Song Index: An Index to More than 12,000
      Songs in 177 Song Collections Comprising 262 Volumes, and
      Supplement, 1934.   N. p.:   Shoe String Press, 1966.
A facsimile reproduction of the Song Index (1926) and Supplement
(1934) originally published by H. W. Wilson Company as two separate
volumes.   The Song Index includes a classified list of collections
indexed, giving bibliographic information and a list of contents of
each collection; a list of collections indexed with key to symbols;
the index itself, which includes in one alphabet entries for title
(main entry), composer, author of words, references from first
lines to titles, and references from alternative titles and translations
of titles.   The title entries give symbols for collections in which the
songs appear.   Composer entries include a listing of titles of their
songs.   Author entries include title of poem and composer's name.
Songs from foreign languages are included.   The supplement is an
index to more than 7,000 songs in 104 collections comprising 124
volumes.   Arrangement is the same as in the main volume.

Speeches

456   Sutton, Roberta B.   Speech Index: An Index to 259 Collections
      of World Famous Orations and Speeches for Various Occa-
      sions.   4th ed.   Rev. and enl.   Metuchen, N. J.:   Scare-
      crow Press, 1966.   Supplement, 1966-1970, by Roberta B.
      Sutton and Charity Mitchell, 1972.   Supplement, 1971-1975,
      by Charity Mitchell, 1977.

An index to speeches of famous orators from earliest times to the present, and to types of speeches. All collections indexed in the first volume were published in English, 1900-1965. Entries by author, subject, type of speech, and cross-references are in one alphabet. References to collections are given by symbols. List of Books Indexed, giving bibliographic information for each book and a key to symbols, precedes the index. An appendix, Selected List of Titles, is a listing of titles with no resemblance to the subject and therefore difficult to locate without the author. The author's name is given for each title for reference to the main section. The 1966-1970 supplement indexes speeches in 58 collections. The 1971-1975 supplement indexes speeches in 33 collections.

Essays

457   Essay and General Literature Index. New York: H. W. Wilson, 1900-. Semiannual with cumulations.
An author and subject index to collections of essays with emphasis on materials in the humanities and social sciences. In author entries the author's works are listed first, then works about her or him, followed by criticism of individual works. Under subject headings authors and their works are listed alphabetically. A list of books indexed, with complete bibliographic information for each book, follows the index. Published semiannually with annual and five-year cumulations. Essay and General Literature Index Works Indexed 1900-1969, published 1972, lists all the 9,917 titles analyzed in the seven cumulations by author and title. Author entries give bibliographic information and reference to the cumulative volume in which the book was analyzed. Title entries refer to author or editor entries.

Reviews

458   Children's Book Review Index. Edited by Gary C. Tarbert. Detroit: Gale Research, 1975-. 3 issues per year with annual cumulations.
Cites reviews of children's books that have appeared in more than 300 periodicals. Reviews cited in CBRI are also cited in Book Review Index. Each entry gives author's name, book title, abbreviation for the reviewing publication, volume number, date, and page number for the review. A list of publications indexed, with their identifying abbreviations, follows the introduction. The main section is arranged alphabetically by author. There is a title index beginning with the 1976 cumulative volume.

459   Children's Literature Review: Excerpts from Reviews, Criticisms, and Commentary on Books for Children and Young People. Detroit: Gale Research, 1976-. Semiannual.
Reviews and criticism of the works of today's authors, with some current criticism of earlier authors. Each semiannual volume presents criticism of about 40 authors and includes excerpts from more than 45 books and 35 periodicals. Complete references are given to sources. Brief information, including nationality, principal genre, and major awards, is given for each author. Cross-references

are given to Contemporary Authors and to Something About the
Author. The listings consist of general commentary on the author,
excerpts from reviews of individual titles, and references to other
review information. Each volume contains cumulative indexes to
authors, titles, and critics.

460   Hall, H. W., ed. Science Fiction Book Review Index. Detroit:
        Gale Research, 1975.
Indexes reviews in science fiction magazines, 1923-1973, and in
selected general magazines, 1970-1973. The Author Entries section
gives for each book author, title, publication data, and citations
to reviews. The Title Entries section is a short list of books without authors. Publication data and citations to reviews follow the
titles. Also includes a directory of magazines indexed divided into
(1) science fiction magazines, and (2) general magazines, library
magazines, and fanzines; a list of indexes to science fiction
magazines; an editor index; and a title index.

Magazines

461   Subject Index to Children's Magazines. Madison, Wis., 1948-.
        Monthly except June and July.
A subject index to approximately 60 magazines primarily for grades
1-8.

Biography

462   Author Biographies Master Index: A Consolidated Guide to
        Biographical Information Concerning Authors Living and
        Dead as It Appears in a Selection of the Principal Bio-
        graphical Dictionaries Devoted to Authors, Poets, Journalists,
        and Other Literary Figures. Edited by Dennis La Beau.
        2 vols. Detroit: Gale Research, 1978.
An index to 416,000 sketches on 238,000 authors in 150 biographical
dictionaries and other sources in English. Includes authors from
every country from the earliest times to the present. Emphasis is
on American and British authors from Anglo-Saxon times to the
present. Includes minor and little-known writers, and illustrators
of children's books. Entries give birth and death dates and code for
sources of biographical sketches. The biographical dictionaries are
listed with brief annotations and the codes used in references to them.

463   Biographical Dictionaries Master Index. Edited by Dennis La
        Beau and Gary C. Tarbert. 3 vols. Detroit: Gale Re-
        search, 1975. First Supplement, 1977.
An index to more than 725,000 entries in more than 50 Who's Whos
and other current works of collective biography, including American
Men and Women of Science, Contemporary Authors, Current Biography, Congressional Directory, Directory of American Scholars, New
York Times Biographical Service, and Something About the Author,
etc. Entries give name, date of birth, and code for the sources of
the biographical information. Sources and their code letters are
listed in the front of the first volume, and on the inside front cover

of all three volumes.   The first biennial supplement indexes more
than 150,000 sketches in 38 biographical sources not covered in the
base set.   The second supplement will cumulate all citations in the
first supplement and will add 150,000 new citations.

464   Biography Index.   New York: H. W. Wilson, 1946-.   Quarterly
        with cumulations.
An index to biographical material in more than 2,400 periodicals,
books of individual and collective biographies, biographical material
in nonbiographical books, and juvenile literature.   Material indexed
includes diaries, memoirs, collections of letters, obituaries, and
bibliographies.   For general and scholarly needs.   In the main section entries are arranged alphabetically by names of biographees.
Information on each entry includes full name, nationality if not
American, dates, occupation or profession, and a list of citations
to biographical material.   A separate section, Index to Professions
and Occupations, lists names under each profession or occupation.
Also includes a checklist of composite books analyzed.

465   Chicorel Index to Biographies.   Edited by Marietta Chicorel.
        Chicorel Index Series, Vols. 15 and 15 A.   New York:
        Chicorel Library Publishing, 1974.
Includes 21,000 references to biographies in books.   Arranged by
professions, occupations, nationalities, historical periods, activities,
and names of biographees.   Bibliographic data and price are given
for each entry.   Includes a list of biographees and a list of subject
indicators.

466   Children's Authors and Illustrators: An Index to Biographical
        Dictionaries.   Edited by Adele Sarkissian.   2d ed.   Detroit:
        Gale Research, 1978.
Includes 55,000 citations to biographical sketches of more than 15,000
children's authors and illustrators in 190 sources.   The alphabetically
arranged entries give the name of the author or illustrator, birth and
death dates, and an alphabetically arranged list of references to
sources of biographical information.   Includes a key to title abbreviations for the reference sources.   Emphasis is on authors and illustrators of this century.

467   Havlice, Patricia P.   Index to Literary Biography.   2 vols.
        Metuchen, N. J.:   Scarecrow Press, 1975.
Locates biographical information on 68,000 authors from antiquity to
the present.   Authors are listed alphabetically.   Each entry gives
author's name, pseudonym, birth and death dates, nationality, type
of writing, and a letter code referring to the volumes in the bibliography that contain the author's biography.   The sources in the bibliography are arranged alphabetically with author, title, place, publisher,
date, and letter code given for each source.

468   Kerr, Laura J.   Who's Where in Books: An Index to Biogra-
        phical Material.   Ann Arbor: Michigan Association of
        School Librarians, 1971.
An index to 4,000 biographies in 551 collective biographies.   Part I

is a list of the collective biographies arranged by author or editor.
Entries give title, publisher, date, and a letter-number symbol.
Part II is an alphabetical list of subjects and biographees, with
symbols for each entry referring to the books in Part I.   For elementary and junior and senior high school levels.

469   Nicholsen, Margaret E.   People in Books: A Selective Guide
      to Biographical Literature Arranged by Vocations and Other
      Fields of Reader Interest.   New York: H. W. Wilson,
      1969.   First Supplement,   1977.
The main section is arranged by vocations or fields of activity.
Under each vocation or activity, entries are arranged first by
country, then by century.   Entries give name, birth and death dates
of the biographee, and citations to biographies and collective
biographies, with indication of sources of recommendation and grade
level according to the sources.   Collective biographies precede
entries for individuals under the vocational or field of activity
headings.   Other sections are: Country-Century List, a list of
biographees arranged by country and century; Autobiographies,
Letters, and Personal Accounts, arranged alphabetically by author;
an alphabetical index of names; and a directory of publishers and
distributors.

470   Silverman, Judith.   Index to Young Readers' Collective Biogra-
      phies: Elementary and Junior High School Level.   2d ed.
      New York: R. R. Bowker, 1975.
An index to biographies of 5, 833 people in 720 collections.   The
two main sections are: Alphabetical Listing of Biographees, giving
for each entry dates of birth and death, nationality, field of activity,
and symbols for collective biographies in which information can be
found; and Subject Listing of Biographees, which lists these persons
under fields of activity and nationalities, giving symbols for collections for each name.   Other sections are a list of books indexed,
with symbols; Indexed Books by Title, listing names of biographees
contained in each book; a directory of publishers; and an index of
subject headings.

471   Stanius, Ellen J.   Index to Short Biographies: For Elementary
      and Junior High Grades.   Metuchen, N. J.:   Scarecrow Press,
      1971.
An index of 455 collections.   The main section is arranged alphabetically by names of biographees.   Entries give nationality and
occupation of biographee, and author, title, and paging of sources
of biographical information.   The Title List, arranged alphabetically
by author, gives bibliographic information and indication of grade
level for the sources of the biographies.

B.   Textbooks

472   El-Hi Textbooks in Print.   New York: R. R. Bowker, 1970-.
      Annual.

The 1978 edition is a listing of 31, 569 elementary, junior high, and senior high school textbooks and pedagogical books from 419 publishers. It also includes some reference books, maps, teaching aids, and programmed learning materials in book form. In four parts: Subject Index, Author Index Title Index, and Series Index. In the Subject Index, 21 major categories with subdivisions are arranged alphabetically, with titles listed alphabetically under each heading. Information on each entry includes: title, author, grade level, publication date, price, ISBN, related teaching materials, and publisher. Books in series are listed under the series title. Entries in the Author and Title Indexes refer to the Subject Index. The Series Index is arranged by subject categories with full information on each series. Also included is a directory of publishers.

C.   Instructional Materials: Print and Nonprint

Reference and Selection Aids

473   Limbacher, James L.   A Reference Guide to Audiovisual Information.   New York: R. R. Bowker, 1972.
Contains an annotated list of 400 reference books; a list of 100 periodicals with descriptive information on each title; a list of reference works by subject; a glossary of 350 audiovisual terms; addresses of publishers; and a selected bibliography of other audiovisual books not primarily for reference.

474   Perkins, Flossie L.   Book and Non-Book Media: Annotated Guide to Selection Aids for Educational Materials.   Urbana, Ill.:   National Council of Teachers of English, 1972.
An annotated bibliography of more than 250 selection aids for books, pamphlets, and audiovisual materials for elementary through college and adult level. Arranged alphabetically by title. Information on each entry includes author, publisher, edition, publication date, purpose, scope, subject headings, similar tools, special features, usefulness, and cost. Also included are selection lists for children, for teenagers, for college students and adults, for teacher-parent background, and for librarians. Title and author-publisher indexes.

475   Rufsvold, Margaret I.   Guides to Educational Media: Films, Filmstrips, Multimedia Kits, Programmed Instruction Materials, Recordings on Discs and Tapes, Slides, Transparencies, Videotapes.   4th ed.   Chicago: American Library Association, 1977.
Describes 245 educational media catalogs, indexes, and reviewing services published 1972-1976. Information on each includes bibliographic data, scope, arrangement, entries, and special features. For all grade levels preschool through university and adult. General index.

476   Sive, Mary R.   Selecting Instructional Media: A Guide to Audiovisual and Other Instructional Media Lists.   Littleton, Colo.:   Libraries Unlimited, 1978.

A selective, annotated guide to 428 published lists of audiovisual and other instructional media, plus 132 additional lists mentioned in the text.   Includes in-print lists published in the United States, 1973-1977.   Includes separately published mediagraphies and catalogs, periodicals carrying reviews of instructional media, mediagraphies on special topics that appear in periodicals and in books, indexes to periodicals and media reviews in periodicals, and ERIC documents. Material covered is appropriate for grades K-12.   Arranged in three major sections: I, Comprehensive Lists, covering more than one subject and format; II, Lists by Subjects; and III, Lists by Media. Information on each entry includes title, compiler, publisher, address, date, price, purpose, grade level, arrangement, subjects covered, number of entries, indexes, period covered, revision and updating, media represented, producers, features, and subject terms.   An Introduction to Media Selection discusses problems of selection, reviews, selection aids, selection criteria, and recommendations for media selection.   Indexes by subject, media, instructional level, title, and name of compiler.

477   U. S. Office of Education.   Aids to Media Selection for Students
        and Teachers.   Compiled by Kathlyn J. Moses and Lois B.
        Watt.   Washington, D. C.:   Government Printing Office,
        1976.
A selected list of bibliographies and journals that review books, periodicals, and audiovisual materials relevant to the elementary and secondary school curriculum.   Emphasis is on tools published since 1970, but also included are older publications considered valuable in developing a media collection.   In three sections: book selection sources; sources of audiovisual materials; and sources of multiethnic materials.   Author-title index.

Directories

478   Audio Visual Market Place: A Multimedia Guide.   New York:
        R. R. Bowker.   Annual.
The 1978 edition is in 25 sections grouped into three major areas: AV Software, AV Hardware, and Reference.   AV Software is divided into sections on producers and distributors; production companies; production services; public radio and TV program libraries; and AV cataloging services.   AV Hardware is divided into sections on AV equipment manufacturers and AV equipment dealers.   Divisions of Reference are: calendar of meetings and conventions; reference books and directories; periodical and trade journals; advertising rate schedules; associations; state AV administrators; funding sources; awards and festivals; and glossary.   Entries include addresses; telephone numbers; key personnel; product lines; services; activities; and other appropriate information.   Five classification indexes are included within the volume: producers and distributors indexed by media and by subject area; production companies indexed by media; manufacturers by product, and reference books by areas of user interest.   General index at end of volume.

479 Children's Media Market Place.   Edited by Deirdre Boyle and
       Stephen Calvert.   Syracuse, N. Y. :   Gaylord Professional
       Publication, 1978.
The first edition, 1978, is a directory of sources of children's
materials listed in 20 categories: publishers; AV producers and
distributors; periodicals for children; periodicals for professionals
and parents; review journals and services; reviewers; wholesalers;
bookstores; book clubs; agents; children's TV stations; children's TV
program distributors; organizations; public library coordinators; state
school media officers; examination centers; federal grants; calendar
of events and conferences; awards; bibliography of selection tools.
Information for sources includes address, telephone number, types
of materials, intended audience, and discounts.   Some sections have
subject and special interest indexes.   Also includes, at the end of
the volume, an index to all personal and firm names with addresses
and telephone numbers.

480 Index to Instructional Media Catalogs: A Multi-Indexed Directory
       of Materials and Equipment for Use in Instructional Programs.
       New York: R. R. Bowker, 1974.
A guide to 631 catalogs of media producers, publishers, and manufacturers of about 40 types of media in 150 subject areas.   The first
section lists materials by subject giving for each entry name of
producer or publisher, type of media, grade level, and indication of
whether the material is basal, supplemental, or a teacher aid.   The
second section is a product and service index, listing alphabetically
about 80 types of equipment and services with name of company for
each one.   Also includes a directory of the companies represented.

481 Publisher Source Directory.   3d ed.   Columbus: Ohio State
       University, National Center on Educational Media and
       Materials for the Handicapped, 1977.
A directory of more than 1, 600 publishers, producers, and distributors of instructional materials and other educational aids, devices,
and media.   Includes several Canadian and European publishers as
well as those in the United States.   The first section is an alphabetical listing of publishers and producers with addresses and code
numbers to correspond to types of instructional aids and media that
each produces, distributes, sells, or loans.   The second section is
a Rotated Index listing all the firms under 74 subject headings.   Also
includes a list of changes since the previous edition, a form for submitting entries, and a list of definitions and codes.

482 Sources: A Guide to Print and Nonprint Materials Available
       from Organizations, Industry, Government Agencies, and
       Specialized Publishers.   Syracuse, N. Y. :   Gaylord Bros.
       in association with Neal-Schuman Publishers, 1977-.   3
       issues per year.
The first issue lists 600 sources and more than 4, 000 titles, covering
approximately 100 subject areas.   Arranged alphabetically by agency.
Information on each source includes address, telephone number,
purpose, information services, and a listing of available print and
nonprint materials.   Cumulative subject index.   Title indexes are
divided according to format.

Types of Media

Multimedia

483   Aubrey, Ruth H.   Selected Free Materials for Classroom
        Teachers.   6th ed.   Belmont, Calif.:   Fearon-Pitman
        Publishers, 1978.
A guide to more than 500 sources for free materials for use for all
grade levels from kindergarten through college and adult education.
Items are listed by curriculum area and indexed by subject and
source.   Grade level is indicated for each entry.

484   Brown, Lucy G., and Betty McDavid.   Core Media Collection
        for Elementary Schools.   2d ed.   New York: R. R. Bowker,
        1978.
An annotated list of more than 3,000 titles of nonprint media of all
types, for grades K-8.   Arranged by subject.   Emphasis is on
titles published since 1971, but classic titles from the first edition
are also included.   Also includes a list of recommending sources,
a producer/distributor directory, and title and media indexes.

485   Brown, Lucy G.   Core Media Collection for Secondary Schools.
        2d ed.   New York: R. R. Bowker, 1979.
A selected list of 3,000 titles of nonprint media in all formats and
covering a variety of subjects and ability levels, appropriate for
grades 7-12.   Arranged by subject.   Each entry gives a description
of contents, grade level, producer or distributor, order information,
Dewey classification, release date, price, and recommending source.
Includes a media index by title, a list of recommending sources, and
a directory of producers and distributors.

486   Educators Grade Guide to Free Teaching Aids.   Randolph,
        Wis.:   Educators Progress Service.   Annual.
An annotated list of bulletins, pamphlets, books, maps, charts, and
exhibits, arranged by subject area.   Also includes special sections
on teacher reference and professional growth materials, and illustrative units.   Indexes by title, subject, and source.   For elementary
and junior high school levels.

487   Educators Index of Free Materials.   Randolph, Wis.:   Educators
        Progress Service.   Annual.
The 86th edition, 1977, contains 3,000 entries for free and inexpensive publications, graphic materials, maps, etc., from 800 commercial, government, and academic producers.   Arranged in eight
subject groupings including curricular subjects.   For secondary
level.   Index of sources.

        Elementary School Library Collection.   11th ed.   Edited by
          Phyllis Van Orden and Lois Winkel.   Newark, N.J.:   Bro-
          Dart Foundation, 1977 (see No. 304).

488   George Peabody College for Teachers.   Free and Inexpensive
        Learning Materials.   Nashville, Tenn.:   Incentive Publica-
        tions.   Biennial.

The 19th edition, 1979, lists more than 3,000 instructional aids from 800 distributors.   Includes books, pamphlets, catalogs, maps, charts, and posters.   Classified under 82 subject headings that parallel subject fields, courses, and unit topics in elementary and secondary schools.   Information in entries includes name of the item, size, price, name and address of distributor, and brief descriptive annotation.   The table of contents lists subject headings alphabetically. Subject headings in the body of the book are cross-referenced to related headings.

489   International Index to Multi-Media Information.   Edited by
        Wesley A. Doak and William J. Speed.   Pasadena, Calif.:
        Audio Visual Associates, 1970-.   Quarterly.
An index to media reviews in 100 periodicals by title, type of media, personal names, series, and subject in one alphabet.   Entries give type of media, distributor, format, quotes from reviews, release date, price, age and grade level.   Also contains a Source Index and a Producer and Distributor Section.   Supersedes Film Review Index, 1970-72.

490   Media Review Digest.   Ann Arbor, Mich.:   Pierian Press,
        1970-.   Annual with semiannual supplements.
An index to and digest of reviews, evaluations, and descriptions of all forms of nonbook media appearing in 150 periodicals and reviewing sources.   The four main sections are: films and videotapes; filmstrips; records and tapes; and miscellaneous media.   Special features sections are: film awards and prizes; mediagraphies; and books.   Also includes an index section and a directory of producers and distributors.   The 1977 edition contains 40,000 citations and cross-references.   Entries give description of format, running time, producer, release date, sale or rental price, note on contents, citations of reviews, and grade level.   The indexes include general subject indicators, classified subject index, alphabetical subject index, and reviewers index.   Supersedes Multi Media Review Index, 1970-76.

        National Information Center for Educational Media.   Los
        Angeles: NICEM, University of Southern California.
Publishes comprehensive, frequently revised lists of media of different types and on various subjects.   Each volume consists of an alphabetical guide, a subject guide, and a producer-distributor code section.   The alphabetical section gives a descriptive annotation, technical information, audience or grade level, and producer-distributor code for each entry.   Listed below are titles, editions, and dates of volumes published.

491   Index to Educational Audio Tapes.   4th ed.   1977.

492   Index to Educational Overhead Transparencies.   5th ed.   1977.

493   Index to Educational Records.   4th ed.   1977.

494   Index to Educational Slides.   3d ed.   1977.

495   Index to Educational Video Tapes.   4th ed.   1977.

496   Index to Free Educational Materials: Multimedia.   1978.

497   Index to 16 mm Educational Films.   6th ed.   1977.

498   Index to 35 mm Filmstrips.   6th ed.   1977.

499   Index to 8 mm Motion Cartridges.   5th ed.   1977.

500   Index to Black History and Studies: Multimedia.   2d ed.   1973.

501   Index to Environmental Studies: Multimedia.   1977.

502   Index to Health and Safety Education: Multimedia.   3d ed.
          1977.

503   Index to Psychology: Multimedia.   3d ed.   1977.

504   Index to Vocational and Technical Education: Multimedia.
          3d ed.   1977.

505   NICEM Catalog to Special Education Non-Print Materials.   1978.

506   U. S. National Archives and Records Service.   National Audio-
          visual Center.   A Reference List of Audiovisual Materials
          Produced by the United States Government.   Washington,
          D. C.:   Government Printing Office,   1978.
Contains more than 6, 000 audiovisual items, produced by 175 government agencies, in 30 major subject areas.   The two main sections
are a subject listing and a title listing.   Entries in the title section
include descriptive information according to the type of material, the
government agency producer, date of issue, availability, price, and
annotation.

507   Wasserman, Paul, and Esther Herman, eds.   Museum Media:
          A Biennial Directory and Index of Publications and Audio-
          visuals Available from United States and Canadian Institu-
          tions.   Detroit: Gale Research, 1973.
A listing of print and nonprint publications of 732 national, state,
and local museums, art galleries, art institutes, and related institutions.   The main section is an alphabetical listing of institutions with
the publications of each institution listed in the following categories:
books, booklets, and monographs; catalogs of exhibits, collections,
and showings; films; filmstrips; pamphlets and leaflets; other
media available.   Bibliographic information is given for each item
listed plus terms of availability, sale price, or rental fee.   Other
sections are: Title and Keyword Index; Subject Index, a listing of
institutions under subjects; and Geographic Index, a listing of institutions by states and Canadian provinces.   Biennial publication was
planned but no editions have been issued between 1973 and 1978.

Films

508   Aros, Andrew A.   Title Guide to the Talkies, 1964 Through
      1974.   Metuchen, N. J.:   Scarecrow Press, 1977.
Lists American films and numerous foreign films distributed in this
country.   Arrangement is alphabetical by title of film.   Entries give
distribution company, year of film's release, name of director, and title
of the novel, play, or nonfiction work on which the film was based.
Index of personal names.

509   Dimmitt, Richard B.   Title Guide to the Talkies: A Compre-
      hensive Listing of 16,000 Feature Length Films from
      October, 1927 Until December, 1963.   2 vols.   New York:
      Scarecrow Press, 1965.
An alphabetical listing of films by title.   Entries give copyright date,
production company, name of producer, and title of novel, play,
poem, short story or screen story on which the movie was based,
with author's name, place of publication, publisher, date, and
pagination.   For works not published separately, reference is given
to the collections in which they appear.   If the movie has a different
title from the book, a cross-reference is given from the original
title to the movie title.   Index of personal names.

510   Educators Guide to Free Films.   Randolph, Wis.:   Educators
      Progress Service.   Annual.
A listing by curriculum areas giving for each film: title, description of contents, size, sound or silent, date, running time, name
and address of distributor, and terms of loan.   Indexes by title,
subject, and source.

511   Gaffney, Maureen, comp.   More Films Kids Like: A Catalog
      of Short Films for Children.   Chicago: American Library
      Association, 1977.
An annotated list of 200 16 mm films for children age 3-12.   Each
entry gives running time, distributor, technique, production data,
synopsis of the film, and reactions of children in three age ranges.
Also contains a section on methods used to determine children's
reactions, and information on a program of film activities for children.   The subject index covers both this volume and Films Kids
Like, edited by Susan Rice, A. L. A., 1973 (see No. 517).

512   Guide to Government Loan Films.   2 vols.   Alexandria, Va.:
      Serina Press, 1976.
Vol. 1, The Civilian Agencies; Vol. 2, The Defense Agencies.   Includes several thousand entries arranged by issuing agency.   Most
of the films were produced in the 1960s and 1970s.   Information on
each film includes running time, release date, a description of contents, and distributor.   For all grade levels.   Subject index.

513   Limbacher, James L., ed.   Feature Films on 8 mm and 16
      mm: A Directory of Feature Films Available for Rental,
      Sale, and Lease in the United States and Canada.   5th ed.
      New York: R. R. Bowker, 1977.

Lists more than 16, 000 feature films alphabetically by title.   Includes commercial productions, documentaries, experimental films,
and animations, ranging from early silent classics through 1975.
Information on each film includes title, releasing company or country
of origin, date of release, running time, sound or silent, black and
white or color, subtitled or dubbed, name of director, names of
cast members and code for distributor.   Also includes a listing of
serials, an index of directors with titles of films they directed, a
list of film reference works, addresses of film companies and
distributors, and a list of companies and distributors by geographical
area.

> National Information Center for Educational Media.   Index to
> 16 mm Educational Films.   6th ed.   Los Angeles: NICEM,
> University of Southern California, 1977 (see No. 497).

514   Parlato, Salvatore J. , Jr.   Films Too Good for Words: A
      Directory of Nonnarrated 16 mm Films.   New York: R. R.
      Bowker, 1972.
Lists and describes 1, 000 nonnarrated educational films for elementary to adult levels.   Arranged under 13 subject headings, with
titles listed alphabetically within each subject grouping.   Information
on each film includes producer or distributor, running time, color
or black-and-white, sound or silent, copyright date, awards, and a
descriptive annotation.   Also includes a title index, a subject index,
and a directory of producers and distributors.

515   Parlato, Salvatore J. , Jr.   Superfilms: An Annotated Guide
      to Award-Winning Educational Films.   Metuchen, N. J. :
      Scarecrow Press, 1976.
A directory of almost 1, 500 nontheatrical prize winning films, most
of which were released between 1955 and 1975.   Arrangement is
alphabetical by title.   Entries give release date, running time,
producer, distributor, awards, viewer level, and descriptive annotation.   Festivals and competitions are identified by a keyword system.
Subject and distributor indexes.

516   Rehrauer, George.   The Short Film: An Evaluative Selection
      of 500 Recommended Films.   New York: Macmillan Infor-
      mation, 1975.
An alphabetical list of 16 mm short films with a multipurpose use
and with running time of 60 minutes or less, issued from the early
1920s to the 1970s.   Each entry includes title, release date, producer or distributor, running time, indication if animated or without
words, black-and-white or color, brief descriptive annotation, suggested audience, subject area use, and sources of recommendation.
Other sections are a list of evaluative sources, additional sources,
selected film periodicals dealing with short films, a list of distributors, and subject listings.

517   Rice, Susan, ed.   Films Kids Like: A Catalog of Short Films
      for Children.   Chicago: American Library Association, 1973.

An annotated list of 229 short films for children up to age 12.   Arranged alphabetically by title.   Each entry gives title, technical description, distributor, country of origin, and annotation.   A preliminary section describes the program of the Children's Film Theatre, and methods and techniques of showing films to children. Includes a key to distributors (see also No. 511).

Filmstrips

518   Educators Guide to Free Filmstrips.   Randolph, Wis.:   Educators Progress Service.   Annual.
A listing by curriculum area, giving for each filmstrip: title, date, sound or silent, description of contents, number of frames or running time, source, and terms of loan.   Indexes by title, subject, and source.

> National Information Center for Educational Media.   Index to 35 mm Filmstrips.   6th ed.   Los Angeles: NICEM, University of Southern California, 1977 (see No. 498).

Records and Tapes

519   Educators Guide to Free Audio and Video Materials.   Randolph, Wis.:   Educators Progress Service.   Annual.
The 24th edition, 1977, lists 1,496 items, including videotapes, audiotapes, phonograph records, scripts, and other materials from 80 producers.   Arranged by 17 curriculum areas and alphabetically within each area.   Information on each item includes title, type of media, format, equipment required, running time, descriptive annotation, and source.   Production date and grade level are given for some items.   Title, subject, and source indexes.   Former title: Educators Guide to Free Tapes, Scripts and Transcriptions.

> National Information Center for Educational Media.   Index to Educational Audio Tapes.   4th ed.   Los Angeles: NICEM, University of Southern California, 1977 (see No. 491).

> National Information Center for Educational Media.   Index to Educational Records.   4th ed.   Los Angeles: NICEM, University of Southern California, 1977 (see No. 493).

> National Information Center for Educational Media.   Index to Educational Video Tapes.   4th ed.   Los Angeles: NICEM, University of Southern California, 1977 (see No. 495).

Illustrations

520   Index to Art Reproductions in Books.   Compiled by the professional staff of the Hewlett-Woodmere Public Library under the direction of Elizabeth W. Thomson.   Metuchen, N. J.: Scarecrow Press, 1974.
Contains 7,000 entries on graphic art, paintings, sculpture, photography, stage design, and architecture.   Covers 65 art books pub-

lished 1956-1971. The main listing is a name index of artists and their works. Entries include the artist's dates, title of the work, location of the reproduction, measurements of the reproduction, and indication of whether in color or black-and-white. Title index.

521 Vance, Lucile E., and Esther M. Tracey. Illustration Index.
      2d ed. Metuchen, N. J.: Scarecrow Press, 1966.
A subject index to illustrations in periodicals and books, published 1950-1963. Most illustrations indexed are photographs, but charts, drawings, paintings, lithographs, and decorative maps are also included. Arrangement of entries under each subject is chronological. References to periodicals give abbreviated title, volume, page, date, and indication if in color. For illustrations in books, references include abbreviated title of book and page. Costume, projects useful to teachers, interests of hobbyists, subjects of scientific interest, and history and culture of peoples and countries of the world are emphasized. Includes a list of books and periodicals indexed.

522 Greer, Roger C. Illustration Index. 3d ed. Metuchen, N. J.:
      Scarecrow Press, 1973.
Continues the scope and pattern of indexing of the second edition. Covers the period, July 1, 1963-December 31, 1971.

Games

523 Belch, Jean, comp. Contemporary Games: A Directory and
      Bibliography Covering Games and Play Situations or Simula-
      tions Used for Instruction and Training by Schools, Colleges
      and Universities, Government, Business, and Management.
      2 vols. Detroit: Gale Research, 1973-74.
Vol. 1, Directory, is an alphabetically arranged guide to more than 900 educational games and simulations. Entries include information on subject area, age or grade level, number of players, materials required, playing time, mode of play, date originated, designer, publisher or distributor, price, description of the game, and references to descriptive and evaluative information. Also includes a guide to subject areas; a list of the games by age and grade level from early childhood through college and adult; and an index of publishers and distributors including addresses and the games available from each company. Vol. 2, Bibliography, contains 2,375 references to books, articles, reports, and study units on gaming, published 1957-1973, covering games and simulations for education, business, and government. Arranged in sections on games in the classroom; business games and management simulations; conflict resolutions; land use and resource allocation; research employing or evaluating games and simulations; directories, bibliographies, and lists. Brief annotations. Author, institution, game, and subject indexes.

524 Zuckerman, David W., and Robert E. Horn. Guide to
      Simulations/Games for Education and Training. With a
      Basic Reference Shelf on Simulations and Gaming, by Paul
      A. Twelker and Kent Layden. Lexington, Mass.: Infor-
      mation Resources, 1973.

The main section contains descriptions of 613 games and simulations arranged by subject. Information on each entry includes title, name of the creator or developer, date originated, age level, number of players, playing time, preparation time, materials, comment, roles, objectives, decisions, purposes, cost, and producer. Also includes five articles about simulations and games; a bibliography of books and articles; a list of games not described; games listed by creators or producers; and an index of titles of games.

Programmed Instruction and Computer-Assisted Instruction

525   Lekan, Helen A., ed.   Index to Computer Assisted Instruction. 3d ed.   New York: Harcourt Brace Jovanovich, 1971.
A list of 1, 272 CAI programs, with descriptive data on each, available from 137 sources, including elementary and secondary schools, colleges and universities, military installations, and industry.   Indexes by subject, central processor, instructional logic, programming language, and source.

526   Programmed Learning and Individually Paced Instruction: Bibliography.   5th ed.   Bay City, Mich.:   Carl H. Hendershot, 1973.   Supplements 1-5, 1974-78.
The Subject section lists 3, 000 units under 213 subjects, for preschool to college and adult level.   Entries give title, author, publisher, time, number of pages or frames, level, price, and other brief information.   The Publisher section lists units by publisher and by subject under each publisher.   The Devices section lists and describes devices, teaching machines and equipment used in the preparation or presentation of individually paced instruction. Listing is alphabetical by manufacturer.   Also included is a list of references and resources on programmed learning arranged by subject.

Media for Special Subjects

Adult Education

527   Florida.   State Department of Education.   Division of Vocational, Technical, and Adult Education.   A Selected Annotated Bibliography of Instructional Literacy Materials for Adult Basic Education.   Tallahassee: State of Florida, Department of Education, 1974.
In four parts: I, Communication Skill Building Materials; II, Tests Designed for Adult Basic Education Students; III, Mathematics Skills and Concepts; IV, Consumer and Family Education Skills.   Materials are listed alphabetically within each division.   Entries give publisher and address; title of book; series; test, kit, or other; date of issue; price; and descriptive annotation including readability level.

528   Thomas, Myra H.   Books Related to Adult Basic Education and Teaching English to Speakers of Other Languages: A Bibliography from the Educational Materials Center.   Washington, D. C.:   Government Printing Office, 1970.

A briefly annotated list of 250 references to materials published 1964-1970, specifically for teaching skills of reading, writing, arithmetic, community living, and citizenship.

Community Education

529   Schwartz, Beverly, and Fran M. Spinelli, comps.   Community Education Bibliography.   Upper Montclair, N. J.:   National Multimedia Center for Adult Education, Department of Adult Continuing Education, Montclair State College, 1977.
An annotated bibliography of multimedia materials on community education in two parts.   The first part is a list of media for workers in community education and in community colleges.   The second part is the 1977 list of acquisitions of the National Multimedia Center/ National Adult Education Clearinghouse.   Each part is arranged by subjects, including facilities, program development, library services, and citizen action.   Includes books, pamphlets, teaching guides, and multimedia items.   No index.

530   U. S. Office of Education.   Federal Community Education Clearing-House.   Catalog of Resource Material on Community Education.   Developed by Informatics, Washington, D. C.: Government Printing Office, 1977.
A list of 973 books, articles, pamphlets, and reports covering various subjects pertaining to community education, and a separate listing of 11 audiovisual items.   Entries give author and affiliation, title, date of publication, type of format, paging, price, source, and a summary of contents.   Indexes of subjects, titles, personal name authors, and institutional authors.

Early Childhood and Elementary Education

531   Harbin, Gloria, and Lee Cross, comps.   Early Childhood Curriculum Materials: An Annotated Bibliography.   New York: Walker, 1976.
A guide to 75 curricular programs for early childhood education. Arranged by developmental areas.   Information on each program includes source, price, and a descriptive annotation including purpose and content.   Programs for handicapped children are included.   Also includes an author index, a chart of developmental skill sheets, and a glossary of developmental terms.

532   Harris, Charles M., and Nancy D. Gardenhour.   Developmental Tasks Resource Guide for Elementary School Children. Metuchen, N. J.:   Scarecrow Press, 1976.
An annotated guide to books, films, filmstrips, records, transparencies, audiotapes and videotapes.   Part I, Tasks for Self Development, contains entries related to independence, values, self-esteem, and physical skills.   Part II, Tasks for Social Development, contains entries related to communication concepts, peer relations, social roles, and social groups.   Part III contains author, subject, and title indexes and a list of publishers.

533   Monahan, Robert.   Free and Inexpensive Materials for Pre-
           school and Early Childhood.   Belmont, Calif.:   Fearon-
           Pitman Publishers, 1977.
Lists more than 600 items, including books, films, pamphlets, and
posters that teachers may obtain free or at low cost.   Arranged
under 30 subject headings.   Audiovisual materials are listed separately.   Includes a section on exceptional children.   Entries include
order information and a brief note on contents.

Guidance

534   Educators Guide to Free Guidance Materials: A Multimedia
           Guide.   Randolph, Wis.:   Educators Progress Service.
           Annual.
Arranged in sections by type of media: films; filmstrips and slides;
tapes, scripts, and transcriptions; printed materials.   Within each
section are subsections on career planning materials, social-personal
materials, responsibility to self and others, and use of leisure time.
Descriptive information and source are given for each item.   Title
index, subject index, and source and availability index.

Health, Safety, and Physical Education

535   Educators Guide to Free Health, Physical Education, and Rec-
           reation Materials: A Multimedia Guide.   Randolph, Wis.:
           Educators Progress Service.   Annual.
The 9th edition, 1976, includes 2,500 items from more than 600
institutional and government producers.   Arranged in 12 categories
by media and subject.   Includes films, filmstrips, slides, transparencies, audio recordings, video recordings, free and inexpensive publications, and government publications.   For all grade levels.   Title
and subject indexes.

           National Information Center for Educational Media.   Index to
           Health and Safety Education: Multimedia.   3d ed.   Los
           Angeles: NICEM, University of Southern California, 1977
           (see No. 502).

Language Arts

536   Bibliography of Language Arts Materials for Native North
           Americans: Bilingual, English as a Second Language, and
           Native Language Materials, 1965-1974.   Los Angeles:
           American Indian Studies Center, University of California,
           1977.
A bibliography of 1,000 works useful for native and bilingual education.   Includes introductory sections on specific linguistic difficulties
and cultural differences with suggestions for improvements in teaching
techniques, and a survey of Indian languages with indication of how
many grammars, dictionaries, and adult reading books are available
for each language.

537   National Council of Teachers of English.   NCTE Guide to

Teaching Materials for English, Grades 7-12.   Urbana, Ill.:
The Council, 1974.   Supplement, 1975.
An annotated listing of 550 anthologies, textbooks, workbooks, multimedia packages, and other instructional materials from 50 publishers.
Arranged in 16 subject areas.   Within each section or subsection
entries are arranged by title.   Entries give title, author, editor,
publisher, copyright date, edition number, prices for paperbound and
hardbound editions, teachers' manuals, supplementary materials,
number of pages, ISBN number, order information, primary audience,
extended audience, reading level, accelerated and remedial ability
level notations where appropriate, description of the text, series, or
package components, and references to reviews in NCTE journals.
Also includes a directory of publishers, ability level indexes, author-
editor index, and title index.   The 1975-76 supplement contains 260
additional entries representing 19 publishers, arranged according to
the plan of the original volume.   Title, author, and ability level
indexes in the supplement cover all entries in both the first volume
and the supplement.   Price changes and out-of-print designations for
entries in the first volume are entered in the title index to the supplement.   Further supplements are planned.

Literature

538   Chicorel Index to Poetry: Poetry on Discs, Tapes, and Cas-
      settes.   Edited by Marietta Chicorel.   Chicorel Index
      Series, Vol. 4. New York: Chicorel Library Publishing,
      1972.
Analyzes 700 collections of recorded poetry on more than 1,800 discs
and tapes.   Includes in one alphabet 25,000 entries by title, first
line, poet, performer, director, editor, and titles of albums, audio-
and videotapes, and cassettes.   Complete information, including
listing of contents, is given for the collection title entries.   Other
types of entries refer to the collection titles.   Includes poetry from
various countries of the world from ancient times to the present.
Also contains a subject indicator section with title references, an
author list, an album title list, a listing of poems by title and first
line, a performer list, a director-editor list, a list of Shakespeare's
sonnets, a producer-distributor directory, and a glossary of technical
terms.

539   Chicorel Index to the Spoken Arts on Discs, Tapes, and Cas-
      settes.   Edited by Marietta Chicorel.   Chicorel Index
      Series, Vols. 7, 7A, 7B. New York: Chicorel Library
      Publishing, 1973-74.
Locates, analyzes, and indexes plays, short stories, novels, speeches,
commentaries, documents, conversations, poems, and prose readings
on more than 1,200 recorded media.   Includes discs, tapes, and
video play performances.   The three volumes contain a total of
23,000 entries.   Each volume includes in one alphabet entries by
title of play, poem, novel, etc., album title, author, actors, per-
formers, readers, directors, and editors.   Entries for album titles
include label and number, length of recording, release date, price,
subject indicators, list of contents, note on printed text, and pro-

ducer or distributor.   Includes U. S. and foreign productions.   Other
sections are an album title list, author list, list of poems by title
and first line, spoken arts title list, editor-director list, performer
list, a list of subject indicators, subject indicators with album title
references, names of producers and directors, and a glossary of
technical terms.

540   Emmens, Carol A. Short Stories on Film.   Littleton, Colo.:
        Libraries Unlimited, 1978.
Lists 1, 300 movies produced 1920-1976, based on short stories by
American authors and well-known foreign authors.   Arranged alphabetically by author.   Entries include author's name, story title,
film title, technical information, credits, and brief summary of the
plot.   Index of film titles.

        Greene, Ellin, and Madalynne Schoenfeld, comps. and eds.   A
        Multimedia Approach to Children's Literature: A Selective
        List of Films, Filmstrips, and Recordings Based on Chil-
        dren's Books.   2d ed.   Chicago: American Library Associa-
        tion, 1977 (see No. 308).

541   Selected Sound Recordings of American, British, and European
        Literature in English.   By Homer E. Salley.   Toledo,
        Ohio: Technological Media Center, University of Toledo,
        1976.
Contains 1, 365 entries arranged in 12 subject categories.   Includes
dramatizations, readings, criticism, and sound tracks from films.
Entries give author, title, label and number, playing time, and release date.   No index.

Multicultural Education

542   Black Experience in Children's Audiovisual Materials.   Compiled
        by Diane De Veaux, Marilyn B. Iarusso, and Viola J. Clark.
        New York: New York Public Library, 1973.
A list of audiovisual materials depicting black life, for primary and
intermediate grades.   Supplements Rollock, Black Experience in
Children's Books (see No. 381).   Includes more than 200 entries in
sections on records and cassettes, films, filmstrips, and multimedia
kits.   Entries give descriptive information and evaluative comment.
Includes a directory of sources.

        Buttlar, Lois, and Lubomyr R. Wynar.   Building Ethnic Col-
        lections: An Annotated Guide for School Media Centers and
        Public Libraries.   Littleton, Colo.:   Libraries Unlimited,
        1977 (see No. 363).

543   Cartel: Annotations and Analyses of Bilingual and Multicultural
        Materials.   Austin, Texas: Dissemination and Assessment
        Center for Bilingual Education, 1973-.   Quarterly.
An annotated list of books, curriculum guides, and multimedia
materials on the Spanish speaking, American Indians, French, Portu-

guese, Chinese, and Russians in the United States.   For preschool
through scholarly level.   Arranged by title.   Entries include format
description, release date, price, grade level, and a descriptive and
evaluative annotation.   Includes a list of publishers and distributors,
and a subject index.

544   Cyr, Helen W.   A Filmography of the Third World.   Metuchen,
        N. J.: Scarecrow Press, 1976.
An annotated list of more than 2, 000 16 mm films that describe
countries and peoples in Africa, the Middle East, Asia, Latin America, and the Pacific, and Third World ethnic groups in North America and Europe.   Includes a title index; a distributors list; and a list
of directors, cinematographers, scenarists, and composers.

545   Goodman, R. Irwin.   Bibliography of Nonprint Instructional
        Materials on the American Indian.   Provo, Utah: Institute
        of American Indian Studies, Brigham Young University,
        1972.
Lists 1, 400 audiovisual items, most of which were produced in the
1960s.   Includes material on Eskimos, Pre-Columbian peoples,
history, art, music, and legends.   Entries, arranged by title, give
media description, producer, release date, age and grade level, and
summary of contents.   Includes a directory of distributors and a
subject index.

546   Johnson, Harry A. , ed. and comp.   Ethnic American Minori-
        ties: A Guide to Media and Materials.   New York: R. R.
        Bowker, 1976.
In five major sections: I, The Afro-American in the Melting Pot, by
Harry A. Johnson; II, Asian-Americans, by Minako K. Maykovich;
III, The Native Indian American, by S. Gabe Paxton, Jr. ; IV, The
Spanish-Speaking American, by Lourdes M. King; and V, Other
Ethnic Minorities on the American Scene, by Harry A. Johnson.
Each section contains a discussion of historical perspective, educational and cultural needs, bibliographic notes and/or a bibliography,
and an annotated list of media and materials, including 16 mm films,
filmstrips, slides, transparencies, audio recordings and cassettes,
videocassettes, and study prints, pictures, posters, and graphics.
Entries include publisher or distributor, grade level, release date,
technical information, purchase and rental prices, and a brief
description of contents.   Includes a directory of producers and
distributors, a title index of media, and a subject index.

547   Johnson, Harry A. , ed.   Multimedia Materials for Afro-
        American Studies: A Curriculum Orientation and Annotated
        Bibliography of Resources.   New York: R. R. Bowker,
        1971.
Part One consists of four papers on the need for adapting educational
technology to the needs of minority students, a discussion of sociological and psychological needs, black studies in the curriculum, and
needs in Negro history for integration.   Part Two is a bibliography
of multimedia materials on the Afro-American culture and heritage
including films, audiotapes, filmstrips, multimedia kits, recordings,

slides, study prints, transparencies, videotapes, telecourses, kine-
scopes, and a classified list of 100 paperback books.   Entries in
all sections are annotated.   Part Three is a briefly annotated bibliography of multimedia materials on the peoples of Africa, their culture,
and their contributions.   Also includes a directory of producers and
distributors of nonprint materials, a list of publishers of paperbound
books, and an author and subject index.   For elementary school
through university level.

548   Multicultural Education: A Functional Bibliography for Teachers.
       Edited by James Giese, Milton J. Gold, and Carl A. Grant.
       Omaha: Teachers Corps, Center for Urban Education,
       University of Nebraska at Omaha, 1977.
A selective bibliography arranged by ten ethnic groups: blacks,
Chinese and Asian, Eastern European, Italian, Japanese, Jewish,
Mexican, American Indian, Northern European, and Puerto Rican;
and categories for multicultural materials, and prejudice and dis-
crimination.   Entries include a descriptive annotation, indication of
appropriate audience, and grade level.   No index.

549   Multi-Ethnic Media: Selected Bibliographies in Print.   David
       Cohen, Coordinator, Task Force on Ethnic Materials Infor-
       mation Exchange, Social Responsibility Roundtable.   Office
       for Library Service to the Disadvantaged.   Chicago: Ameri-
       can Library Association, 1975.
A brief listing in three sections: bibliographical essays; bibliographies (bibliographic materials to be used with children and young
adults); and sources of information on materials available for ethnic
groups.   Includes material on blacks, American Indians, Eskimos,
Mexican Americans, Puerto Ricans, and Chinese Americans.   Entries
are annotated.   Intended as an aid in developing ethnic collections
in public schools.

       National Information Center for Educational Media.   Index to
       Black History and Studies: Multimedia.   2d ed.   Los
       Angeles: NICEM, University of Southern California, 1973
       (see No. 500).

550   Nichols, Margaret S. , and Margaret N. O'Neill.   Multicultural
       Bibliography for Preschool through Second Grade in the
       Areas of Black, Spanish Speaking, Asian American, and
       Native American Cultures.   Stanford, Calif.:   Multicultural
       Resources, 1972.
An unannotated bibliography in sections on Black Cultures, Spanish
Speaking Cultures, Asian American Cultures, Native American
Cultures, Multicultural, Pictures and Posters, Material for Teachers
and Parents, and Multi-Ethnic Bibliographies.   Entries give author,
title, publisher, date, and price.   Also includes a directory of
publishers and a title index.

       Recommended East Asian Core Collection for Children's, High
       School, Public, Community College, and Undergraduate
       College Libraries.   Compiled by the East Asian Bibliographic

Group and edited by William H. O. Scott. Seattle: University of Washington Libraries, 1974 (see No. 378).

551 Reilly, Robert P.   A Selected and Annotated Bibliography of Bicultural Classroom Materials for Mexican American Studies.   San Francisco: R & E Research Associates, 1977.
Part I contains three chapters: an introduction with statements of the problem of Mexican American education; the purpose, goals, and background of the study; definition of terms; limitations and organization of the study; a review of the literature; and a chapter on the research methodology of the study, conclusions, and recommendations.   A bibliography follows the third chapter.   Part II is the Selected and Annotated Bibliography of 233 references to printed materials and 45 references to audiovisual aids, arranged in sections by curriculum subjects, professional teacher resources, and bibliographies.   Three appendixes are a list of 25 books and four audiovisual items not available for review; a list of Chicano journals and newspapers; and a list of publishers and distributors of multicultural materials.   No index.

552 U. S. Office of Child Development.   A Bibliography of Bilingual-Bicultural Preschool Material for the Spanish Speaking Child.   Washington, D. C.: Government Printing Office, 1977.
A bibliography of materials prepared by teachers and other workers in early childhood education programs.   Arranged in three major categories: curriculum guides, instructional materials, and supplemental materials.   Index.

Science

553 AAAS Science Film Catalog.   Ann Seltz-Petrash, project editor and compiler, and Kathryn Wolff, managing editor, AAAS Publications Program.   Prepared with the assistance of the National Science Foundation.   Washington, D. C.: American Association for the Advancement of Science, 1975.
An annotated list of 5, 600 16 mm films in the sciences and social sciences, in two sections, one for junior high school and adult levels, and one for elementary school level.   Each section is arranged by subject (by the Dewey Decimal classification system), with an alphabetical, cross-referenced list of subject headings.   Information on each film includes whether black-and-white or color, intended audience, running time, rental and sale prices, description, release date, order number, and a distribution code.   Also includes a directory of producers and distributors, and a title index.

554 Educators Guide to Free Science Materials: A Multimedia Guide.   Randolph, Wis.: Educators Progress Service.   Annual.
Arranged in sections by type of media: films; filmstrips, slides, and transparencies; tapes, scripts, and transcriptions; charts, exhibits, magazines, and posters.   Each section is subdivided by subject area.   Descriptive information and source are given for each

item.   Includes a section on illustrative units.   Indexes by title, subject, and source and availability.

555   Higgins, Judith H.   Energy: A Multimedia Guide for Children
         and Young Adults.   Santa Barbara, Calif.:   American
         Bibliographical Center - Clio Press, 1979.
An annotated list of 433 references.   Part One is arranged by energy source, divided into print and nonprint sections.   Part Two lists curriculum guides and other instructional materials.   Part Three lists selection aids.   Part Four lists other sources of information on energy.

         National Information Center for Educational Media.   Index to
            Environmental Studies: Multimedia.   Los Angeles: NICEM,
            University of Southern California, 1977 (see No. 501).

         Science Books and Films.   Washington, D. C.:   American
            Association for the Advancement of Science.   1965-.
            Quarterly (see No. 395).

Social Studies

556   Educators Guide to Free Social Studies Materials: A Multimedia
         Guide.   Randolph, Wis.:   Educators Progress Service.
         Annual.
Arranged in sections by type of media: films; filmstrips and slides; tapes, scripts, and transcriptions; printed materials.   Each section is subdivided by areas of social studies.   Descriptive information and source are given for each item.   Indexes by title, subject, and source and availability.

Special Education

557   Anderson, Robert M. , Robert E. Hemenway, and Janet W.
         Anderson.   Instructional Resources for Teachers of the
         Culturally Disadvantaged and Exceptional.   Springfield,
         Ill.:   C. C. Thomas, 1969.
An annotated list of instructional materials arranged by curriculum area.   In each area are listed texts and workbooks, teaching aids, and teacher resources.   Information on each item includes author, publisher, type of material, interest level and difficulty level, descriptive annotation, and price.   Includes a directory of publishers.

558   Instructional Materials for the Handicapped: Birth Through
         Early Childhood.   Arden R. Thorum, project director.
         Salt Lake City: Olympus Publishing Company, 1976.
Includes materials for the handicapped child and general developmental aids for early childhood or elementary school programs. Chapter 1 gives criteria for selection of toys and games, and includes a directory of more than 600 manufacturers.   Chapter 2 reviews research reports and guides relating to the use of educational kits in developmental education, and includes guidelines for analyzing kits and learning materials, and a chart that analyzes 270 commercially produced instructional kits in terms of cost, appropriate

age, developmental skills areas, subject areas, and format and components.   Chapter 3 is an annotated bibliography of 92 curriculum and activity guides for early childhood education.

National Information Center for Educational Media.   NICEM Catalog to Special Education Non-Print Materials.   Los Angeles: NICEM, University of Southern California, 1978 (see No. 505).

National Information Center for Special Education Materials. Los Angeles: NICSEM, University of Southern California. Publishes lists of large print and Braille books, audiovisual materials, and equipment and adaptive devices related to all educational levels of the handicapped, primarily to children.   Items are annotated. Listed below are titles of volumes published.

559   Index to Assessment Devices, Testing Instruments, and Parent Materials.   1978.

560   Index to Media and Materials for the Deaf, Hard of Hearing, Speech Impaired.   New ed.   1978.

561   Index to Media and Materials for the Visually Handicapped, Orthopedically Impaired, Other Health Impaired.   1978.

562   Index to Mentally Retarded, Specific Learning Disability, Emotionally Disturbed.   1978.

563   Special Education Index to Learner Materials.   1979.

Speech and Communication

564   Buteau, June D.   Nonprint Materials on Communication: An Annotated Directory of Select Films, Videotapes, Videocassettes, Simulations and Games.   Metuchen, N. J.: Scarecrow Press, 1976.
An annotated list of 2, 236 items from more than 1, 400 sources. Classified in three major sections--films, videotapes and videocassettes, and simulations and games--and further subdivided into 27 subject categories and subcategories.   For secondary and adult levels.   Information on each entry includes title; producer/vendor/ sponsor; distributor/releasing agent; date produced and/or released; running time and other technical data; availability; audience level; series reference and/or revision information; awards; and synopsis. Also includes a directory of sources and a cross-category index.

565   Feezel, Jerry D. , Kent R. Brown, and Carol A. Valentine, comps.   Selected Print and Nonprint Resources in Speech Communication: An Annotated Bibliography K-12.   Falls Church, Va.:   Speech Communication Association; Urbana, Ill.:   ERIC Clearinghouse on Reading and Communication Skills; distributed by National Council of Teachers of English, 1976.
A bibliography of 201 entries for resources in speech communication,

most of which were issued since 1965.   Arranged in four categories:
Print; Nonprint; Multimedia; and Major Sources (publishers, distributors, catalogs, etc.).   Each category is subdivided by grade level
and coded for content area.   Entries give title, author or editor,
place, publisher or distributor, date, and price.   Form is given for
nonprint items.   Annotations include suggestions for class use.
Index by content area.

Vocational Education

National Information Center for Educational Media.   Index to
Vocational and Technical Education: Multimedia.   3d ed.
Los Angeles: NICEM, University of Southern California,
1977 (see No. 504).

566   Reinhart, Bruce, ed.   Vocational-Technical Learning Materials:
Books and Manuals for Schools and Community Colleges.
2d ed.   Williamsport, Pa.:   Bro-Dart Publishing Co., 1974.
A classified, annotated list of books, periodicals, programmed
materials, etc., arranged alphabetically by title under each subject.
Price and grade level are given for most items.   Recommendation
for first, second, or third purchase is given for each title.   Author
and subject indexes.

567   Schuman, Patricia.   Materials for Occupational Education: An
Annotated Source Guide.   New York: R. R. Bowker, 1971.
A directory of 600 professional and trade associations, government
agencies, and private businesses that publish books, periodicals,
manuals, multimedia aids, and other instructional items useful as
curriculum and training materials in occupational education.   Arranged by occupational field.   Entries give name of organization,
address, type of material published, and titles of publications with
prices.   Also includes lists of background readings, curriculum
guides, further sources of occupational information, and organizations included with addresses.   Index of occupational categories.

D.   Tests and Measurements

568   Buros, Oscar K., ed.   Eighth Mental Measurements Yearbook.
2 vols.   Highland Park, N. J.:   Gryphon Press, 1978.
In three main parts: Tests and Reviews, Books and Reviews, and
Indexes.   The Tests and Reviews section lists 1,184 tests, 898
test reviews, 140 excerpted test reviews from 29 journals, and 17,481
references.   Information for individual tests includes title, acronym,
grade level, copyright dates, part scores, manual, instructions,
price of test and manual, time required for test, author, and publisher.   This information is followed by a list of references on
construction, use, and validity of the test, and by a review article
covering structure, purpose, technical information, usefulness, and
evaluation, or by one or more excerpted reviews from journals.
The Books and Reviews section lists 576 books on testing, most of
which were published 1970-1977.   Included are 381 excerpted book

reviews from 46 journals for 229 of the books listed.   The Indexes
section includes: Periodical Directory and Index, which lists 50
journals from which excerpts of reviews are reprinted; Publishers
Directory and Index, a list, with addresses, of the 456 publishers
of tests and books listed in the first two sections; Index of Book
Titles, listing the 576 books on testing in the Books and Reviews
section; Index of Test Titles, including tests listed in this yearbook
and in Tests in Print II; Index of Names, indicating authorship of
tests, test reviews, measurement books, excerpted reviews, and
references dealing with specific tests; Scanning Index, an expanded
table of contents for the Tests and Reviews section, presenting
titles of all tests in each classification plus titles in Tests in Print
II, giving for each test information on whether new, revised, or un-
changed since last listed, population for which test is intended, range
of copyright dates, number of reviews, excerpts, and references in
this yearbook, Tests in Print II, and in earlier publications.

569   Buros, Oscar K., ed.   Tests in Print II: An Index to Tests,
        Test Reviews, and the Literature on Specific Tests.
        Highland Park, N.J.:   Gryphon Press, 1974.
A comprehensive bibliography of all known tests published as
separates for use with English speaking subjects.   It also serves
as a master index to the contents of all Mental Measurements Yearbooks.   It includes entries for 2,467 tests in a classified arrangement.   Information for entries includes test title, population for
which it is suitable, range of copyright dates, acronym, part scores,
manual, updating of test materials, authors, publisher, country if
not the United States, and cross-references to Mental Measurements
Yearbooks.   This information is followed by a list of references on
construction, use, and validity through 1971, and a cumulative name
index for each test with references.   Also includes a reprinting of
the 1974 ADA-AERA-NCME Standards for Educational and Psychological Tests; a publishers directory with a listing of each publisher's
test titles; an index of titles, an index of names, and a classified
scanning index with indication of grade level for each test.

570   Compton, Carolyn.   A Guide to 65 Diagnostic Tests for Special
        Education.   Belmont, Calif.:   Fearon-Pitman Publishers,
        1979.
Evaluates the strengths and limitations of 65 diagnostic tests commonly used to assess students from kindergarten through grade 8.
Includes academic tests, language tests, perception and memory
tests, gross motor tests, general intelligence tests, and developmental skills tests.   A special section covers preschool and bilingual
tests.   Sample sections of many tests are included.

571   Johnson, Orval G., and James W. Bommarito.   Tests and
        Measurements in Child Development: A Handbook.   San
        Francisco: Jossey-Bass Publishers, 1971.
Contains a listing of 300 tests and measures issued 1956-1965,
covering the age span 0-12.   Arranged in ten categories.   Information for each test or measure includes title, author, age range for
which it is appropriate, variable being measured, type of measure,

source from which the measure can be obtained, description of the
measure including sample items, reliability and validity, and bibliography.   Index of authors, index of measures, subject index, and
general index.

572   Johnson, Orval G.   Tests and Measurements in Child Develop-
        ment: Handbook II.   2 vols.   San Francisco: Jossey-Bass
        Publishers, 1976.
Handbook II lists approximately 900 instruments issued 1966-1974,
from more than 140 journals and other sources.   Age span covered
is 0-18.   Arranged in eleven categories.   Information for each test
is similar to that given in the 1971 volume.   Subject, author, and
measure indexes.

573   Mauser, August J.   Assessing the Learning Disabled: Selected
        Instruments.   San Rafael, Calif.:   Academic Therapy Publi-
        cations, 1977.
Descriptions of more than 300 tests for evaluating children and adults
with learning disabilities.   Tests are grouped in 11 categories: preschool readiness; motor, sensory, and language; reading readiness;
diagnostic reading; survey tests; oral reading; math abilities; creativity tests; social adjustment; vocational; and miscellaneous.   Information on individual tests includes age range, time to administer, and
special features.   Concise annotations are followed by name of
publisher.   Also includes a list of selected readings, and an alphabetical index to tests.

574   National Council of Teachers of English.   Committee to Review
        Standardized Tests.   Reviews of Selected Published Tests
        in English.   Edited by Alfred H. Grommon.   Urbana, Ill.:
        The Council, 1976.
Part One is a discussion of statewide accountability programs of
testing and assessment, by Alfred H. Grommon.   Part Two includes
reviews of 51 tests including description and evaluation of each test.
Test reviews are grouped into five sections: Language Development
and Its Evaluation, by Walter Loban; Elementary School Language
Tests, by Walter A. Jenkins; Tests on the English Language, by
J. N. Hook; Evaluation of Writing Tests, by Richard Braddock; and
Literature Tests, by Alan C. Purves.   Part Three summarizes some
of the problems in educational accountability and makes recommendations to teachers.   Includes an alphabetical index of tests reviewed.

        National Information Center for Special Education Materials.
        Index to Assessment Devices, Testing Instruments, and
        Parent Materials.   Los Angeles: NICSEM, University of
        Southern California, 1978 (see No. 560).

VI.   OTHER TYPES OF REFERENCE MATERIALS

The bibliographies and indexes listed in Sections I-V are sources for finding references to various types of material.   In this section sources of factual information are listed, such as encyclopedias, dictionaries, thesauri, handbooks, statistical sources, directories, and biographical sources.

A.   Encyclopedias, Dictionaries, and Thesauri

The most comprehensive and useful general encyclopedia in this field is:

575   Encyclopedia of Education.   Edited by Lee C. Deighton.   10
        vols.   New York: Macmillan, 1971.
A comprehensive, scholarly work containing more than 1,000 signed articles covering every major subject area in the field of education. Most articles include bibliographies.   Deals primarily with American education, but a considerable number of articles concern international education, comparative education, exchange programs, and educational systems of more than 100 countries.   Articles on individuals present their contributions to educational thought and practice rather than biographical information.   In Vols. 1-9, articles are arranged alphabetically.   Vol. 10, index volume, contains a directory of contributors; a guide to articles, arranged under broad headings; and an alphabetical topical index with related articles listed under topical headings.

Other Encyclopedias of Education

576   Anderson, Scarvia B., and others.   Encyclopedia of Educational Evaluation.   San Francisco: Jossey-Bass Publishers,
        1975.
Major categories of articles are: evaluation models, functions and targets of evaluation, program objectives and standards, social context of evaluation, planning and design, systems technologies, variables, measurement approaches and types, technical measurement considerations, reactive concerns, and analysis and interpreta-

tion.   Includes a 26-page bibliography, a name index, and a subject
index.

577   Blishen, Edward, ed.   Encyclopedia of Education.   New York:
      Philosophical Library, 1970.
A one-volume encyclopedia including information on educational
administration, teaching methods, legislation, examinations, teaching
aids, primary schools, secondary schools, further and higher education, and history and philosophy of education.   Lists for further
reading are included with many articles.   British emphasis.

Encyclopedia of Educational Research.   Edited by R. L. Ebel.
      4th ed.   New York: Macmillan, 1969 (see No. 269).

578   International Encyclopedia of Higher Education.   10 vols.   San
      Francisco: Jossey-Bass Publishers, 1977.
Covers all major aspects of international higher education, including
national systems; academic fields of study; educational associations;
research centers, institutes, and documentation centers; academic
and administrative policies and procedures; and current issues and
trends in higher education.   Does not include biographical entries or
entries for individual colleges and universities.   Vol. 1 includes an
alphabetical listing of entries of Vols. 2-9, a classification of entries,
a list of contributors, a list of acronyms, and a glossary of terminology.   Vols. 2-9 contain 1, 300 entries arranged alphabetically.
Most articles are signed and include bibliographies.   Name and
Subject Indexes make up Vol. 10.

579   Monroe, Paul, ed.   Cyclopedia of Education.   5 vols.   New
      York: Macmillan, 1911-13.   Reprint ed.   Detroit: Gale
      Research, 1968.
Includes information on all countries and periods, with fullest treatment given to American subjects.   Signed articles by specialists.
Analytical index in Vol. 5 groups articles by broad subjects.   Includes bibliographies and illustrations.   Still useful for biographical
and historical material.

Encyclopedias Covering All Social Sciences Fields
Including Education

580   Encyclopedia of the Social Sciences.   15 vols.   New York:
      Macmillan, 1930-35.
A comprehensive encyclopedia of the whole field, covering political
science, economics, law, anthropology, sociology, penology, and
social work, and the social aspects of ethics, education, philosophy,
psychology, biology, geography, art, etc.   Includes many biographies.

581   International Encyclopedia of the Social Sciences.   17 vols.
      New York: Macmillan, 1968.   8 vol. edition, 1977.
A comprehensive, scholarly work that complements the earlier
Encyclopedia of the Social Sciences.   A majority of the articles are
devoted to the concepts, theories, and methods of the disciplines of

anthropology, economics, geography, history, law, political science, psychiatry, psychology, sociology, and statistics.   Many articles present modern social thought about the arts, religions, and the professions.

Dictionaries

582   Barnard, Howard C. , and J. A. Lauwerys.   Handbook of
        British Educational Terms.   London: Harrap, 1963.
"Terms used in the general processes of education and teaching techniques, in educational organization and administration--frequently with a historical reference--and also words in common use in ordinary school, college, and university life in Britain. "--Preface. Also includes an outline of the British educational system.

583   Bush, Clifford L. , and Robert C.   Andrews.   Dictionary of
        Reading and Learning Disability Terms.   Matawan, N. J. :
        Educational and Psychological Associates Press, 1973.
Defines more than 2, 100 terms in reading and learning disabilities and related terms from linguistics, medicine, and psychology.   Appendixes list ERIC clearinghouses, publishers, and a classified list of tests for this field.

584   Collins, K. T. , and others.   Key Words in Education.   London:
        Longman Group, 1973.
Defines words that are most frequently needed by education students. References to standard works are cited with most of the definitions. Names of educators and organizations are included in addition to educational terms.

585   Educational Technology: Definition and Glossary of Terms.
        AECT Task Force on Definition and Terminology.   2 vols.
        Washington, D. C. :   Association for Educational Communica-
        tions and Technology, 1977-.
Vol. 1 defines terms dealing with development and production of learning resources.   Vol. 2 will define terms relating to their management.   The first part of Vol. 1 discusses theory, intellectual techniques, and practical applications of educational technology. The second part contains separate glossaries for theory, research, design, production, evaluation and selection, materials, devices, and techniques.   Alphabetical index.

586   Gatti, Daniel J. , and Richard D. Gatti.   Encyclopedic Dic-
        tionary of School Law.   Englewood Cliffs, N. J. :   Parker
        Publishing, 1975.
Contains 250 alphabetically arranged terms covering a wide range of topics in school law.   Entries include cross-references to related topics.   Includes a categorical index listing all entries by 14 major subject areas, and a detailed subject index.

587   Good, Carter V.   Dictionary of Education.   3d ed.   New York:
        McGraw-Hill, 1973.

A scholarly dictionary defining more than 30, 000 technical and professional terms and concepts in the entire area of education.   Special sections for terms in Canada, England, and Wales.

588   Kelly, Leo J.   Dictionary of Exceptional Children.   New York:
      MSS Information, 1972.
Concise definitions, descriptions, or information for the most commonly used terms and the best-known organizations concerning exceptional children.   Each definition or description is written with emphasis on the special meaning relative to exceptional children.   Includes a list of references on special education.

589   Page, Graham Terry, and J. B. Thomas, with A. R. Marshall.
      International Dictionary of Education.   London: Kogan Page;
      New York: Nichols Publishing, 1977.
Defines more than 10, 000 expressions and specialized terms of the international language of education from preschool to postdoctoral levels.   Includes entries on famous educationalists and educational thinkers and their contribution to the field.   Also includes a wide coverage of international organizations and major national institutions and associations.   Extensive cross-referencing.   Appendix 1 lists abbreviations for associations and organizations found in the Dictionary.   Appendix 2 lists U. S. honor societies, fraternities, and sororities.

590   Schubert, Delwyn G.   Dictionary of Terms and Concepts in
      Reading.   2d ed.   Springfield, Ill.:   C. C. Thomas, 1969.
Defines terms and basic concepts as well as the technical vocabulary employed in the field of reading and related fields.

591   UNESCO.   Terminology: Special Education.   By Lise Brunet,
      and others.   Paris: UNESCO, International Bureau of Education, 1977.
A glossary in four languages: English, Spanish, French, and Russian.   Defines terms and provides their equivalents in the other languages.

592   Van Osdol, Bob.   Vocabulary in Special Education.   Moscow:
      University of Idaho Research Foundation, 1972.
A basic list of current terms related to activities, interests, needs, and concerns in exceptional child education, with definitions.   Appendixes include a list of special education organizations, a list of special education publications, a list of tests, and terms in testing with definitions.

Thesauri

593   Barhydt, Gordon C., and Charles T. Schmidt.   With the as-
      sistance of Kee T. Chang.   Information Retrieval Thesaurus
      of Education Terms.   Cleveland: Press of Case Western
      Reserve University, 1968.

Part One is an alphabetical word list.   Part Two is a faceted or classified array.   Part Three is a permuted list of descriptors. Preliminary sections include: Introduction; Thesaurus Development; Vocabulary Control; Hierarchical and Collateral Relationships; An Example of Faceting and Cross-Referencing; Facet and Subfacet General Headings.

594   Council for Exceptional Children, Information Services.
      Thesaurus for Exceptional Child Education.   Washington,
      D. C.:   Council for Exceptional Children, 1975.
Contains indexing terms (descriptors) selected from the ERIC Thesaurus for indexing and retrieving in the Council for Exceptional Children's data base.   The main section is the Alphabetical Listing of Descriptors, in which terms, with scope notes where applicable, are given, related terms are identified, and previously used descriptors are listed.   Other sections are Search Saves, a listing of descriptors under broader subjects; and a Rotated Index.   Preceding the main section are Age List, Exceptionality List, and Format List.

595   Thesaurus of Psychological Index Terms.   2d ed.   Washington,
      D. C.:   American Psychological Association, 1977.
In three sections: 1, Relationship Section, in which terms are listed alphabetically, cross-referenced, and displayed with broader, narrower, and related terms; 2, Rotated Alphabetical Terms Section, in which preferred Thesaurus terms are listed in alphabetical order by each word contained within them; 3, Postable Terms and Term Codes Section, which lists Thesaurus terms in alphabetical order to facilitate rapid selection of search terms and verification of spelling. Includes all the preferred terms listed in the Relationship Section. Numerical codes preceding each term provide access points for users of the computer readable version of Psychological Abstracts.   New terms are so indicated in footnote references with the year in which they were first used.

596   UNESCO: IBE Education Thesaurus.   Paris: UNESCO; In-
      ternational Bureau of Education, 1977.
A faceted list of terms for indexing and retrieving documents and data in the field of education.   A revised English version with French and Spanish equivalents.   Covers all aspects of education.   Sections provide general headings for fields, facets and subfacets; an alphabetical array of descriptors and identifiers; a faceted array of descriptors and identifiers; and a rotated list of descriptors.

597   UNESCO Thesaurus: A Structured List of Descriptors for
      Indexing and Retrieving Literature in the Fields of Educa-
      tion, Science, Social Science, Culture, and Communication.
      Compiled by Jean Aitchison.   2 vols.   Paris: UNESCO,
      1977.
A tool for the indexing and retrieval of information handled by the UNESCO Computerized Documentation System and by other indexing-retrieving systems whose documentation coverage is closely related to UNESCO's.   Vol. 1 contains an introduction, classified thesaurus, permuted index, and hierarchical display of descriptors.   Vol. 2 is

the alphabetical thesaurus.   Entries include the topic's number in the
classified thesaurus, scope notes, "use for" notes, narrower term,
broader term, related term, and class numbers for cross-references.

598   U. S. Educational Resources Information Center.   Thesaurus of
      ERIC Descriptors.   With a special chapter, "The Role and
      Function of the Thesaurus in Education," by Frederick Good-
      man.   7th ed.   New York Macmillan Information, 1977.
Represents the vocabulary of the field of education.   The main section lists descriptors, which are authoritative terms acceptable for
indexing and searching in the ERIC system, and synonyms and near
synonyms with notations indicating "used for," "narrower term,"
"broader term," and "related term."   Scope notes, brief statements
of restricted usage, are given for some descriptors.   "Use" entries
refer from synonyms to preferred descriptors.   Other sections are:
Rotated Descriptor Display, Two-Way Hierarchical Term Display,
Descriptor Groups, Descriptor Group Display, and Bibliography.

                        B.   Handbooks

General

599   Bowen, James.   A History of Western Education.   3 vols.
         London: Methuen & Co. , 1972-.
Vol. 1, 1972, Ancient World, Orient and Mediterranean, 2000 B. C. -
A. D. 1054.   Vol 2, 1975, Civilization of Europe: Sixth to Sixteenth
Century.   Vol. 3 will cover the modern period in Europe and its
extension to the world outside.   Includes illustrations and maps.
Index in each volume.

600   Cohen, Sol.   Education in the United States: A Documentary
         History.   5 vols. New York Random House, 1974.
Includes the text of the most significant documents in the field of
American education from the 16th and 17th century English and
European background and the earliest colonial beginnings to the
present.   The documents are arranged chronologically.   Book One,
The Planting, 1607-1789; Book Two, The Shaping of American Edu-
cation, 1789-1895; Book Three, The Transformation of American
Education, 1895-1973.   Each book is divided into sections, and is
prefaced with an historical overview.   Index.

601   Council of Chief State School Officers.   Education in the States.
         Edited by Jim B. Pearson and Edgar Fuller.   2 vols.
         Washington, D. C. :   National Education Association, 1969.
The first volume, Historical Development and Outlook, traces developments since 1900 in each of the 50 state departments of education and
the central school agencies of the territories.   The second volume,
Nationwide Development Since 1900, contains 16 sections dealing with
areas of concern to state departments of education, including the
legal basis for state action, state departments of education within
state governments, service and leadership to local schools, state
financing of education, curriculum, the world of work, adult educa-

cation, pupil personnel services, teacher education and certification, educational facilities, federal programs, food services, rehabilitation, the organized teaching profession, higher education relationships, and public relations. Bibliographies and statistical tables are included.

602   Handbook on Contemporary Education. Compiled and edited by
        Steven E. Goodman. New York: R. R. Bowker, 1976.
Includes 118 articles arranged in eight parts: Part I, Educational Change and Planning; Part II, Administration and Management of Education; Part III, Teacher/Faculty Issues; Part IV, Education and Training of Teachers and Administrators; Part V, Students and Parents; Part VI, Special Interest Groups; Part VII, Teaching and Learning Strategies; Part VIII, Some Alternatives and Options in Education. Each article gives "state-of-the-art" information, and includes specific programs and projects, and references to further sources of information. Keyword index, and author index.

603   Kawakami, Toyo S. Acronyms in Education and the Behavioral
        Sciences. Chicago: American Library Association, 1971.
Restricted to American, British, and Canadian terms, and acronyms for international organizations that have English as one of their official languages. Arranged alphabetically with address and zip code, and, when feasible, a source or authority. Separate sections are a list of sources as listed in the entries, verification sources, and a reverse-order index (by full name of organization).

604   Standard Educational Almanac. Chicago: Marquis Academic
        Media, Marquis Who's Who. Annual.
Current information, with detailed statistical data, on all aspects of education from more than 60 sources. The 11th edition, 1978-79, is in eight parts: Part One, Education (General); Part Two, Elementary and Secondary Education; Part Three, Higher Education; Part Four, Career and Adult Education; Part Five, Equal Educational Opportunity; Part Six, Educational Resources; Part Seven, Related Statistics; Part Eight, Subject, Organization, Personnel, and Geographic Indexes. The first three parts cover enrollment, instructional and administrative staff, revenues and expenditures, educational achievement, and Canadian schools at the various levels, and include directories of education associations and agencies, a poll of public attitudes toward education, and a guide to U. S. Office of Education programs. Part Four gives a profile of programs and participants in career, occupational, and adult and continuing education. Part Five includes research reports on problems of inequality in the education of minorities and statistics of educational achievement. Part Six gives statistics on holdings, staffing, and finances of public and private libraries, and directories of publishers, public TV stations, audiovisual producers, and ERIC clearinghouses. Part Seven includes background material on population, employment, and foreign education, and a list of international education associations.

605   World Survey of Education. 5 vols. Paris: UNESCO, 1955-72.
Vol. 1, Handbook of Educational Organization and Statistics, 1955, gives descriptive and statistical material on all aspects of national

school systems of all countries of the world.   Vol II, Primary Education, 1958, Vol. III, Secondary Education, 1961, and Vol. IV, Higher Education, 1966, treat these levels of education in relation to each national system of education as a whole.   Vol. V, Educational Policy, Legislation and Administration, 1971, includes aims of education and policy, local basis of the educational system, and educational administration for each country.   Each volume includes descriptive text, statistical tables, diagrams, glossaries, and bibliographies.

Special Subjects

606   Education Funding Research Council.   Federal Funding Guide
         for Elementary and Secondary Education.   Washington, D. C. :
         Education Funding Research Council.   1975-.   Annual.
The 1978 edition, the fourth annual guide, is in six main sections. Section I, Federal Aid to Education, includes the 1978 education budget and appropriations, regulations, the legislative process, an annotated list of government publications for educators, general provisions for programs, and a glossary of budget terms.   Section II, Legislation, is a report on the status of all important education legislation in Congress as of January 1, 1978.   Section III lists Congressional committees and subcommittees for Education.   Section IV is a directory of the U. S. Office of Education and its divisions, and of the National Institute of Education.   Section V, Federal Aid Programs, is the main section, providing information on individual programs administered by USOE and other agencies, including aid to educationally disadvantaged children, aid to the handicapped, desegregation programs, impact aid, vocational education, right to read, bilingual education, teacher training, cultural programs, drug and alcohol abuse education and prevention, adult education, environmental education, child development and early childhood education, social service grants to states, food programs, special projects, Indian education, educational research, guidance and counseling, and shared revenues.   Section VI is a deadline date calendar reminder for closing dates for application for grants programs, with titles of programs listed alphabetically.   Index.

607   Encyclopedia of Careers and Vocational Guidance.   3d ed.
         Edited by William E. Hopke.   2 vols.   Chicago: J. G.
         Ferguson Publishing; distributed by Doubleday, 1975.
Vol. I, Planning Your Career, contains articles on 71 broad career fields, giving general descriptions of fields or groups of occupations. Vol. II, Careers and Occupations, contains articles on 220 specific occupations, giving for each a definition, history, information on nature of the work, educational and special requirements, opportunities for experience and exploration, method of entry, advancement, employment outlook, earnings, conditions of work, social and psychological factors, and sources for additional information.

608   Handbook of Adult Education in the United States.   Edited by
         Robert M. Smith, George F. Aker, and J. R. Kidd.   New
         York: Macmillan, 1970.

In three major parts: I, Forms, Function, and Future; II, Some
Institutions and Organizations; III, Some Program Areas.   Each part
consists of several chapters written by specialists in the adult education field.   Appendixes include a Directory of Participating Organizations of the Committee of Adult Education Organizations; General
Information Sources in Adult Education, an annotated list; The Changing Focus: Contents of Past Handbooks.   This handbook and its four
predecessors, published 1934-1960, trace the evolution of the field
of adult education.

609   Knowles, Asa S.   Handbook of College and University Adminis-
      tration.   2 vols.   New York: McGraw-Hill, 1970.
Vol. I, General, covers legal aspects of general administration;
governing boards; general administration; planning, space requirements, and institutional research; public relations, development, and
alumni relations; nonacademic personnel administration, physical
plant administration, and business and financial administration.   Vol.
II, Academic, covers administrative programs that are the responsibility of officers concerned with academic programs: legal aspects of
academic administration; academic affairs administration; admissions;
learning resources--library and instructional resources; adult education; academic personnel administration; student personnel administration; athletics administration; health programs; religion on the campus;
and campus community facilities and enterprises.

610   Manual on Standards Affecting School Personnel in the United
      States.   By T. M. Stinnett.   Washington, D. C. :   National
      Education Association, Instruction and Professional Develop-
      ment, 1974.
Information on certification requirements for teachers, supervisors,
administrators, and special school personnel, arranged by state.
An introductory section is a summary of standards and practices in
teacher education, certification, and accreditation, with tables.   Also
includes tabular information on teacher education institutions and approved programs, arranged by state.   Title of previous editions: A
Manual on Certification Requirements for School Personnel in the
United States.

611   Remmlein, Madaline K. , and Martha L. Ware.   School Law.
      3d ed.   Danville, Ill. :   Interstate Printers and Publishers,
      1970.
In two major sections: Problems of Teacher Personnel and Problems of Pupil Personnel.   Each chapter consists of Editorial Comment, explaining the legal principles involved in the subject; Statutory
Material and Case Material, excerpts from laws and court decisions;
and Sources of Further Information.   Appendixes include legal research tools, glossary of legal terms, and selected bibliography.

612   Requirements for Certification of Teachers, Counselors, Li-
      brarians, Administrators for Elementary Schools, Secondary
      Schools, Junior Colleges.   By Elizabeth H. Woellner.
      Chicago: University of Chicago Press.   Annual.
Certification requirements are given in outline form for each state.

Preliminary sections include recommendations of regional and national accrediting associations; and sources of information regarding teacher applications in the U. S. possessions and territories.

613   Sourcebook of Equal Educational Opportunity.   2d ed.   Chicago: Marquis Academic Media, Marquis Who's Who, 1977.
Detailed statistical and narrative data from government and private sources tracing the struggle for equal access and quality education. Part One, Equal Educational Opportunity, General (subsections on population characteristics, melting pot vs. cultural pluralism, and sexism and racism); Part Two, American Indian/Native Alaskan; Part Three, Asian American/Pacific Islander; Part Four, Black; Part Five, Disadvantaged/White Ethnic; Part Six, Hispanic; Part Seven, Women; Part Eight, Indexes (subject and geographic).   The first edition was published in 1975 with the title, Yearbook of Equal Educational Opportunity.

614   U. S. Department of Labor.   Bureau of Labor Statistics.   Occupational Outlook Handbook.   Washington, D. C.:   Government Printing Office.   Biennial.
The 79th edition, 1978, contains 300 occupational briefs grouped into 13 broad clusters of related jobs, with subdivisions, and 36 industrial briefs.   Includes a section on Education and Related Occupations. Information on each occupation includes nature of the work, places of employment, training and other qualifications needed, advancement, employment outlook, earnings, working conditions, and sources of additional information.   Includes a dictionary of occupational titles index, and an alphabetical index to occupations and industries.   Kept up to date between biennial editions by Occupational Outlook Quarterly.

C.   Statistical Sources

615   American Council on Education.   Fact Book on Higher Education.   Washington, D. C.:   American Council on Education, 1958-.   4 issues per year.
Condenses data related to higher education into figures and tables that emphasize trends and relationships.   Data are collected from documented sources.   Subjects regularly covered include demographic and economic data relevant to higher education; enrollment data; data concerning numbers and characteristics of institutions, faculty and staff, and students; and earned degrees conferred by colleges and universities.   Index in each issue.

616   Hamilton, Malcolm C.   Directory of Educational Statistics: A Guide to Sources.   Ann Arbor, Mich.:   Pierian Press, 1974.
A guide to 99 sources of educational statistics, current and historical, on a wide range of topics, some back to 1870.   Includes publications of the U. S. Office of Education, National Education Association of the U. S., U. S. Bureau of the Census, UNESCO, and other government and nongovernment organizations.   Entries are arranged by

broad categories: General Surveys and Summaries; Public Elementary and Secondary Schools; Public School Expenditures and Revenues; Salaries of Public School Professional Personnel; Nonpublic Schools; Institutions of Higher Learning; Degrees and Enrollment in Higher Education; Salaries in Higher Education; International Education; Education in Great Britain; Miscellaneous Educational Statistics.   Title and subject indexes.

617   Harris, Seymour E.   A Statistical Portrait of Higher Education: A Report for the Carnegie Commission on Higher Education.   New York: McGraw-Hill, 1972.
Includes 700 statistical tables and text in five major sections covering problems relating to students, enrollment, faculty, income and expenditures, and productivity and structure.   Also includes an introduction and summary, and a list of references.

618   National Education Association of the United States.   Research Division.   Research Report.   Washington, D. C.:   National Education Association.   Irreg.
A series of reports issued irregularly, several titles per year, including statistical reports on salary schedules for teachers; salary schedules for administrative personnel; faculty salary schedules in community-junior colleges; faculty salary schedules in colleges and universities; staff salaries; state departments of education; teacher supply and demand in public schools; status of the American public school teacher; economic status of the teaching profession; rankings of the states; and estimates of school statistics.   The same titles are revised, some annually, some biennially.

619   Open Doors: Report on International Exchange.   New York: Institute of International Education.   Annual.
Statistical information on foreign students attending schools of higher education in the United States.   The 1975/76-1976/77 edition includes an overview of international student exchange in relation to the United States; tables on the number and location of foreign students in the United States; data on the origin of students; and additional characteristics including distribution by sex, academic level, fields of study (total and by continent), field and level (actual numbers and percentages within field and level).   Appendixes cover foreign enrollment by student, home country, and other criteria.

Standard Educational Almanac.   Chicago: Marquis Academic Media, Marquis Who's Who.   Annual (see No. 604).

620   UNESCO.   Basic Facts and Figures, International Statistics Relating to Education, Culture, and Mass Communication.   Paris: UNESCO, 1952-61.   Annual.
Statistical information on education, libraries, museums, book production, newspapers and periodicals, films, and radio and television broadcasting for more than 200 countries.   Superseded by UNESCO, Statistical Yearbook, 1964-.

621   UNESCO.   Statistical Yearbook.   Paris: UNESCO, 1964-.   Annual.

Extensive statistics from more than 200 countries on population,
education, science and technology, libraries and museums, book
production, newspapers and other periodicals, film and cinema, radio
broadcasting, and television.   In English, French, and Spanish.

622   UNESCO.   Statistics of Educational Attainment and Illiteracy,
        1945-1974.   Statistical Reports and Studies, No. 22.   Paris:
        UNESCO, 1978.
Worldwide statistics on levels of educational achievement and illiteracy, covering 179 countries and territories over a period of 30 years.
Tables include classification by age groups; population subgroups;
classification by level of educational attainment; educational attainment by age and sex from 1945; summaries of statistics on educational attainment and on illiteracy.

623   UNESCO.   Statistics of Students Abroad, 1969-1973.   Paris:
        UNESCO, 1976.
A statistical analysis of international trends of students studying
abroad.   Includes a methodological introduction and analysis of
recent trends.   Country tables present statistics of students abroad
according to host countries and fields of study.   Also includes a
statistical comparison with other time periods; a run-down of countries covered and data availability; and tables on interregional movement of students.   Statistics for 1962-1968 were covered in a volume
with the same title published in 1972.

624   U. S. Bureau of the Census.   Statistical Abstract of the United
        States.   Washington, D. C.:   Government Printing Office,
        1878-.   Annual.
The 1978 edition is in 33 sections.   Section 5, Education, includes
statistical tables on public and private schools, enrollments, finances,
illiteracy, school years completed, employment, dropouts, elementary
and secondary schools, Catholic schools, minority groups, teachers
(employment, salaries), pupil transportation and absenteeism, graduates and school retention rates, higher education (enrollments,
salaries, finances, degrees conferred), libraries, and vocational
training.

625   U. S. National Center for Educational Statistics.   Digest of
        Educational Statistics.   Washington, D. C.:   Government
        Printing Office, 1962-.   Annual.
An abstract of statistical information covering the entire field of
education from kindergarten through graduate school.   Contains
statistics on the number of schools and colleges, enrollments, teachers, graduates, educational attainment, finance, federal funds, libraries, international education, research and development, and equal
educational opportunity.   Includes historical statistics.   Preceded by
U. S. Office of Education, Biennial Survey of Education, 1919-1960
(see No. 629).

626   U. S. National Center for Educational Statistics.   Historical
        Educational Statistics of the United States.   4 vols.   Wash-
        ington, D. C.:   Government Printing Office.   (In preparation.)

To be published in four volumes: (1) Enrollment; (2) High School Graduates and Earned Degrees; (3) Instructional Staff; (4) Expenditures.   Each volume will present state by state data on elementary, secondary, and higher education.   Statistical information back to 1870 will be included.

627   U. S. National Center for Educational Statistics.   Projections of Educational Statistics.   Washington, D. C. :   Government Printing Office.   Annual.
Ten-year projections of statistics for elementary and secondary schools and institutions of higher education, including enrollments, graduates, teachers, and expenditures.   Includes information about projected changes and the assumptions on which they are based.

628   U. S. National Center for Educational Statistics.   Statistics of State School Systems.   Washington, D. C. :   Government Printing Office, 1958-.   Biennial.
Provides statistics on the organization, staff, students, and finances of public elementary and secondary schools in 50 states, the District of Columbia, and outlying districts.   Includes historical trend data in addition to current statistics.   Some statistics are given back to 1870.

629   U. S. Office of Education.   Biennial Survey of Education.   Washington, D. C. :   Government Printing Office, 1919-60.
Statistics on all aspects of education in the United States.   Includes chapters on summary of education, state school systems, city school systems, higher education, special education, libraries, etc.   Superseded by U. S. National Center for Educational Statistics, Digest of Educational Statistics (see No. 625).

630   U. S. Office of Education.   Statistics of Public Elementary and Secondary Day Schools.   Washington, D. C. :   Government Printing Office, 1954-.   Annual.
Statistics on local school districts, instructional and noninstructional staff, pupils, pupil-teacher ratio, pupils in curtailed sessions, high school graduates, schools by levels, instruction rooms, expenditures, and large city data.

World Survey of Education.   5 vols.   Paris: UNESCO, 1955-72 (see No. 605).

Numerous statistical reports on various aspects of education are issued by federal agencies, state agencies, and UNESCO.   They can be located through the lists and indexes described on pages 61-64.

D.   Directories

General

631   Klein, Barry T.   Guide to American Educational Directories. 4th ed.   Rye, N. Y. :   Todd Publications, 1975.

Lists 2, 700 directories under 100 subjects.   Entries give title of the
directory, bibliographic data, price, and a descriptive annotation.
Includes state directories of public schools, fraternity and alumni
association directories, and other education related directories.
Index of titles.

632   Norback, Peter G. , and Craig T. Norback. Educational
         Market Place.   New York: McGraw-Hill, 1977.
A directory and source book covering accreditation boards, architects,
associations and organizations, book publishers, bookstore equipment
and supplies, colleges and universities, consultants, Department of
Health, Education and Welfare (National Institute of Education and
Office of Education), educational films, educational radio and television stations, fellowships, scholarships, grants and loans, fund
raising, government education assistance programs, music publishers,
periodical publications, school equipment and supplies, shows and
conventions, and teaching abroad.

633   Patterson's American Education.   Mount Prospect, Ill. :   Educa-
         tional Directories.   Annual.
The 75th edition, 1979, is in two main sections: I, School Systems,
and II, Schools Classified.   Part I is a geographical listing of public,
private, and endowed schools and colleges in the United States and
territories.   Gives names and addresses of officials of state, county,
and city educational systems.   Also includes sections on Diocesan
Superintendents, Lutheran Superintendents, General Conference of
Seventh Day Adventists, and Educational Associations and Societies.
In Part II schools are listed by state within each classification.
Index of schools.

Adult Education

634   Jensen, Jo.   College by Mail.   New York: Arco Publishing,
         1972.
A guide to more than 10, 000 correspondence courses for high school
diplomas, college degrees, and advanced graduate work, offered by
64 colleges and universities that are members of the National University Extension Association.   Part I gives general information on
correspondence study.   Part II is a numbered list of colleges and
universities with correspondence programs, with numerical codes
for types of courses offered and enrollments accepted.   Arrangement is by state.   Part III lists elementary and high school courses,
college level courses (undergraduate and graduate), college certificate courses, and college noncredit courses, with numbers referring
to the institutions in Part II.   Part IV includes a glossary of terms
and a bibliography.   No index.

635   Jones, John H.   Correspondence Educational Directory: A
         Directory of Higher Adult Education at Lower Cost, Certi-
         ficate, Diploma, Degree.   2d ed.   Oxnard, Calif. :   Racz
         Publishing, 1978.
Lists correspondence programs in a variety of subject areas from

high school through adult level.   Includes 60 American college and
university correspondence programs offering credit toward degrees,
32 English and 11 Canadian correspondence schools, and 158 American trade, technical, and professional correspondence schools.   Also
lists external programs, contract degree programs, special undergraduate centers in the United States, and British examination centers
and professional institutes.   Includes brief descriptions of three proficiency examinations (CLED, USAFI, and Advanced Placement), and
a list of accrediting agencies.

636   Munzert, Alfred W.   National Directory of External Degree
        Programs.   Machias, N. Y.:   Hemisphere Publications;
        distributed by Hawthorn Books, 1976.
Part I, Questions and Answers on External Degree Programs, includes sections on proficiency exams, credit for life experience,
credit for noncollegiate sponsored instruction, and correspondence
study.   Part II, Existing External Degree Programs, describes
programs of individual institutions listed by state.   Information includes fields and degrees offered, requirements, cost, and address
for further information.   General index.

637   New York Times Guide to Continuing Education in America.
        Prepared by the College Entrance Examination Board.
        Edited by Frances C. Thomson.   New York: Quadrangle
        Books, 1972.
The main section consists of course listings by 2, 098 accredited
institutions that offer adult classroom instruction.   Descriptive information, including admissions requirements, is given for each
institution.   Arranged alphabetically by state, and within each state,
alphabetically by name of the institution.   Includes four-year and
two-year colleges, proprietary schools, and independent study plans,
and a separate list of correspondence schools.   Also includes a
descriptive list of organizations active in continuing education, and
an annotated bibliography.

638   Sandri-White, Alex.   Worldwide Register of Adult Education.
        Central Valley, N. Y.:   Aurea Publications, 1973.
A directory of university extension facilities, correspondence schools,
and testing centers, covering institutions in many countries throughout the world.

639   UNESCO.   Adult Education.   Paris: UNESCO, 1966.
The first section lists 43 international nongovernmental organizations.
The main section lists 900 official, semiofficial, and private agencies
in 86 countries concerned with adult education.   Each entry includes
name, address, name of director, year founded, number on staff,
objectives, activities, and publications.

Associations

640   Encyclopedia of Associations.   13th ed.   3 vols.   Detroit:
        Gale Research, 1979.

Vol. 1, National Organizations of the United States, is arranged in
17 major subject categories.   Section 5, Educational Organizations,
includes accreditation, administration, admissions, adult education,
alternative education, black students, cooperative education, counseling, curriculum, extension education, financial aid, foreign students,
gifted children, graduate schools, humanities, independent colleges
and schools, integration, international exchanges, junior colleges, research, retired teachers, scholarship, special education, technical
schools, testing, and urban schools organizations.   Entries give official name of the organization, popular name, acronym, founding
date, address, telephone number, chief executive, number of members and staff, purpose, activities, committees, publications, and
convention and meeting schedule.   Vol. 2 contains a Geographic
Index, which lists associations with address and officials' names
under states and cities; and an Executive Index, an alphabetical listing
of names of executives with title, name of organization, address,
and telephone number for each name listed.   Each listing in both
indexes gives the entry number of the organization in Vol. 1.   Vol.
3, New Organizations, is a periodical supplement that gives descriptions of newly formed organizations.   Cumulatively indexed.

641   National Education Association of the United States.   NEA
        Handbook.   Washington, D. C.:   The Association.   Annual.
Basic information on the Association, its policy documents, governing
bodies, goals and objectives, programs and administrative structure,
and component parts; other organizations; state affiliates; nongovern-
ance affiliates.   Also includes a staff listing, membership figures,
a list of NEA presidents, list of convention cities, calendar of
governance meetings, NEA Service Officers, and important telephone
numbers at NEA Headquarters.   Index of Names and Index of Subjects.

642   UNESCO.   Teachers' Associations.   2d ed. rev.   Paris:
        UNESCO, 1971.
The first part is a directory of 28 international and regional organizations.   The main part is a directory of 801 national organizations
listed under 91 countries and territories.   Information on each entry
includes: name of the organization, address, title of official to whom
correspondence is sent, year of foundation, number of members,
budget, functions, relations with educational authorities, and publications.   Subject index.   An appendix contains the text, in English,
French, Russian, and Spanish, of the Recommendations Concerning
the Status of Teachers, adopted by the Special Intergovernmental
Conference on the Status of Teachers, Paris, October 5, 1966.

643   U. S. Office of Education.   Directory of Education Associations.
        Washington, D. C.:   Government Printing Office, 1977.
In sections on National and Regional Education Associations; College
Professional Fraternities and Sororities, Honor Societies, and Recog-
nition Societies (National); State Education Associations; Foundations;
Religious Education Associations; and International Education Associations.   Arrangement within each section is alphabetical by name of
association.   Information on each association includes address, telephone number, chief officers, and publications.   Index by keyword in
name of association and index by subject.

Colleges and Universities--U. S.

644   American Council on Education.   Accredited Institutions of
         Postsecondary Education: A Directory of Accredited Insti-
         tutions, Professionally Accredited Programs, and Candidates
         for Accreditation.   Published for the Council on Postsecond-
         ary Accreditation by the American Council on Education.
         Washington, D. C.   Annual.
The 1978 edition includes a listing by states of institutions accredited
by national and regional accrediting groups.   Institutions are listed
alphabetically by name under each state.   Information on each includes address, control, type of institution, accrediting agency, date
of first accreditation, branch campuses or affiliated institutions, type
of academic calendar, level of degrees, specialized accreditation of
professional programs, name of chief executive officer, enrollment,
and telephone number.   Other sections are a listing of major changes
in four-year and two-year institutions; and a listing by state of institutions that are candidates for accreditation, with the same type
of information on each that is given in the first section.   Appendix
A, The Accrediting Process; Appendix B, Accrediting Groups; Appendix C, Statement Regarding Accreditation and Transfer of Academic Credit.   Institutional index.

645   American Universities and Colleges.   11th ed.   Washington,
         D. C. :   American Council on Education, 1973.
Descriptive data on more than 1, 440 institutions including address,
control, accreditation, history, calendar, admission and degree requirements, fees, student services, staff, distinctive programs, enrollment, library, publications, finances, buildings and grounds, and
administrative officers.   Introductory chapters on higher education
in the United States, and a separate section on professional education, which includes a listing of accredited schools for each profession.

646   Barron's Handbook of College Transfer Information.   2d ed.
         By Nicholas C. Proia and Barbara J. Drysdale.   Woodbury,
         N. Y. :   Barron's Educational Series, 1975.
Gives information in chart form on 1, 300 colleges and universities.
Information on each institution includes address, control, admissions
officer, admissions criteria, examinations and recommendations required, housing requirements, financial aids, application date and
calendar, special and graduate programs, evaluation of transfer
credit officer, enrollment, summer session, etc.   Arranged alphabetically by state, and by institution under each state.   Index of
names of institutions.

647   Barron's Profiles of American Colleges.   11th ed.   Woodbury,
         N. Y. :   Barron's Educational Series, 1978.
A directory of accredited four-year colleges arranged alphabetically
by state, then by institution.   Each profile includes name of institution, address, telephone number, enrollment statistics, application
deadline, admissions rating and requirements, faculty, student-
faculty ratio, student life, programs of study, required courses,

special studies, and admissions standards, procedure, and transfer. Also includes a "College Admissions Selector," listing colleges in categories according to competition in admissions requirements; a glossary of terms; and an alphabetical index to institutions.

648   Cass, James, and Max Birnbaum.   Comparative Guide to American Colleges for Students, Parents, and Counselors. 8th ed.   New York: Harper & Row, 1977.
The main section is a listing of institutions alphabetically by name, giving for each: address, enrollment, affiliation, and information on admission requirements, academic environment (degrees, special programs, graduate or professional study, calendar), graduate career data, faculty, student body, campus life, and annual costs. Also includes a state index, a selectivity index, a religious index, and a list of institutions conferring the largest number of baccalaureate degrees in selected fields.

649   College Blue Book.   16th ed.   3 vols.   New York: Macmillan Information,   1977.
Vol. 1, U.S. Colleges: Narrative Descriptions, lists more than 3,000 colleges and universities by state.   Information on each institution includes address, control, enrollment, type of program, number of faculty, degrees granted, entrance requirements, costs, collegiate environment, and community environment.   Includes a map of each state.   Vol. 2, U.S. Colleges: Tabular Data, lists colleges alphabetically by state, with tabular information on location, telephone number, names of chief administrator and registrar, entrance requirements, affiliation, accreditation, costs, scholarships, calendar system, enrollment, and faculty.   In Vol. 3, Degrees Offered by College and Subject, Part 1 lists colleges by state, with subject areas and degrees offered listed under each college; Part 2 is an alphabetical listing of more than 2,000 subject areas for which degrees are granted, with names of institutions listed under the subjects by state.   An alphabetical list of colleges precedes Part 1.

650   College Entrance Examination Board.   A Chance to Go to College: A Directory of 800 Colleges That Have Special Help for Students from Minorities and Low Income Families. New York: College Entrance Examination Board, 1971.
The main section is a listing of colleges by state.   Information on each institution includes location, type, control, enrollment, housing, admission requirements, date for application for admission, type of financial aid available, date for aid application, and name of official to contact for further information.   There is an introductory article on choice of a college, applying for admission, expenses and financial aid, followed by a list of other books about college and financial aid.   A Quick Guide to the 829 Colleges, with information in chart form, precedes the main section.   Alphabetical index of colleges gives state location for each college listed.

651   College Entrance Examination Board.   College Handbook.   New York: The Board, Biennial.
The 16th edition, 1977, contains descriptions of 2,878 colleges, ar-

ranged by state and alphabetically by name under state.   Information
on each college includes type of institution, enrollment, calendar,
curriculum (degrees, fields of study, graduate programs, special
academic programs, special remedial services), academic regulations, admission requirements, student life, expenses, financial aid,
and address for correspondence.   Introductory sections include "De-
ciding Where to Go to College, " a glossary of terms, and an annotated list of other books about college.   Index of names of institutions.

652   College Entrance Examination Board.   College Handbook Index
      of Majors.   New York: The Board,   1977.
Organized by major fields of study, with subdivisions by specific
curriculum fields.   Under each of 350 fields colleges offering a
major in that field are listed by state.   Level of degrees offered is
indicated for each college.   Includes all colleges listed in the College Handbook, 1977.   Also includes an alphabetical list of colleges
by state.

653   Gollay, Elinor, and Alwina Bennett.   College Guide for Students
      with Disabilities: A Detailed Directory of Higher Education
      Services, Programs, and Facilities Accessible to Handi-
      capped Students in the United States.   Cambridge, Mass. :   Abt
      Publications; Boulder, Colo. :   Westview Press, 1976.
Descriptions of 500 two- and four-year colleges and universities, including details of services and policies, with information on enrollment (total vs. disabled), number of buildings with special facilities,
special counseling programs, and special educational resources.
Also includes summary information in tabular form; an essay on
legal rights of disabled students; a list of financial and educational
aids; descriptions of admission testing programs; federal and state
referral agencies; and an annotated bibliography.

654   Gourman, Jack.   The Gourman Report: A Rating of American
      and International Universities.   2d ed.   Los Angeles: Na-
      tional Education Standards, 1977.
Part 1 is a discussion of Objectives and Procedures for Comparative
Assessment in Higher Education; Part 2 is a rating of 68 under-
graduate programs in the United States; Part 3, A Rating of Prelegal
and Premedical Education in the United States; Part 4, A Rating of
University Administrative Areas; Part 5, A Rating of Foreign/Inter-
national Universities; Part 6, A Rating of Law Schools: Foreign/
International and the United States; Part 7, A Rating of Medical
Schools: Foreign/International and the United States; Part 8, A
Rating of Dental Schools in the United States.   Appendixes include
statistical tables of ratings, and listings by states and countries of
the institutions rated in the body of the Report.

655   Hawes, Gene R.   Hawes Comprehensive Guide to Colleges.
      New York: New American Library, 1978.
Sections 1 and 2 explain the use of the guide and types of ratings.
Section 2 includes lists of top social prestige colleges, top social
achievement colleges, and top faculty salary colleges in nationwide
rank order.   In Section 3, Arrays by States, the main section, four-

year colleges "are grouped under headings designed to answer your prime questions" rather than alphabetically.   Under each state is a career-preparation majors index; a listing of fields of study, with names of institutions under each field; followed by information on individual institutions grouped as "best to good buys, " and by ratings for social prestige, social achievement, expenses, admissions, and faculty salaries.   Also lists church-related colleges, black colleges, and two-year private colleges.   Other information on individual institutions includes enrollment, average income of students' families, majors offered, basic information, student life, costs, scholarships, admission for freshmen, and admission for transfers.   Section 4 is a "locator" listing of two-year community colleges by states; Section 5, Other Reference and Information Sources; Section 6, Index to Four-Year Colleges.

656   Higher Education Exchange: Directory, Marketplace, Almanac.
         Edited by Janet A. Mitchell.   Princeton, N. J.:   Peterson's
         Guides and J. B. Lippincott, 1978.
In three major parts.   The Directory includes a listing by state of 3, 200 institutions of higher education with lists of administrative heads, academic heads, athletic coaches, and campus facilities for each institution; a list of 2, 500 accredited postsecondary proprietary institutions, in nine categories each divided by state; a list by state of 200 institutions that offer independent study opportunities; a list by institution of university presses; a list by institution of college and university radio stations; a list of 1, 300 education agencies and associations; and a list of funding sources (government agencies and private foundations).   The Marketplace lists 4, 000 companies and their sales contacts in categories for media and publishing, consultants and services, and manufacturers and suppliers of equipment and systems.   The Almanac includes statistical information in tabular form arranged under Institutional and Financial Data; Faculty and Student Profiles; and Related Information (Senate and House education related committees, education periodicals, education guides and directories, a summary of data on higher education institutions, and a summary count of marketplace companies by product category). Index to Higher Education Institutions and Index to the Marketplace.

657   Insider's Guide to the Colleges.   Compiled and edited by the
         staff of the Yale Daily News.   New York: Berkley Pub-
         lishers, 1978.
The 1978-79 edition contains profiles of 230 colleges and universities in the United States.   Brief information is given on location, classification (urban, suburban, rural), enrollment, annual expenses, percentage of entering class receiving financial aid, number of volumes in the library, student-faculty ratio, number of transfer students, percentage of students belonging to fraternities and sororities, requirements for admission tests, and application deadline. This information for each institution is followed by an informal description written by students attending the colleges, and covering the campus, the community, the best departments and programs, cultural and recreational opportunities, housing, and characteristics of the student body.

658   Lovejoy, Clarence E.   Lovejoy's College Guide.   New York:
        Simon and Schuster.   Biennial.
The 13th edition, 1976, is a guide to 3,600 American colleges and
universities.   Section 1 is an article covering expenses, financial
aid, admissions, choice of a college, and college religious groups.
Section 2 contains a list of 500 professional curricula and a list of
22 special programs and the institutions in which they are offered.
Section 3, the main section, contains capsule descriptions and ratings
of colleges and universities listed alphabetically under states and
U. S. dependencies.   Includes an alphabetical index of institutions.

659   Peterson's Annual Guide to Undergraduate Study.   Princeton,
        N. J.:   Peterson's Guides.   Annual.
The 1979 edition, in two volumes, gives information on 2,900 two-
year and four-year colleges and universities of the United States and
Canada.   Vol. 1, College Descriptions and Profiles, is in three
sections: (1) profiles, brief data on general information, enrollment,
special programs, campus life, expenses, admissions, athletics,
majors and degrees, and name and telephone number of the director
of admissions;   (2) two-page descriptions including academic programs,
facilities, costs, financial aid, off-campus study, campus life,
majors and degrees, faculty, and student government; (3) special
section on campus ROTC programs.   Vol. 2, Standardized Test
Scores and Majors, is in two sections: (1) table of required tests
and 1977 freshman score ranges at each college; (2) directory of
266 majors listing colleges that offer them at the associate and baccalaureate levels.

660   Songe, Alice H.   American Universities and Colleges: A Dic-
        tionary of Name Changes.   Metuchen, N. J.:   Scarecrow
        Press, 1978.
An alphabetical list of all the four-year, degree-granting universities
and colleges in the United States and outlying territories that have
undergone name changes since they were founded.   Each entry includes location, type of institution, the former names and the years
in which these names were adopted.   References are given from
former names to present names.   Also listed are institutions that
have closed since 1964-65, with date of closing.   An appendix, Location of Academic Records for Institutions Listed as Closed, is arranged by state and gives name and address of institution and/or
agency to contact for locating records.

661   U. S. National Center for Educational Statistics.   Education
        Directory: Colleges and Universities.   Washington, D. C.:
        Government Printing Office.   Annual.
A listing by state of institutions in the United States and its outlying
areas that offer at least a two-year program of college level studies
in residence, or if nonresident, that are accredited by an agency
recognized by the U. S. Commissioner of Education.   Information on
each institution, in the 1977-78 edition, includes address, congressional district and county where located, telephone number, FICE
identification code, entity number, date established, fall 1976 enrollment, undergraduate tuition and fees, sex of student body, calendar

system, control or affiliation, highest level of offering, type of program, accreditation, names and titles of principal officers, and a coded classification of principal officers by functional area of responsibility. Index of institutions. Appendixes: A, Changes; B, State-wide Agencies of Postsecondary Education; C, Higher Education Associations; D, Reproduction of Questionnaire Form; E, Reproduction of Sample Computer Printout; F, Abbreviations; G, FICE Codes; H, FICE Code Changes; I, Administrative Officers, Descriptions and Codes. Also includes statistical tables and charts.

Two-Year Colleges

662   American Junior Colleges. 8th ed. Washington, D. C.: American Council on Education, 1971.
Descriptive information on institutions accredited by the six regional accrediting agencies. In two parts: Public Institutions, listed by state; and Private Institutions, listed alphabetically by name. Each part includes introductory essays. Information on each institution includes address, telephone number, history, control, buildings and grounds, administrative officer, calendar, admission, programs, teaching staff, degrees, special facilities, enrollment, student life, fees, student aid, and finances. Appendixes include a list of institutions that offer programs in various occupational fields, a list of two-year programs offered by four-year institutions, and a list of church-related colleges.

663   Barron's Guide to Two-Year Colleges. 2 vols. Woodbury, N. Y.: Barron's Educational Series, 1978-79.
Vol. 1 lists 2, 300 colleges in three sections: (1) Directory of Two-Year Colleges; (2) Directory of Residential Colleges; (3) Directory of Four-Year Colleges and Universities offering Two-Year Transfer Programs. Information for individual colleges in Section 1 includes address, affiliation, environment, enrollment, admissions, degrees, special programs, calendar, student-teacher ratio, accreditation, expenses, and financial aid. Sections 2 and 3 give the same information plus programs of study, learning environment, student life, and off-campus facilities. Vol. 2 is an occupational program selector for the colleges listed in Vol. 1. Lists more than 180 programs of study. (Annotation is for the 1972 edition.)

664   Cass, James, and Max Birnbaum. Comparative Guide to Two-Year Colleges and Career Programs. New York: Harper & Row, 1976.
Includes descriptions of 1, 740 community colleges, junior colleges, technical schools, and four-year colleges and professional schools that offer less than a four-year program. Institutions are listed by state. Information for each one includes location, admission requirements, degrees and programs offered, calendar, costs, and basic information on campus life for institutions that provide residential facilities. Indexes include: Guide to Post-Secondary Technical/Vocational/General Education and Training Programs--a listing of institutions under 200 fields of study, and by state under each field; a list of programs offering above average job opportunities; and a religious index, a listing of institutions by denominations.

665   Community, Junior, and Technical College Directory.   Washing-
          ton, D. C. :   American Association of Community and Junior
          Colleges.   Annual.
Information on two-year colleges in table form.   The 1979 edition
contains four tables: I, Directory of Community, Junior, and Technical Colleges, arranged by state with institutions listed alphabetically
by name under each state and directory-type information in table
form for each institution;   II, Summary by States - All Two-Year
Colleges;   III, Summary by States - Public Colleges;   IV, Summary by
States - Independent Junior Colleges.   Also includes a directory of
community, junior, and technical college organizations;   a list of state
administrators;   and an alphabetical list of two-year colleges.   Former
titles: Junior College Directory and Community and Junior College
Directory.

Graduate and Professional Schools

666   American Council on Education.   Guide to Graduate Study:
          Programs Leading to the Ph. D. Degree.   4th ed.   Edited
          by Robert Quick.   Washington, D. C. :   The Council, 1969.
Lists graduate schools offering programs leading to the Ph. D. degree,
giving for each: description, admission requirements, fees and
financial aid, and fields of study.   Also includes introductory sections
on objectives of graduate study, selection of and admission to graduate school, and financing, and a bibliography.   Institutional Index
and Index to Ph. D. Programs.

667   Graduate and Professional School Opportunities for Minority
          Students.   Princeton, N. J. :   Educational Testing Service.
          Biennial.
The 5th edition, 1973-74, contains information in tabular form in
sections on graduate schools, listed alphabetically by name of institution, with name and address of official to contact, application fee,
tests used, application dates, number of students, and percentage of
minority students;   graduate departments, arranged by names of departments, with institutions listed under them with the same type of
information as given for graduate schools.   Also contains sections
on law schools, business schools, and medical schools, listed by
name of institution in each section, with the same type of information as given for graduate schools.   Preliminary sections are on
sources of funds for minority students, and qualifying examinations
for entrance to graduate and professional schools.   Includes a bibliography and a list of sources of information on the guaranteed loan
program for students.   Index.

668   Livesey, Herbert B. , and Harold Doughty.   Guide to American
          Graduate Schools.   3d ed.   New York: Viking Press, 1975.
Information on more than 600 institutions in the United States providing graduate and professional study.   Includes programs in all
areas of the liberal arts and sciences, education, medicine, dentistry,
veterinary medicine, pharmacy, nursing, law, social work, agriculture, theology, applied arts, engineering, and business.   Arrangement is alphabetical by name of institution.   Information on each

institution includes admission and degree requirements, standards, enrollment and faculty figures, tuition, financial aid opportunities, fields of study, research and housing facilities.   Indexes: Location of Institutions by State; Fields of Study; and Institutional Abbreviations.

669   Peterson's Annual Guides to Graduate Study.   Princeton, N. J.:
      Peterson's Guides.   Annual.
The 1979 edition, in five volumes, covers 1, 350 institutions.   Book 1, Graduate Institutions in the United States and Canada, is in four sections: (1) Profiles of Institutions Offering Graduate Work, giving for each entry brief information on control, enrollment, tuition, financial aid, research affiliations, a listing of schools and colleges within the university with number of graduate students, entrance requirements, degrees offered, and name of dean for each; (2) Directory of Graduate Program Distribution, a list of 200 fields and institutions offering graduate work in each field; (3) Directory of Institutional Offerings, an alphabetical listing of institutions with graduate programs listed under each; (4) Graduate School Descriptions, one- to two-page descriptions of 160 institutions, which present an overview of the school, including information on programs of study, research facilities, financial aid, cost of study, cost of living, student groups, the community, the university, application for admission, name and address for correspondence, and names of faculty chairmen of graduate programs and their fields of specialization.   Index to full descriptions and abstracts.   Books 2-5 give program directory and full descriptions of universities under each specialized subject field. Book 2, Humanities and Social Sciences; Book 3, Biological, Agricultural, and Health Sciences; Book 4, Physical Sciences; Book 5, Engineering and Applied Sciences.   Each volume contains an index to full descriptions and an index to directories and subject areas.   A separate index volume, covering all seven volumes of the guides to undergraduate and graduate study, contains Index to Contents of the 1979 Guides; Index to Graduate Directories and Subject Areas; and Index to Institutional Descriptions, Announcements, and Abstracts.

Colleges and Universities--Foreign

670   Association of African Universities.   Directory of African Uni-
      versities.   2d ed.   Prepared with the assistance of UNESCO.
      Accra, Ghana: Association of African Universities, 1976.
Covers 59 universities in 36 African countries.   The first part, in English, contains information on Anglophone universities.   The second part, in French, contains information on Francophone universities. Information on each institution includes history; principal officers; composition of the University Council; number of administrative, technical, and academic staff; student enrollment; a listing of faculties and departments with names of heads; institutes with names of deans; degrees, admission requirements, financial requirements, student facilities, library, publications, and programs of university cooperation.

671   Commonwealth Universities Yearbook. London: Association of
        Universities of the British Commonwealth.   Annual.
A directory of universities of all the nations of the Commonwealth,
giving for each institution teaching and administrative staff, and
general information.   An introductory essay and a directory to fields
of study are given for each country.   General Index and Names
Index.

672   Directory of Canadian Universities.   Ottawa: Statistics Canada,
        Education, Science and Culture Division; Association of Uni-
        versities and Colleges of Canada.   Annual.
Former title: Universities and Colleges of Canada.   The 20th edition,
1977, describes 71 universities and colleges arranged alphabetically
by name.   Information on each institution includes address, telephone
number, telex number, names of chief administrator and registrar,
enrollment, number of faculty, finances, history and governance,
buildings and grounds, student housing, libraries, student life and
services, calendar, grading system, student awards and financial
assistance, fees and costs, admission requirements, courses and
degrees, extension programs, research institutes, and affiliated
institutions.   An introductory article, "The Universities of Canada,"
by David Munroe, traces history and development, structure, organization, curriculum, instruction, staff, students, and university-
government relations.   Other sections include a bibliography; an
alphabetical list of universities, with a map showing location; a listing
of undergraduate and graduate diploma and degree programs by subject fields; and a general index.

673   International Association of Universities.   World List of Uni-
        versities.   Paris: International Association of Universities.
        Biennial.
The 13th edition, 1978, is a directory of more than 6, 000 universities and other institutions of higher education in 151 countries and a
guide to principal national and international organizations concerned
with higher education, including bodies that have special responsi-
bilities for interuniversity cooperation and for facilitating exchange
of academic staff and students.   Part One, Institutions and National
Organizations, is a listing by country.   The first section for each
country is a listing of universities and other institutions that gives
brief information on each, including address, date of founding, note
on composition by faculties, schools, departments, or institutes.
The second section lists national academic and student associations,
giving information on membership, meetings, publications, names
of executive officers, and address.   Explanations are given in both
English and French.   Part Two, International and Regional Organizations, gives information in English and French on history, control,
membership, purpose, activities, congresses and conventions, publications, accomplishments, officers, and address for each organization.   The Appendix, International Association of Universities, lists
officers, members of the administrative board, member institutions
listed by country, and publications.   The Index, Part 1, is an alphabetical listing of countries, and a separate listing of international
institutions; Part 2 is an alphabetical listing of international and
regional organizations.

674 International Handbook of Universities and Other Institutions of
        Higher Education. 7th ed. Paris: International Association
        of Universities, 1978.
Covers institutions in 110 countries and territories, excluding the
United States and the British Commonwealth. Arranged alphabetically
by countries. Information on each institution includes organization,
admission requirements, fees, degrees, library, staff, enrollment,
and publications. Index of institutions. Published every three years.

675 UNESCO. World Guide to Higher Education: A Comparative
        Survey of Systems, Degrees and Qualifications. Epping,
        Eng.: Bowker; Unipub/Unesco Press, 1976.
Provides a country-by-country survey of systems of higher education and of degrees awarded in each country. An introduction offers
an analysis of problems encountered in evaluating studies and degrees
for study abroad, supplies criteria for recognizing degrees and
diplomas, and suggests creation of means of comparison and decision
making.

676 World Guide to Universities. 2d ed. Compiled by Michael
        Zils. Munich: Verlag Dokumentation; distributed by R. R.
        Bowker, 1977.
Part I, Europe; Part II, Africa, The Americas, Asia, Oceania,
Index. A listing by country of 638 accredited universities and 5,000
colleges and institutes that offer doctoral degrees and postdoctoral
studies. Information on institutions includes name, address, telephone number, year founded, student enrollment, names of administrators, director of library, a list of each university's schools and
departments, and names and specialties of professors. More than
95,000 faculty members are indexed by name, and the institutions
are indexed by 276 subject fields.

677 World of Learning. London: Europa Publications. Annual.
The 29th edition, 1978, is in two volumes. Vol. 1 covers international educational, scientific, and cultural organizations, and
countries arranged alphabetically from Afghanistan to Kuwait. Vol.
2 covers countries from Laos to Zambia. Information on international organizations includes address, date of founding, membership, purpose, names of officials, and publications. Listings for
countries include learned societies and research institutes, libraries,
museums, art galleries, colleges and universities, technical colleges,
and other institutions of higher education. Gives date of founding,
administrative officers, and faculties of most institutions. An index
of institutions is included at the end of Vol. 2.

Research and Information

678 ALSED Directory of Specialists and Research Institutions.
        Paris: UNESCO, 1974.
A directory of "scholars, groups and agencies actively dealing with
the socio-cultural and linguistic adaptation of the content and methodology of education." Includes a list of specialists arranged by coun-

try, and a list by research group and institution. Information on each entry includes address, telephone number, name of project, name of director, financial support, and publications. Country index.

679 Directory: Educational Documentation and Information Services. Paris: UNESCO; International Bureau of Education, 1977. Lists educational documentation services in 76 countries, and regional and international services. Resource organizations and institutions are listed by country. Information on each entry includes types of activities, people served, services given, fields covered, size of collections, and publications. In English and French. A new edition will be issued every two years.

International Guide to Educational Documentation, 1955-1960. Paris: UNESCO, 1963 (see No. 17).

International Guide to Educational Documentation, 1960-1965. Paris: UNESCO, 1971 (see No. 18).

680 Research Centers Directory. 6th ed. Detroit: Gale Research, 1979. A guide to university-related and other nonprofit research organizations established on a permanent basis and carrying on continuing research programs. In sections covering 15 subject areas. Section 5, Education, includes research organizations concerned with testing, teaching materials, reading, continuing education, adult and special education, and school planning. Information on each entry includes name of the research unit, affiliation, address, telephone number, name of director, year established, present status, source of support, staff, volume of research, principal fields of research, special research facilities, media in which results are published, serial publications and frequency, seminars and conferences, and library facilities. Institutional index, alphabetical index of research centers, and subject index.

681 Wanger, Judy, comp. Directory of Educational Information Resources. New York: CCM Information, 1971. A revised edition of Directory of Educational Information Centers (U. S. Office of Education, 1969). Section I, Local Resources, is arranged by state. Centers are listed alphabetically by name under each city. Lists 163 centers including state education agencies; Research Coordinating Units for Vocational and Technical Education; state education associations; and local, county, and regional centers. Information on each entry includes name, address, name of director, telephone number, year established, sponsor, purpose, services and products, users, and holdings. Section II, National Resources, includes agencies that serve a multistate area or the nation, such as ERIC, U. S. Office of Education Regional Offices, U. S. Office of Education Sponsored Programs (regional educational laboratories, research and development centers, special education regional instructional materials centers), national associations, and national information centers. The same type of information is given as in Section I. Section III is an

annotated bibliography of directories and guides that list specialized information centers and education and education-related organizations, and some secondary sources for listing of other directories and guides.

Scholarships, Fellowships, Grants, and Loans

682   Annual Register of Grant Support. Chicago: Marquis Academic
         Media, Marquis Who's Who. Annual.
Provides details of grant support programs of government agencies, public and private foundations, corporations, community trusts, unions, educational and professional associations, and special interest organizations. Entries give name of organization, address, telephone number, year founded, areas of interest, name of program, type, year program started, purpose, eligibility, financial data, number of applicants and number of awards in most recent year for which statistics are available, application information, address for information, and special stipulations. The 12th edition, 1978-79, contains more than 2,000 entries divided into 11 major areas with subdivisions for specific fields. Subdivisions of the section for Education are: Educational Projects and Research (general); Elementary and Secondary Education; Higher Education; Scholar Aid Programs (all disciplines). Subject index; organization and program index; geographic index; and personnel index.

683   Barron's Handbook of American College Financial Aid. By
         Nicholas C. Proia and Vincent M. DiGaspari. Woodbury,
         N.Y.: Barron's Educational Series, 1978.
Information in chart form on more than 1,200 four-year colleges, arranged by state. Each chart indicates grants and loans available, application date, eligibility, and name and address of official responsible for financial aid. Similar information is given for two-year colleges in Barron's Handbook of Junior and Community College Financial Aid, 1977.

684   College Blue Book: Scholarships, Fellowships, Grants and
         Loans. Edited by Lorraine Mathies and Elizabeth I. Dixon.
         New York: Macmillan Information, 1975.
Awards of financial assistance granted at the level of high school senior through advanced professional programs. Arranged in seven subject areas: General; Humanities; Social Sciences; Sciences; Health and Medical Sciences; Area Studies; Specialized Programs. Within each division listing is by the sponsoring association, society, or agency. Information on each entry includes name, address, and telephone number of the sponsoring agency; title of award; area, field, or subject; level of education at which award or loan is granted; number, amount, and type of awards or loans; method of disbursement, and method of repayment, if loan; qualifications; additional information; application date; and address for information or application. Also includes a list of acronyms and abbreviations, a list of additional resources, and an index.

685   Directory of Research Grants. Phoenix: Oryx Press. Annual.

The 1978 edition gives information about grant, contract, and fellowship support programs available from federal and state governments,
private foundations, associations, and corporations for research,
training, and innovative efforts. Principally a guide to programs in
the United States, but some sponsored by other countries are included. Programs are arranged by academic discipline or subject.
Each entry gives name of fellowship or grant, purpose, requirements, restrictions, amount, date application is due, and name, address, and telephone number of sponsoring agency. Indexes of grant
names; sponsoring organizations listed alphabetically; and sponsoring
organizations listed by type (business and professional organizations
and foundations, and government agencies).

686 Feingold, S. Norman. Scholarships, Fellowships and Loans.
     6th ed. Boston: Bellman Publishing, 1977.
An alphabetical list of administering agencies, giving for each:
name, address, qualifications for scholarships, fellowships, and
loans, funds available, and special fields of interest. Index by
fields of interest.

687 Grants Register. New York: St. Martin's Press. Biennial.
Primarily for students at or above the graduate level, or for all
requiring further professional or advanced vocational training. Lists
grants and awards from government agencies, and international, national, and private organizations, including: scholarships, fellowships, and research grants; exchange opportunities, vacation study
awards, and travel grants; grants-in-aid, including equipment, publication and translation grants, and funds for attending conferences,
seminars, and courses; grants for artistic or scientific projects;
competitions, prizes, and honoraria; professional and vocational
awards including opportunities for academic and administrative staff
of educational institutions; special awards for minority groups and
refugees; and funds for students in financial difficulties. The 6th
edition, 1979-81, lists 2,181 awards alphabetically by name of
sponsoring organization. Information on entries includes sponsor,
name of award, purpose, subject, number offered, value, duration,
eligibility, closing date, and address for further information. A
subject index precedes the listing of awards. Also includes an index
of awards and awarding bodies, and a bibliography.

688 Keeslar, Oreon. Financial Aids for Higher Education. 8th ed.
     Dubuque, Iowa: Wm. C. Brown, 1977.
Lists more than 4,400 programs alphabetically by program title.
Information on each includes name and address of agency offering
the scholarship, description, restrictions, field of specialization,
value, eligibility, basis of awards, and application procedures.
Introductory sections include: How to Seek a Scholarship; College
Entrance Examination Board Tests; College Scholarship Service;
American College Testing Program; NASSP Advisory List of National
Contests and Activities; Pointers for the Scholarship Counselor; Ad-
ditional Books on Colleges and Financial Aids; and Program Finder.
General Index.

689   Schlachter, Gail A.   Directory of Financial Aids for Women.
      Los Angeles: Reference Service Press,   1978.
In five sections: a list of scholarships, fellowships, loans, grants,
internships, awards and prizes designed primarily or exclusively for
women, with descriptive information on each; a list of women's credit unions, with address and telephone number for each; a list of state
sources of educational benefits, with addresses; an annotated bibliography of 74 general financial aid directories;   and three indexes:
sponsoring organization index, geographic index, and subject index.

690   Searles, Aysel, Jr., and Anne Scott.   Guide to Financial Aids
      for Students in Arts and Sciences for Graduate and Profes-
      sional Study.   Rev. ed.   New York: ARCO Publishing,
      1974.
Lists scholarships, fellowships, traineeships, grants, loans, and
other aids.   In sections on Study Abroad; Arts and Sciences; Social
Services; Professional Study in Health Related Fields; Other Fields
of Professional Study (Business and Public Administration, Education,
Journalism, Law, Library Science, Theology, Urban Planning);
Financial Aid Available Only to Members of Minority Groups; and
Sources of Financial Aid Unrestricted as to Field of Study.   Entries
in each section are listed by sponsoring agency and give address,
description of award, value, qualifications, application deadline and
address for correspondence.   Index.

691   UNESCO.   Study Abroad: International Scholarships, Inter-
      national Courses.   Paris: UNESCO.   Biennial.
The 22nd edition, 1979-81, lists and describes more than 200,000
scholarships, assistantships, travel grants, courses and seminars
at postsecondary level, in all academic and professional fields,
available in 107 countries under the auspices of 1,000 national and
100 international organizations.   Text is in English, French, and
Spanish.   In two main parts: I, Scholarships, and II, International
Courses.   Part I is divided into sections on scholarships offered
by international organizations and by national institutions.   Information on scholarships includes sponsoring agency, address, number
of scholarships and type, subjects, eligibility, amount, closing date
and address for application.   Part II is also divided into sections
for international organizations and national institutions.   Information
on courses includes sponsoring agency, address, type of course,
eligibility, where held, duration, fees, scholarships offered, and
closing date and address for application.   Index of international
organizations; index of national institutions, by countries; and index
to subjects of study.

Schools, Public and Private

692   Early Childhood Education Directory: A Selected Guide to
      2,000 Preschool Educational Centers.   Edited by E. R. La
      Crosse, Jr.   New York: R. R. Bowker, 1971.
Centers are listed by states and alphabetically by cities under each
state.   At the beginning of each state section there is a condensation

of state credentialing laws for teachers in early childhood education. This is followed by the Office of Child Development's region number and the regional director's name and address.   Information on each center includes name, address, telephone number, year established, statement of educational philosophy, and brief information on calendar, admission, administration and staff, curriculum, fees, enrollment, finances, and facilities.   Also includes a list of Head Start Regional Offices, with address and names of regional director and assistant regional director for each office.   Alphabetical index.

693   Guide to Summer Camps and Summer Schools.   20th ed.
       Boston: Porter Sargent Publishers, 1977.
Descriptions of more than 1, 100 programs arranged by type, specialty, and individual features.   Includes academic programs; programs for perceptual, learning, and reading disabilities; summer study and travel abroad; music and arts; student travel tours; adventuring and pioneering; specialized sports; programs for the handicapped and maladjusted; boys' camps, girls' camps, and Canadian camps.   Also includes a listing of programs by subjects or activities emphasized. Information on individual programs includes location, enrollment, director's winter address, fees, and duration of program.   Alphabetical index.

694   Handbook of Private Schools: An Annual Descriptive Survey of
       Independent Education.   Boston: Porter Sargent Publishers.
       Annual.
The 58th edition, 1977, contains information on 1, 900 elementary and secondary boarding and day schools in the United States.   The main section, Leading Private Schools, is arranged by region.   Information on each school includes entry number, school name, category, address and telephone number, names of academic head and admissions officer, grades offered, academic orientation and curriculum, number of new students admitted yearly, admissions tests required, enrollment, faculty, number of graduates in the preceding year and number entering college, tuition, scholarships, summer session, plant evaluation and endowment, year established, type of calendar, association membership, and paragraph description including the school's history and significant features of its program. Other sections are: Schools Classified; Private Schools Illustrated; Select Directory of Summer Academic Programs and Summer Camps; Concise Listing of Schools; Other Schools; and Directories of Firms and Agencies of Interest to Educators.   Alphabetical index of schools.

695   Private Independent Schools.   Wallingford, Conn.:   Bunting and
       Lyon.   Annual.
The 31st edition, 1978, gives information on 1, 200 schools, including day, boarding, coeducational, single-sex, church-related, military, and international schools.   Most are college preparatory, but schools for special needs and interests are also included.   In the main section long descriptive articles (each including an illustration) on 363 schools are arranged by state.   An alphabetical index of institutions precedes the main section.   Other sections are a listing by state of all 1, 200 schools, with brief descriptions; and an alphabetical listing

of educational associations, giving address, telephone number, chief
officers, purpose, membership, and meetings for each association.
Alphabetical index of schools, and a geographical and classified
index of schools.

696   Schools Abroad of Interest to Americans.   3d ed.   Edited by
         Anne Maher.   Boston: Porter Sargent Publishers, 1975.
The main section is a directory of 700 private elementary and
secondary schools in 115 countries and territories.   Arranged by
continent and country.   Information on each school includes location,
program offerings, language of instruction, international aspects of
enrollment and faculty, brief description of the school, facilities,
school history, and costs.   Other sections include an introduction
on education abroad and types of schools available; a list of additional schools; a finding list; postsecondary, special, and summer
programs; a glossary; a general index; and an index of associations,
consultants, foundations, and societies.

697   U. S. National Center for Educational Statistics.   Directory:
         Public Elementary and Secondary Day Schools.   5 vols.
         Washington, D. C.:   Government Printing Office, 1968-70.
Vol. I, North Atlantic Region; Vol. II, Great Lakes and Plains
Region; Vol. III, Southeast Region; Vol. IV, West and Southwest;
Vol. V, Nonpublic Elementary and Secondary Day Schools.   Lists
all elementary and secondary schools in the United States.   Information for each school includes name, address, grade span, number
of students and teachers by levels, number of graduates, type of
program, and district name.

698   U. S. National Center for Educational Statistics.   Education
         Directory: Public School Systems.   Washington, D. C.:
         Government Printing Office.   Annual.
The main section of the 1978 edition gives names and other information on local public school systems listed by states and outlying
territories.   Gives name of each unit, location of superintendent,
zip code, county name, grade span, number of pupils, and number
of schools.   Also includes a ranking by enrollment of school systems
with enrollments of 10, 000 or more.   Gives rank, name of unit,
city and state, and enrollment.   Also includes five tables: (1) Distribution of local public school systems by size of system;   (2) Number of local public school systems by grade span and size of system;
(3) Number of local public school systems by grade span and state;
(4) Number of local public school systems by size of school system
and state; (5) Number of operating and nonoperating public school
systems and pupils and schools by state and outlying area.

Special Education

699   Academic Underachiever: A Handbook of Preparatory, Tutorial,
         Remedial, and Diagnostic Resources in Independent Schools,
         Alternate Programs, and Clinics.   2d ed.   Boston: Porter
         Sargent Publishers, 1970.

A directory arranged in five sections: Academic Schools, Specialized Schools, Alternative Programs, Clinical Facilities, and Specialized Clinics. Entries are arranged geographically within each section. Information on entries includes type of institution, address, telephone number, name of director, grades offered, number of faculty or staff, ratio of faculty to students, enrollment, programs or services, tuition or fees, summer program, and a paragraph description. Information for alternative programs includes name, address, and telephone number only. Contains a list of Facilities Classified by Special Features. Also includes illustrated announcements, a list of agencies and organizations at the national level, and an index of institutions.

700   Axford, Lavonne B.   A Directory of Educational Programs for the Gifted. Metuchen, N. J.: Scarecrow Press, 1971. Public and private schools and summer programs are listed under each state. Information on individual schools includes name of director, address, whether for boys or girls or coed, ages, grade levels, boarding or day, enrollment, tuition, scholarships, faculty-student ratio, average class size, school year, accreditation, religious affiliation, IQ required for entrance, foreign, minority, or physically handicapped accepted, student activities, and size of library. Includes a bibliography, pp. 261-279.

701   Directory for Exceptional Children: A Listing of Educational and Training Facilities. 8th ed. Boston: Porter Sargent Publishers, 1978. A directory of more than 3,000 educational and training facilities and organizations in the United States. Arranged in categories by types of facilities: academic programs for the learning disabled; private, state, and public facilities for the emotionally disturbed and socially maladjusted; psychiatric and guidance clinics; residential and day facilities for orthopedic and neurological handicaps; private residential and private day facilities for the mentally retarded; state and public facilities for the mentally retarded; schools for the blind and partially sighted; schools for the deaf and hard of hearing; schools for the speech handicapped; and speech and hearing clinics. Arrangement within each category is by state. Description of each facility includes address, telephone number, tuition and rates, population served, and type of program. Also includes a list of associations, societies, and foundations (U. S. and Canadian); and a list of federal and state agencies and personnel (U. S. and Canadian). Index of institutions and organizations.

702   Ellingson, Careth C., and James Cass. Directory of Facilities for the Learning-Disabled and Handicapped. New York: Harper & Row, 1972. Descriptive information on institutions in the United States and Canada. Arranged by states and provinces. Information on each institution includes name, address, name of director, type, diagnostic facilities (programs, procedures, fees, faculty, funding), remedial, developmental and therapy programs (diagnostic categories, enrollment, tuition, faculty). Includes an index of institutions and a listing of services by major cities.

703   UNESCO.   Special Education.   International Directories of Edu-
           cation, 5.   Paris: UNESCO, 1969.
A list of special education facilities in 66 countries and territories.
Information for each country includes responsible authority, staff,
institutions, administrative functions of the department, role of local
authorities, publications, and other organizations concerned.   Also
includes a list of international agencies.

Study and Teaching Abroad

704   Garraty, John A. , Lily von Klemperer, and C. J. H. Taylor.
           New Guide to Study Abroad: Summer and Full-Year Pro-
           grams for High School Students, College and University
           Students, and Teachers.   New York   Harper & Row, 1978.
Covers more than 500 programs in Europe, Asia, and Africa.
Major sections are: Planning for Study Abroad; The College and
Graduate Student Abroad; The Secondary and Postsecondary Student
Abroad; The Teacher Abroad; and Foreign Experience Outside the
Classroom.   Information on specific programs includes sponsor,
language requirements, costs, academic credits, and application
procedures.   Includes preliminary chapters on benefits of study
abroad; basic considerations; cost; and higher education systems in
various countries.   Appendixes include a list of organizations and
agencies promoting foreign study and travel, and a currency conver-
sion table.   General index and index to fields of study.

705   Handbook on International Study for U. S. Nationals.   6th ed.
           5 vols. New York: Institute of International Education, 1976-.
A series including volumes on study in Europe; the American Re-
publics Area; Africa South of the Sahara; the Middle East and North
Africa; East and South Asia and Oceania.   The main section of each
volume lists universities and other institutions of higher education
under individual countries.   Information for each country includes a
brief description of the higher education system, language of instruction, academic year, major university degrees, admissions, costs,
and housing, followed by a listing of institutions with brief information for each and an address for obtaining further information.   Other
sections are on fields of study, awards for study and research, study
and exchange programs, volunteer and trainee opportunities, organizations and agencies providing services, and government regulations.
Indexes of institutions; fields of study; organizations and agencies;
and institutions with their major fields.

706   Handbook on U. S. Study for Foreign Nationals.   5th ed.   New
           York: Institute of International Education, 1973.
A guide for foreign nationals on study, training, and other opportuni-
ties in the United States.   Major sections are: Education in the
United States; The Foreign Student in the United States; Fields of
Study; U. S. Colleges and Universities; English Language and Orien-
tation Programs; Awards for Study and Research in the U. S. ; Special
Programs; Organizations and Agencies Providing Services to Foreign
Nationals Coming to the U. S. ; and U. S. Government Regulations Af-
fecting Foreign Nationals.

707   Higher Education in the United Kingdom: A Handbook for
          Students from Overseas and Their Advisers.   Harlow, Eng. :
          Longman Group.   Biennial.
Contains information on courses available; admission of students
from overseas; knowledge of English; money matters; entry to Britain; student life in Britain; a directory of subjects and facilities for
study; addresses of universities, colleges, polytechnics; national and
professional bodies; British council offices overseas and in Britain;
overseas student offices in London; tuition, fees, and other charges;
fees for residential accommodations.   Index.

708   Mathies, Lorraine, and William G. Thomas.   Overseas Oppor-
          tunities for American Educators and Students: Perspectives
          and Possibilities.   New York: Macmillan Information, 1973.
Part I, Perspectives of Overseas Educational Programs and Service,
contains essays describing activities representative of U.S. govern-
ment-affiliated agencies, including ACTION's Peace Corps, the
Institute of International Education, Fulbright Teacher Exchange Program, American university overseas programs, and others.   Part
II, Overseas Study Opportunities for American Youth, contains a
worldwide listing of elementary and secondary schools, including
schools for American dependents; and a list of overseas branches
of U.S. colleges and universities, and study and tour organizations.
Part III, Overseas Educational Employment Opportunities, includes
descriptions of different types of schools and organizations that
sponsor overseas educational programs and have employment opportunities available, and employment opportunities with institutions at
single locations and at multiple locations.   Part IV, Considerations
in Obtaining an Overseas Position, contains two chapters on steps
in the overseas placement process, and benefits, risks, and other
considerations.   Also includes sample forms, a selected bibliography,
and an index.

          Schools Abroad of Interest to Americans.   3d ed.   Edited by
          Anne Maher.   Boston: Porter Sargent Publishers, 1975
          (see No. 696).

709   Summer Study Abroad.   Edited by Gail A. Cohen.   New York:
          Institute of International Education.   Annual.
The 29th edition, 1978, describes 826 programs for precollege students, college students, and teachers.   Programs included are
sponsored by U.S. colleges and universities, and by foreign institutions and private and government organizations and agencies.   Includes professional study opportunities for teachers at all levels,
student teachers, lawyers, medical students, and others.   Program
descriptions are listed geographically by continent or region, subdivided by country and city, then by institution.   Information on each
program includes description, duration, eligibility, credits, teaching
methods, housing, costs, evaluation, deadline for application, and
address.   Appendixes: A, Consortia; B, Publications on Higher
Education Abroad; C, Foreign Exchange.   Indexes by sponsoring
institutions, and by fields of study.

710   Teaching Abroad.   Edited by Gail A. Cohen.   New York   In-
      stitute of International Education, 1976.
Lists more than 150 programs for teachers at all levels, guidance
counselors, and administrative personnel.   Gives information on
qualifications, numbers of positions available, language of instruction, benefits, duration, and application procedures.   Also describes
student teaching opportunities, nonclassroom-teacher-related work,
research grants, and specialized study programs for teachers on
sabbaticals.

UNESCO.   Study Abroad: International Scholarships, Interna-
        tional Courses.   Paris: UNESCO.   Biennial (see No. 691).

711   U. S. College Sponsored Programs Abroad: Academic Year.
      Edited by Gail A. Cohen.   New York   Institute of Inter-
      national Education.   Annual.
Describes more than 700 study abroad programs on the undergraduate
and graduate levels, conducted by U. S. colleges and universities in
countries around the world.   Gives information on courses, credits,
costs, scholarships, housing, and language of instruction.   Includes
suggestions for choosing a program.

Vocational Education

712   Blue Book of Occupational Education.   3d ed.   Edited by Max
      M. Russell.   New York   Macmillan Information, 1977.
Descriptive information on more than 13, 000 occupational schools.
The first part, Occupational Schools of the United States, is a listing
of schools by state and city.   At the beginning of each state section
is a statement of licensing requirements for occupational schools.
Descriptive data on institutions include name, address, classification,
name of school official, telephone number, tuition, enrollment, requirements for admission, degree or certificate awarded, and accrediting or licensing agency.   The second part includes an alphabetical listing of curricula offerings of business, trade, technical,
and vocational schools; and curricula listed by occupational classification, with schools arranged by state under each classification.
The third part is a listing by state of two-year colleges, giving
name and address for each.   The fourth part is a listing by state
of schools approved for veterans' training, giving city of location for
each.   The fifth part consists of descriptions of various occupations
including nature of work, places of employment, training and other
qualifications, employment outlook, earnings, and working conditions.

713   Continuing Education: A Guide to Career Development Pro-
      grams.   Syracuse, N. Y.:   Gaylord Bros. in association
      with Neal-Schuman Publishers, 1977.
A directory of institutions and organizations in the United States that
offer continuing education courses.   Contains a directory of 2, 000
schools, colleges, universities, and other institutions arranged by
state, giving for each entry a description of programs, areas, type
of credit, and special programs available; an alphabetical directory

of organizations offering continuing education opportunities; and a guide to career areas, listing 200 subject and career fields. Appendix material includes a list of television stations, sources of further information on continuing education, and a reprinting of the Directory of the Accrediting Commission of the National Home Study Council. Index of institutions and organizations.

714 Lovejoy, Clarence E. Lovejoy's Career and Vocational School Guide: A Source Book, Clue Book, and Directory of Institutions Training for Job Opportunities. 5th ed. New York Simon and Schuster, 1978.

The main sections are Vocational Career Curricula, a listing by career classification with schools arranged by state under each classification; and Capsule Descriptions of the schools, arranged by state. Information on individual schools includes address, type of school, tuition, length of course, admission requirements, and certificate or diploma. Other sections are a list of 1, 550 career titles; a list of 679 jobs in the Armed Services; and a list of organizations under titles of vocations or professions. An alphabetical index of schools gives state location for each.

715 U. S. Office of Education. Directory of Secondary Schools with Occupational Curriculums: Public-Nonpublic. Washington, D. C.: Government Printing Office, 1973.

Secondary schools that offer vocational curriculums are listed alphabetically by state, city, and name of school. Public and nonpublic schools are listed separately within each state. Information on each school includes address, enrollment statistics, and vocational courses offered.

716 U. S. Office of Education. Directory of Postsecondary Schools with Occupational Programs: Public and Private. Washington, D. C.: Government Printing Office, 1977.

A comprehensive listing of postsecondary schools and institutions with occupational programs. Includes public and private noncollegiate vocational schools and two-year and four-year colleges that offer occupational programs that lead to a certificate or degree at a lower level than a bachelor's. Arranged by state and city. Information on each institution includes address, accrediting agency, programs offered, and enrollment statistics. Index of subjects of programs and index of institutions.

Miscellaneous Directories

717 American Council on Education. Overseas Liaison Committee. International Directory for Educational Liaison. Washington, D. C.: American Council on Education, 1973.

A directory of information on higher education in the developing world. The international section lists organizations with a multiregional focus, with information on each organization including administrative structure, personnel, funding sources, and program interests and activities. Geographical sections on Africa, Asia, and

Latin America/Caribbean include descriptions of national and regional organizations, and of universities and research institutes listed by countries.   Each geographical section also lists embassies and consulates, with names, addresses, and telephone numbers, and entry requirements for U. S. nationals.   General index and index of acronyms.

718   Directory of Educational Consultants.   Amsterdam, N. Y. :
        Ralka Press.   Annual.
The main section is a numbered listing of firms with address, telephone number, principal officers, areas of service and specialties, publications, and description of purpose and services of each firm. Preceding the main section is a list of consultants arranged alphabetically by name of chief executive, with address and number and symbol referring to the firm in the main section.

719   Educational Media Organization Directory.   New York: Educational Film Library Association, 1974.
Information on 35 organizations that are concerned primarily or exclusively with media in education, and are national membership organizations or regional organizations with national programs open to applicants in the United States and Canada.   Information on each organization includes name, acronym, address, names of executive officers and of members of the board of directors, number of staff; aims, purposes, objectives; activities, services, periodicals; permanent committees, task forces; and membership requirements.   Appendix A is a list of organizations that responded to the questionnaire but do not meet criteria for inclusion in the main body of the directory.   Address and executive officer's name are given for each organization.   Appendix B is a list of organizations solicited but not responding.   The index is an alphabetical list of all organizations in the main body plus the two appendixes.

720   Johnson, Willis L. , ed.   Directory of Special Programs for
        Minority Group Members: Career Information Services,
        Employment Skills Banks,   Financial Aid Sources.   2d ed.
        Garrett Park, Md. :   Garrett Park Press, 1975.
Lists 1, 340 organizations in four main sections.   Section 1, General Employment and Educational Assistance Programs, includes national, regional, and area scholarship programs, employment services, and other sources of assistance.   Section 2, Federal Programs, lists economic assistance, job retraining, and student financial aid programs operated with federal funds.   Section 3, Women's Programs, details programs that provide information on career counseling and job assistance programs for women.   Section 4, College and University Awards, includes remedial, financial aid, special academic or skills training programs, and other activities for minority group members by individual institutions, listed by state and alphabetically by name of institution within states.   Also includes an alphabetical list of all organizations included in the directory, a program index, and a description of sources of information.   Appendix A, Upward Bound, Talent Search, and Special Services and Special Veterans Programs.   Appendix B, Definitions of Terms used in the directory.

Other Sources of Information is a list of books and other publications providing information on financial aid and career programs.

721   Piele, Philip K. , and Stuart C.   Smith.   Directory of Organiza-
          tions and Personnel in Educational Management.   5th ed.
          Eugene: ERIC Clearinghouse on Educational Management,
          University of Oregon, 1976.
Includes an alphabetical listing of 160 organizations engaged in research and development relating to educational management, and 489
individuals engaged in research relating to educational management.
Information on organizations includes name, address, telephone number, service area, service policy, purpose, subjects of specialization, types of publications, and periodicals issued.   Subject index
and geographic index to organizations.   Information on researchers
includes name, title, address, research subjects, affiliations, and
publications.   Subject index to personnel.

722   UNESCO.   International Directory of Programmed Instruction.
          Paris: UNESCO, 1973.
Arranged by 31 countries, with three sections under each country:
organization and activities; publications; and research and applications.   Lists university research centers, educational laboratories,
publishers of programmed materials, periodicals, professional
organizations, and books and bibliographies.

723   U. S. Office of Education.   Catalog of Federal Education As-
          sistance Programs: An Indexed Guide to the Federal
          Government's Programs Offering Educational Benefits to
          the American People.   Washington, D. C. :   Government
          Printing Office.   Biennial.
"Includes all programs administered by the U. S. Office of Education
as well as programs administered by other federal agencies in support of educational services, professional training, or library services
available to the general public. "--Introd.   Information on each program includes name of agency, authorization, objectives, type of
assistance, uses and use restrictions, and eligibility requirements.
Arrangement is by program number sequence.   In addition to descriptions of programs, this catalog includes an administrative
agency index, authorization index, public law index, U. S. Code index,
general index, beneficiary index, and program name index.   Excerpted from the Catalog of Federal Domestic Assistance, published
annually by the U. S. Office of Management and Budget.

E.   Yearbooks

724   Advances in Child Development and Behavior.   New York:
          Academic Press, 1963-.
Provides scholarly articles on problems of current interest.   A list
of references is given at the end of each article.

725   American Association for Higher Education.   Current Issues in
          Higher Education.   San Francisco: Jossey-Bass Publishers,
          1967-.

Selected papers and speeches of the annual National Conference on Higher Education. Each volume is devoted to a special theme.

726   American Association of Colleges for Teacher Education.   Yearbook.   Washington, D. C. :   The Association, 1948-.
Proceedings of the annual meetings, each with a special theme.   Contains addresses delivered, reports of committees, constitutions and bylaws, and a directory of officers, committees and members.

727   Association for Supervision and Curriculum Development.   Yearbook.   Washington, D. C. :   The Association, 1944-.
Each yearbook consists of several articles by different authors on a central theme.   Articles include lists of references.   Also included are lists of ASCD Board of Directors, Executive Committee, and Headquarters staff.

728   Educational Media Yearbook.   New York: R. R. Bowker, 1973-.
Reports important developments in funding, organizational programs, new media, research and development, and trends in the educational media field.   The 1978 edition is in three major parts.   Part I, The Year in Review, includes sections on Special Education and Media, Instructional Television and Films, Field Reports, Media Professions and Manpower Training, Research and Development, Media Industry, Media in International Development.   Each section is made up of several articles.   Part II, Mediagraphy: Print and Nonprint Resources, is a classified listing of recent resources related to educational communication and technology.   It is in four sections: reference tools, media-related periodicals and newsletters, media about media, and data base resources for library/education institutions.   Part III is a guide to organizations, training programs, and funding sources.

729   International Yearbook of Education.   Geneva: International Bureau of Education; Paris: UNESCO, 1948-69.
Detailed reports on various fields of education and on educational conditions in various countries of the world.   Ceased publication, but may be useful for information for the period covered.

730   International Yearbook of Educational and Instructional Technology.   New York: Nichols Publishing, 1976-.   Biennial.
The 1978-79 edition gives an overview of educational technology and programmed learning worldwide, with emphasis on the United Kingdom.   Includes sections on trends in the technology, covering behavioral sciences, individualized learning, and simulation and gaming; a selected bibliography on educational technology; a review of the current state of the art in the United States, Europe, Asia, Australia, Latin America, the Middle East and Africa; a directory of centers of activity; lists of international organizations and national and international conferences; and reviews of recent models of audiovisual media including filmstrip and slide projectors, tape recorders, language laboratories, and videotape machines.

731   National Council for Social Studies.   Yearbook.   Washington,
      D. C.:   The Council, 1931-.
Each yearbook has a specific theme, with articles written by specialists.   Articles include bibliographies.

732   National Council of Teachers of Mathematics.   Yearbook.
      Washington, D. C.:   The Council, 1926-.
Each volume consists of articles, written by educators, on a particular theme.   Includes bibliographies.

733   National Institute of Adult Education (England and Wales).   Year-
      book.   London: The Institute, 1961-.
Main sections are: A Directory of Organizations, including the
Ministry of Education, local education authorities, providing bodies,
NIAE corporate members, residential education, professional associations, etc.; and Annual Report and Financial Statement.   Also includes "Guides to Studies in Adult Education," a brief, annual bibliography.

734   National Society for the Study of Education.   Yearbook.   Chi-
      cago: University of Chicago Press, 1929-.
Each yearbook is issued in two parts, each part with a different
theme.   Each part consists of several chapters written by specialists.

735   Paedagogica Europaea: The European Yearbook of Educational
      Research.   Amsterdam: Agon Elsevier, 1965-.
Publishes contributions from every field of education.   Each volume
consists of major articles based on research, reports of symposia,
and summaries of problems in various fields of educational activity.
Contributions published in English, French, or German, with summaries in the other two languages.

736   Technician Education Yearbook.   Ann Arbor, Mich.:   Prakken
      Publishers, 1963-.
The 1975-76 edition is in six sections: New Issues, Problems and
Proposals; Case Studies of Programs in Schools; Directories of Institutions and Officials; Occupational Information; Professional Organizations; and Bibliography.   The directory section lists by state
1, 850 schools that offer technician programs.   Information on each
institution includes name, executive officers, enrollment, admission
requirements, accreditation, and areas of specialization.

737   World Yearbook of Education.   New York: Harcourt, Brace,
      1932-74.
Each yearbook is written around a central theme and contains survey
articles on English-speaking countries and the major European countries.   Ceased publication but useful for information for the period
covered.

738   Yearbook of Adult and Continuing Education.   Chicago: Mar-
      quis Academic Media, Marquis Who's Who, 1975-.
Presents government and private agency statistics and descriptive
data on topics related to adult education, including general adult

education, adult basic education, career/vocational education, continuing education, and community education.   In addition to these topics, the first edition includes sections on equal educational opportunity, educational materials, related statistics, adult education and government, and professional education in adult education; and the second edition, a section on teacher training, programs, and organizations.   Includes textual material, tables, charts, and directory lists.   Each volume has subject and geographic indexes.

739   Yearbook of Higher Education.   Chicago: Marquis Academic
         Media, Marquis Who's Who, 1969-.
The 10th edition, 1978-79, is in four parts.   Part One, Directory of Institutions of Higher Education in the United States and Canada, lists 3, 257 U.S. two-year and four-year institutions, and 177 Canadian institutions by state and province.   Information on each institution includes address, telephone number, control, calendar, enrollment, and a listing of administrative personnel, academic deans, and department chairmen.   Part Two, Statistics of Higher Education, covers enrollment, degrees, faculty and staff, facilities, revenue and expenditures.   Part Three, Resource Information in Higher Education, includes directories of ERIC Clearinghouses, educational associations, institutional consortia, and Canadian associations of higher education.   Part Four, Indexes, contains an index of institutions, a subject index to statistics and resource information, and an index of associations.

740   Yearbook of School Law.   Danville, Ill.:   Interstate Printers
         and Publishers, 1950-.
Covers decisions dealing with schools and education, rendered by higher state and federal courts during a twelve-month period.   Also contains a section for particularly significant cases, articles on subjects of timely interest, an annotated bibliography of recent research reports on school law, and an index of cases.

741   Yearbook of Special Education.   Chicago: Marquis Academic
         Media, Marquis Who's Who, 1975-.
The first edition of this yearbook presents government and private agency statistics on educational problems in the field of special education.   The second edition gives evaluative studies related to various handicaps, current status reports of federal and state legislation, and listings of current research.   It also includes a directory of associations concerned with the handicapped, and subject and geographic indexes.   Articles in both editions include statistical tables, charts, and bibliographies.   The third edition updates the most significant statistical material and includes additional evaluative reports.

F.   Biographical Sources

742   Academic Who's Who: University Teachers in the British Isles
         in the Arts, Education and the Social Sciences.   London:
         Adam & Charles Black.   Biennial.

The second edition, 1975-76, includes 7,000 entries for university teachers who have the rank of senior lecturer or above, or have taught for five years or more as a lecturer or assistant lecturer. Arrangement is alphabetical by name. Entries give concise biographical information, including date of birth, date of marriage, number of children, educational background, professional experience including present position, membership in professional organizations, publications, and address.

743 American Men and Women of Science: The Social and Behavioral Sciences. 13th ed. Edited by Jaques Cattell Press. New York: R. R. Bowker, 1978.
Contains brief biographical information for 24,000 scientists actively engaged in teaching or research in the social science fields. Entries give name, date and place of birth, address, marital status, educational background, positions, special fields of interest, and publications.

744 Biographical Dictionary of American Educators. Edited by John F. Ohles. 3 vols. Westport, Conn.: Greenwood Press, 1978.
Brief biographical information on 1,665 educators from colonial times to the 1970s. Includes only persons who had reached the age of 60, retired, or died by January 1, 1975. In addition to well-known national educators, it includes state and regional, women, and minority educators. Information on each entry includes birth and death dates, educational background, professional career, and personal data. Many entries include references to sources for further information. Appendixes include listings according to place of birth, state of major service, and field of specialty; a chronology of birth years; and important dates in American education. General index.

745 Directory of American Scholars. 7th ed. Edited by Jaques Cattell Press. 4 vols. New York: R. R. Bowker, 1978.
Contains information on 39,000 scholars currently active in teaching, research, and writing. Vol. 1, History; Vol. 2, English, Speech, and Drama; Vol. 3, Foreign Languages, Linguistics, and Philology; Vol. 4, Philosophy, Religion, and Law. Entries give name, birthplace, date of birth, citizenship, date of marriage and number of children, discipline, educational background, honorary degrees, professional experience including present position, concurrent appointments, honors and awards, membership in professional societies, chief fields of research interest, major publications, and mailing address. Each volume contains a geographic index listing names by state and city of work location. Vol. 4 also includes an alphabetical list of all names in the directory, indicating the volume in which biographical information is given.

746 International Scholars Directory. Edited by John W. Montgomery. Strasbourg, France: International Scholarly Publishers, 1975.
Inclusion is limited to scholars of international reference interest from countries of the Free World. Each entry includes name, date

of birth, highest degree, institution granting the degree, current position, most significant or latest monograph with year published and reference to a review, total number of monographs and of journal articles published, and references to other bio-bibliographic sources.

747   Leaders in Education: A Biographical Directory. 5th ed.
        Edited by Jaques Cattell Press. New York: R. R. Bowker, 1974.
Contains biographical sketches of 17, 000 American and Canadian educators including officers and deans of accredited institutions of higher learning, professors of education, directors and staff of educational research institutes, state and provincial commissioners of education, leading figures in public and private school fields, officers of foundations concerned with education, officials of the U. S. Office of Education and of major educational associations, and authors of important pedagogical books.   Entries give name, place and date of birth, date of marriage, number of children, degrees, past and present positions, fields of interest, publications, and address.

748   National Faculty Directory. Detroit: Gale Research, 1970-.
        Annual.
The 1979 edition, in two volumes, lists alphabetically 480, 000 teaching faculty members of junior colleges, colleges, and universities in the United States and selected Canadian institutions.   Entries give name, department, institution, and address.   A list of institutions arranged by states and Canadian provinces is given in the first volume.

749   Who's Who Biographical Record: Child Development Profes-
        sionals. Chicago: Marquis Who's Who, 1976.
Brief information on 9, 000 child psychologists, guidance counselors, special education teachers, directors of special programs, educational researchers, and college and university professors of education and psychology.   Information on each entry includes academic background, professional experience, membership in professional associations, area of specialization, and address.

750   Who's Who Biographical Record: School District Officials.
        Chicago: Marquis Who's Who, 1976.
Concise biographical information on 12, 000 district superintendents, principals, administrative personnel, and others providing service at the district level.

VII. THE RESEARCH PAPER

In order to prepare material for a research paper or report, the student must have some knowledge of the methodology of research, including selection of a problem, review of the literature, types of research, tools of research, and data analysis.

Handbooks of form and style should be consulted before writing the paper and while the writing is in progress.

The handbooks listed in this section are recommended for these purposes.

A. Methodology of Research

751 Best, John W. Research in Education. 3d ed. Englewood Cliffs, N. J.: Prentice-Hall, 1977.
A comprehensive, detailed guide written as a basic textbook in an introductory course in educational research and as a reference source for research, thesis writing, or professional study. Contains ten chapters covering the meaning of research, selecting a problem and preparing a research proposal, use of reference materials, experimental research, descriptive studies, the tools of research, descriptive data analysis, inferential data analysis, the research report, and historical research. A summary, suggested exercises or activities, and a bibliography are included at the end of most chapters. Also includes a research methods bibliography; answers to statistics exercises; and eight appendixes including statistical formulas, tables, grouped data computations, research course report evaluation, and federal involvement in educational research. Author and subject indexes.

752 Burroughs, George E. R. Design and Analysis in Educational Research. 2d ed. Birmingham, Eng.: University of Birmingham, School of Education, 1975.
A discussion of the scientific type of investigation in educational research. Covers hypotheses, designing the experiment, sampling, measurement, data collection, data analysis, tabulation and summarization, statistical hypothesis testing, analysis of variance, correlation, factor analysis, multiple regression, and writing the report. Includes a bibliography; two appendixes: I, Some Preliminary Mathematical Skills; II, Tables; and an index.

753   Cook, David R. , and N. Kenneth La Fleur.   A Guide to Edu-
        cational Research.   2d ed.   Boston: Allyn and Bacon,
        1975.
Major sections are: I, A Framework for Understanding Educational
Research; II, The Research Study; III, Historical Research; IV,
Descriptive Research; V, Experimental Research.   Sections III, IV,
and V contain reprints of ten published research studies with an
analysis of each study, in addition to textual material.   Index.

754   Johnson, M. Clemens.   A Review of Research Methods in
        Education.   Chicago: Rand McNally College Publishing,
        1977.
Presents a review of traditional research methods plus less common
and more recent methods.   Chapters 1 and 2 provide an overview of
educational research and related literature, general problems in
designing school studies and in reviewing research literature.   Chapters 3-15 cover uses and interpretations of descriptive statistics,
measurement and test development, sampling problems and surveys,
hypothesis testing, experimental design and problems in conducting
and evaluating studies, use of the computer as a research tool, longitudinal studies and assessment of change, research directed at the
individual, simulation research, research and development projects,
and reading the research report and reacting to it.   Index.

755   Mason, Emanuel J. , and William J. Bramble.   Understanding
        and Conducting Research: Applications in Education and the
        Behavioral Sciences.   New York: McGraw-Hill, 1978.
In 14 chapters: Science and Research; Modes of Research and the
Scientific Method; Making Problems Researchable; Using Experimental
Designs; Using Quasi-Experimental Designs; Evaluation; Some Funda-
mental Quantitative Tools; Making Inferences with Statistics; More
Advanced Concepts in Data Analysis; Observing and Measuring;
Methods of Measuring and Observing Behavior; Guidelines for Con-
ducting Research; But What About the Computer?   Some Perspectives
on Research and Reality.   At the end of each chapter are a sum-
mary, problems for discussion, and a list of references.   Appendixes:
A, Glossary of Terms;   B, Statistical Tables; C, Answers to Selected
Problems.   Index.

756   Mouly, George J.   Educational Research: The Art and Science
        of Investigation.   Boston: Allyn and Bacon, 1978.
Part I, The Scientific Method, contains chapters on the World of
Science; Nature of Scientific Inquiry; Conducting the Research Study;
The Library; Statistical Considerations; and Sampling.   Part II,
Introduction to Research Methods, includes chapters on Historical
Research; The Survey: Descriptive Studies; The Survey: Analytical
Studies; Experimental Method; and Predictive Methods.   Part III,
Overview and Appraisal, is a chapter on Educational Research, A
Review and Evaluation.   Material at the end of each chapter includes
highlights of the chapter, questions and projects, suggestions for
further study, and self-test.   Also includes a key to end-of-chapter
self-tests, a bibliography, and an index.

757   Tuckman, Bruce W.   Conducting Educational Research.   2d ed.
      New York: Harcourt Brace Jovanovich,   1978.
In 14 sections: The Role of Research; Selecting a Problem and
Constructing Hypotheses; Reviewing the Literature; Identifying and
Labeling Variables; Constructing Operational Definitions of Variables;
Identifying Techniques for the Manipulation and Control of Variables;
Constructing Research Designs; Identifying and Describing Procedures
for Observation and Measurement; Constructing and Using Question-
naires and Interview Schedules; Carrying Out Statistical Analyses;
Using Procedures for Data Processing; Writing a Research Report;
Doing Classroom Research; and Conducting Evaluation Studies.
Recommended sources and competency test exercises are given at
the end of each chapter.   Also includes a List of References Cited
in the Text; Appendix A, Sample Studies and a Sample Proposal;
Appendix B, Tables; Answers to Exercises; and an index of names
and titles, and an index of subjects.

758   Wiersma, William.   Research Methods in Education: An In-
      troduction.   2d ed.   Itasca, Ill.:   F. E. Peacock Pub-
      lishers, 1975.
Part One, General Principles of Research, contains chapters dealing
with general concepts, research design, principles, types of research,
measurement, and sampling.   Part Two, Techniques for Hypothesis
Testing, discusses specific procedures for testing hypotheses by
parametric, nonparametric, and correlational techniques.   Part Three,
The Research Literature, deals with searching the literature and
reading research reports critically, and with writing about research,
proposals, and reports.   Suggested study exercises are given at the
end of each of the 13 chapters.   Appendix 1, Solution to Suggested
Study Exercises.   Appendix 2, Tables of Underlying Distributions.
Also includes a Glossary of Research Methods Terms, a selected
bibliography, and author and subject indexes.

                    B.   Form and Style in Research Papers

759   Berry, Dorothea M. , and Gordon P. Martin.   Guide to Writing
      Research Papers.   New York: McGraw-Hill, 1971.
Includes sections on organization and writing of the paper, documentation, tables and illustrations, and typing the manuscript.   Separate
sections cover preparation of theses and dissertations, and scientific
papers.   Sample pages illustrate form.   An appendix covers selection of a subject, outlining, and note taking, and includes an annotated list of sources of information and a list of reference materials in the major academic fields.   Index.

760   Turabian, Kate L.   A Manual for Writers of Term Papers,
      Theses, and Dissertations.   4th ed.   Chicago: University
      of Chicago Press, 1973.
Includes sections covering parts of the paper, abbreviations and
numbers, spelling and punctuation, capitalization, underlining, and
other matters of style, quotations, documentation, public documents,
tables, illustrations, scientific papers, and typing the paper.   Index.

761 Wilson, John A. R. Research Guide in Education. Morristown, N. J.: General Learning Press, 1976.
Part I gives a brief overview of education as a discipline. Part II, How to Research a Paper in Education, includes sections on selecting, defining, and organizing a topic; using the library; and papers in specific fields, with suggested sources. Part III, How to Write a Paper in Education, contains sections on content of the paper, clarity in writing, form of the paper, and documentation. Includes a bibliography and an index.

762 Chicago. University. Press. A Manual of Style. 12th ed. rev. Chicago: University of Chicago Press, 1969.
For authors, editors, and copywriters. Part 1, Bookmaking, covers parts of a book, manuscript preparation, proofs, rights and permissions. Part 2, Style, includes sections on punctuation, spelling, names, numbers, quotations, illustrations, tables, abbreviations, footnotes, bibliography, indexes. Part 3, Production and Printing, contains a section on design and typography, and a glossary of technical terms.

763 National Education Association. NEA Style Manual for Writers and Editors. Washington, D. C. : The Association, 1974.
Covers abbreviations, symbols, capitalization, dates, division of words, foreign words and phrases, italics, lists and enumerations, numbers and figures, plurals, punctuation, titles, tables, bibliographical and footnote references, title page and reverse, and notes on typing copy for the typesetter. Particular attention is given to problems specifically related to publications of the NEA and the field of education.

764 U. S. Government Printing Office. Style Manual. Rev. ed. Washington, D. C. , 1973.
A stylebook based on principles of good usage and custom in the printing trade. Sections of interest to writers of research papers cover capitalization, spelling, punctuation, abbreviations, numerals, signs and symbols, and tables.

APPENDIX: OTHER GUIDES TO REFERENCE MATERIALS

General

765 American Reference Books Annual. Edited by Bohdan S.
      Wynar. Littleton, Colo.: Libraries Unlimited, 1970-.
A comprehensive annual reviewing service for reference books
published in the United States during the year. Entries include
bibliographic information and reviews that are both descriptive and
critical. The 1979 volume is in 42 sections; the section for Education is divided into general works, bibliographies, dictionaries and
encyclopedias, directories, handbooks and yearbooks, biography, and
instructional materials. Also includes references on children's
literature in the Literature section. Subject, author, title index in
each volume. Five-year cumulative subject, author, and title indexes.

766 Sheehy, Eugene P., comp. Guide to Reference Books. 9th
      ed. Chicago: American Library Association, 1976.
A comprehensive guide to scholarly reference works in English and
in foreign languages, published up to 1974. Includes 10,000 entries
in a classified arrangement. Major sections are: General Reference
Works; The Humanities; Social Sciences; History and Area Studies;
Pure and Applied Sciences. All sections are subdivided. Each subdivision includes a selection of basic reference materials in that
field. Entries include bibliographic information and an annotation.
Education, a subdivision of Social Sciences, is further subdivided
for various aspects of the field, and includes guides, bibliographies,
indexes, abstracts, dictionaries, encyclopedias, handbooks, yearbooks, directories, biographical and statistical sources. Author,
title, subject index.

767 Walford, Albert J., ed. Guide to Reference Material. 3d ed.
      3 vols. London: Library Association, 1973-77.
A comprehensive guide to reference works in English and other
languages, with emphasis on British publications. Vol. 1, Science
and Technology; Vol. 2, Social and Historical Sciences, Philosophy and Religion; Vol. 3, Generalities, Languages, The Arts, and
Literature. Vol. 2 contains a section on Education, which includes
references to bibliographies, thesauri, encyclopedias, annuals, com-

parative education, educational documentation, educational research, theory, educational psychology, teaching and training, vocational guidance, programmed instruction, audiovisual aids, adult education, primary, secondary, and higher education, academic dress, further education, and technical education.   Entries include bibliographic information and descriptive annotations.   Author, subject, title index.

Social Sciences

768   White, Carl M., and others.   Sources of Information in the
       Social Sciences: A Guide to the Literature.   2d ed.
       Chicago: American Library Association, 1973.
Major sections are: Social Science Literature; History; Geography; Economics and Business Administration; Sociology; Anthropology; Psychology; Education; Political Science.   The division for Education includes short bibliographical essays, followed by lists of references to books, on several aspects of education, and an annotated bibliography of reference books.   The first part includes sections for Classics; Introductory Works; Educational History; Educational Philosophy; Educational Sociology; Comparative and International Education; Educational Psychology; Measurement and Guidance; Curriculum and Instruction; Preschool and Elementary Education; Secondary Education; Higher Education; Teacher Education; Adult Education; Special Education; Educational Research; Educational Administration and Supervision; and Educational Criticism and Controversy.   Subdivisions of the annotated reference section are: Guides to the Literature; Reviews; Current Research; Current Books; Abstracts and Summaries; Bibliography of Bibliographies; Current Bibliographies; Retrospective Bibliographies;   Directories and Biographical Information; Dictionaries; Encyclopedias; Handbooks; Yearbooks; Statistical Sources; Sources of Scholarly Contributions (journals, monographs, organizations); Sources of Current Information (journals).   Detailed author-title-subject index.

Education

769   Burke, Arvid J., and Mary A. Burke.   Documentation in Edu-
       cation.   New York: Teachers College Press, Columbia
       University, 1967.
A comprehensive guide for documentary and bibliographic work in education.   Part One, Fundamentals of Information and Storage and Retrieval, contains sections on the ability to find information, recording, storing, and retrieving information, with subsections on books of various kinds, different kinds of publications, other records and new media, libraries, access to collections, searching and automation.   Part Two, Locating Educational Information or Data, contains sections on reference books, dictionaries, sources of information on persons, institutions, organizations, places, miscellaneous facts, subject matter, statistics, news items, and audiovisual materials.   Part Three, Bibliographic Searching in Education, includes searching procedures, bibliographies, bibliographic citations, book

reviews, periodicals, abstracts, serial publications, government documents, U. S. Office of Education publications, publications of educational organizations, educational research reports, and new media in education. Index to Sources and Index to Subjects. Not up to date but still useful.

770 Humby, Michael. A Guide to the Literature of Education. 3d ed. Education Libraries Bulletin Supplement 1. London: University of London, Institute of Education Library, 1975.
Based on S. K. Kimmance, A Guide to the Literature of Education, 1961. Includes 572 annotated entries intended as examples of various types of printed material to be found in an education library. Contains sections on guides to the literature of education, bibliographies, educational research, encyclopedias and dictionaries, directories and yearbooks, organizations, periodicals, biographies, official publications, statistics, textbooks and other teaching aids, classification schemes for education, and libraries and information services. Title and author index.

771 Manheim, Theodore, Gloria L. Dardarian, and Diane A. Satterthwaite. Sources in Educational Research: A Selected and Annotated Bibliography. Vol. 1: Parts I-X. Detroit: Wayne State University, 1969.
Part I, Educational Research - General, lists and annotates general education encyclopedias, dictionaries, guides, bibliographies, indexes, research series, yearbooks, handbooks, periodicals, and directories. Parts II-X list the same type of research tools for particular areas of educational research: mathematics education, social studies education, library science, comparative education, science education, music education, instructional technology, and language arts. Future parts are planned to cover educational sociology, business education, industrial education, educational psychology, educational administration, curriculum, and history and philosophy of education.

772 Woodbury, Marda. A Guide to Sources of Educational Information. Washington, D. C.: Information Resources Press, 1976.
An annotated bibliography of more than 600 sources of information. Part I, Effective Research, consists of a chapter on the research process. Part II, Printed Research Tools, contains chapters on dictionaries, encyclopedias, thesauri, directories, yearbooks, monograph series, periodicals, newsletters, bibliographies and review sources, statistical sources, and abstracting, indexing, and current awareness services. Part III, Special Subjects, covers printed sources on funding, legislation, and foundations; educational products and curricular resources, including selecting instructional materials, curriculum materials and activities, guides to nonprint instructional materials, children's books, and tests and assessment instruments. Part IV, Nonprint Sources, includes directory and institutional information sources, sources of government and financial information, institutional sources of product and curricular information, computerized retrieval sources, gaining access to educational information and materials, and state library service to educators. Author, title, subject index.

AUTHOR-EDITOR INDEX

Numbers refer to entries.

TITLE INDEX

Numbers refer to entries.